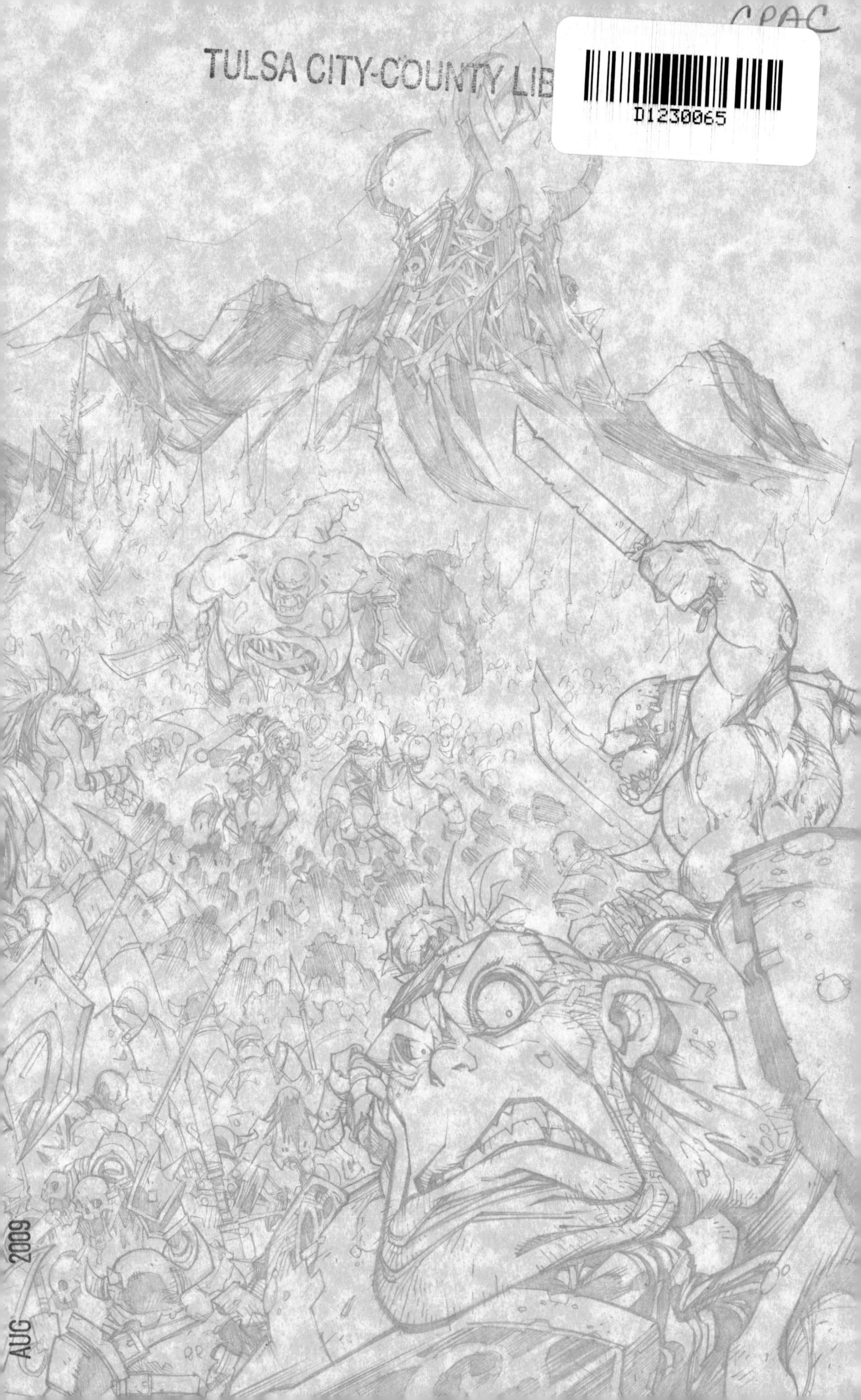

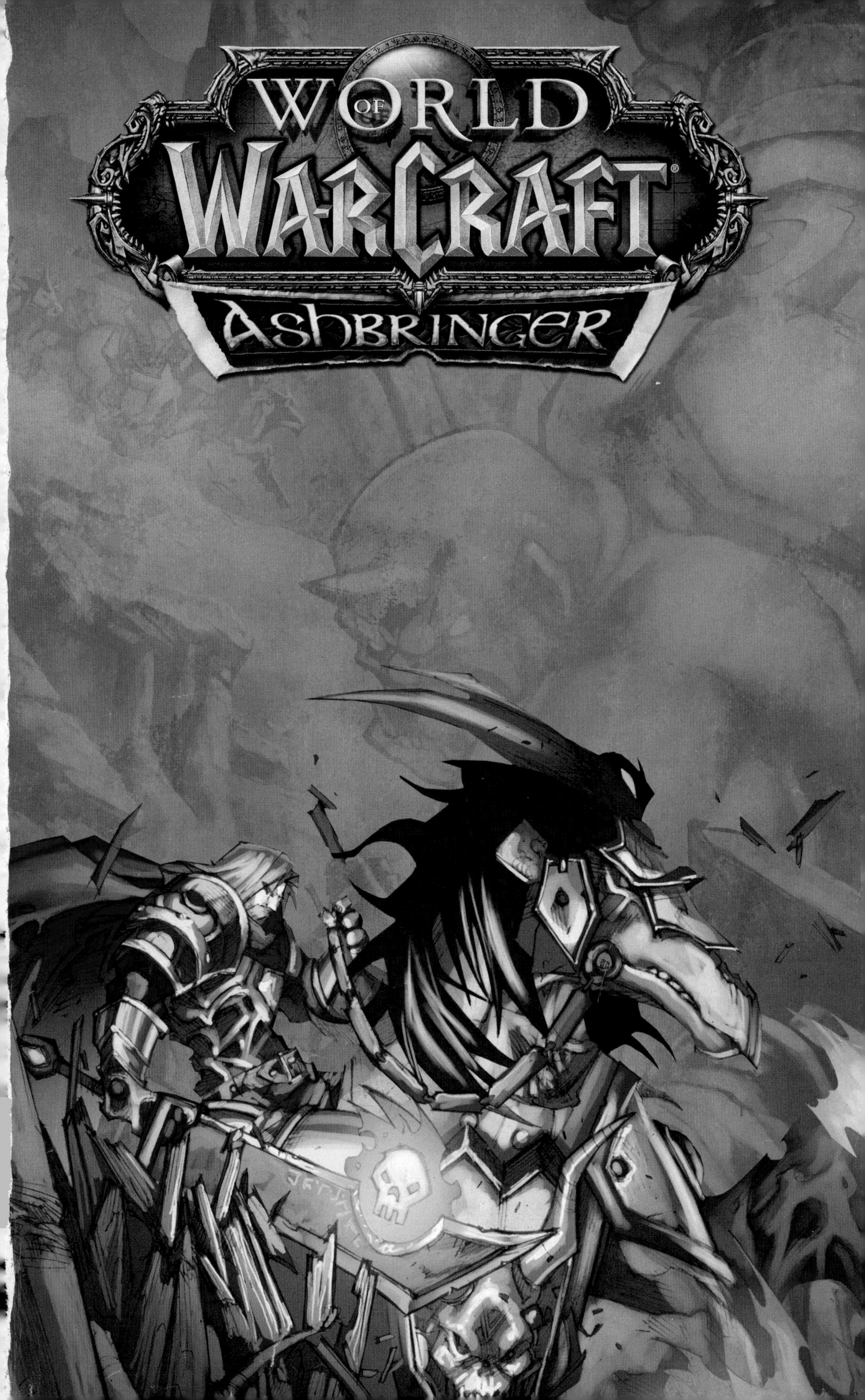
WORLD OF WARCRAFT®
ASHBRINGER

Writer: Micky Neilson
Artists: Ludo Lullabi and Tony Washington
Letterer: Wes Abbott

Story Consultants: Chris Metzen and Alex Afrasiabi
Collected Edition Cover and Original Series Covers by Chris Robinson
Original Series Variant Covers by Ludo Lullabi and Tony Washington

For Blizzard Entertainment:

Chris Metzen, Senior VP—Creative Development
Shawn Carnes, Manager—Creative Development
Micky Neilson, Story Consultation and Development
Glenn Rane, Art Director
Cory Jones, Director—Global Business Development and Licensing
Jason Bischoff, Associate Licensing Manager

Additional Development:
Samwise Didier, Evelyn Fredericksen, Ben Brode, Sean Wang

Blizzard Special Thanks: Brian Hsieh, Gina Pippin

For DC Comics:

Jim Lee, Editorial Director
Hank Kanalz, Editor–Original Series
Kristy Quinn, Editor–Collected Edition
Sarah Gaydos and Kristy Quinn, Assistant Editors–Original Series
Ed Roeder, Art Director
Paul Levitz, President & Publisher
Georg Brewer, VP–Design & DC Direct Creative
Richard Bruning, Senior VP–Creative Director
Patrick Caldon, Executive VP–Finance & Operations
Chris Caramalis, VP–Finance
John Cunningham, VP–Marketing
Terri Cunningham, VP–Managing Editor
Amy Genkins, Senior VP–Business & Legal Affairs
Alison Gill, VP–Manufacturing
David Hyde, VP–Publicity
Hank Kanalz, VP–General Manager, WildStorm
Gregory Noveck, Senior VP–Creative Affairs
Sue Pohja, VP–Book Trade Sales
Steve Rotterdam, Senior VP–Sales & Marketing
Cheryl Rubin, Senior VP–Brand Management
Alysse Soll, VP–Advertising & Custom Publishing
Jeff Trojan, VP–Business Development, DC Direct
Bob Wayne, VP–Sales

Hardcover ISBN: 978-1-4012-2341-0
Softcover ISBN: 978-1-4012-2342-7

LICENSED BLIZZARD ENTERTAINMENT PRODUCT

Cast of Characters

HIGHLORD ALEXANDROS MOGRAINE

A COURAGEOUS AND DEVOTED COMMANDER WITHIN THE KNIGHTS OF THE SILVER HAND. HE DIRECTS HIS FORCES WITH STEADFAST DETERMINATION AND UNWAVERING FAITH.

RENAULT AND DARION MOGRAINE

ALEXANDROS' ONLY SONS. THEIR MOTHER DIED WHEN DARION WAS BORN. FOLLOWING THAT TRAGIC LOSS, EACH OF THEM STRUGGLES TO FIND HIS OWN IDENTITY.

FAIRBANKS

A LOYAL AND DEVOTED FRIEND OF THE MOGRAINE FAMILY. HE IS ALEXANDROS' TRUSTED ADVISOR AND RIGHT HAND IN ALL DIPLOMATIC MATTERS.

SAIDAN DATHROHAN

A DEVOUT PALADIN, RESPECTED LEADER, AND HONORABLE WARRIOR. DATHROHAN IS A MAN OF STRENGTH AND CONVICTION TO WHOM ALL PALADINS LOOK FOR GUIDANCE.

GENERAL ABBENDIS AND LADY BRIGITTE ABBENDIS

THOUGH BOTH ARE OCCUPIED WITH SCOURING EVIL FROM THE WORLD, GENERAL ABBENDIS IS JUST AS OFTEN ENGAGED IN CONTROLLING HIS WILLFUL DAUGHTER'S BEHAVIOR.

ISILLIEN AND DOAN

ISILLIEN THE PRIEST AND DOAN THE MAGE WORK TO MAINTAIN THE "PURITY" OF THE ORDER OF THE SILVER HAND.

MAXWELL TYROSUS

AN OUTSPOKEN DEVOTEE OF THE LIGHT, MAXWELL'S VIEWS OF WHAT IS BEST FOR THE ORDER ARE NOT ALWAYS SHARED BY THE MAJORITY OF HIS COMPANIONS.

CHAPTER I

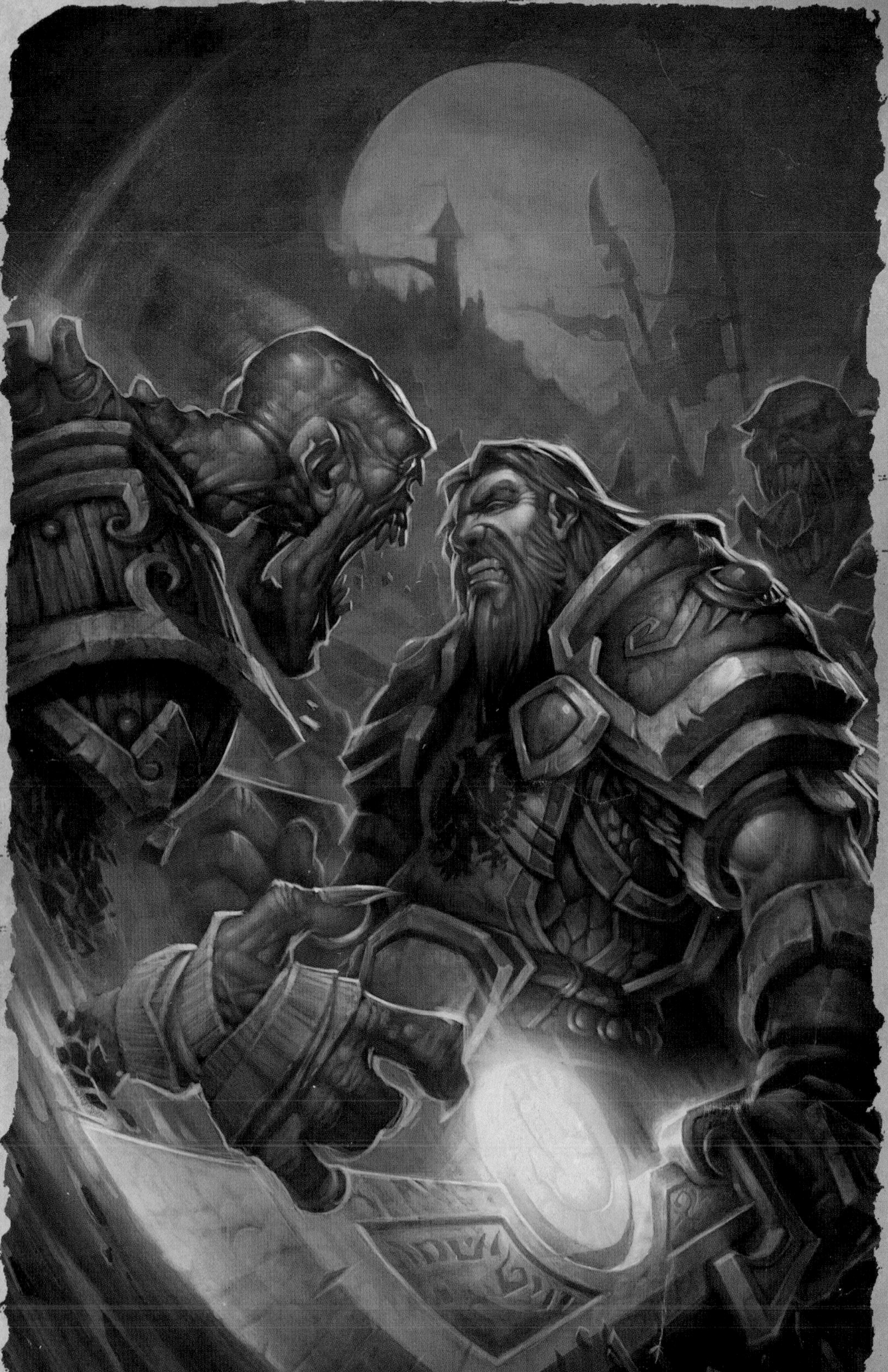

Cover by Chris Robinson

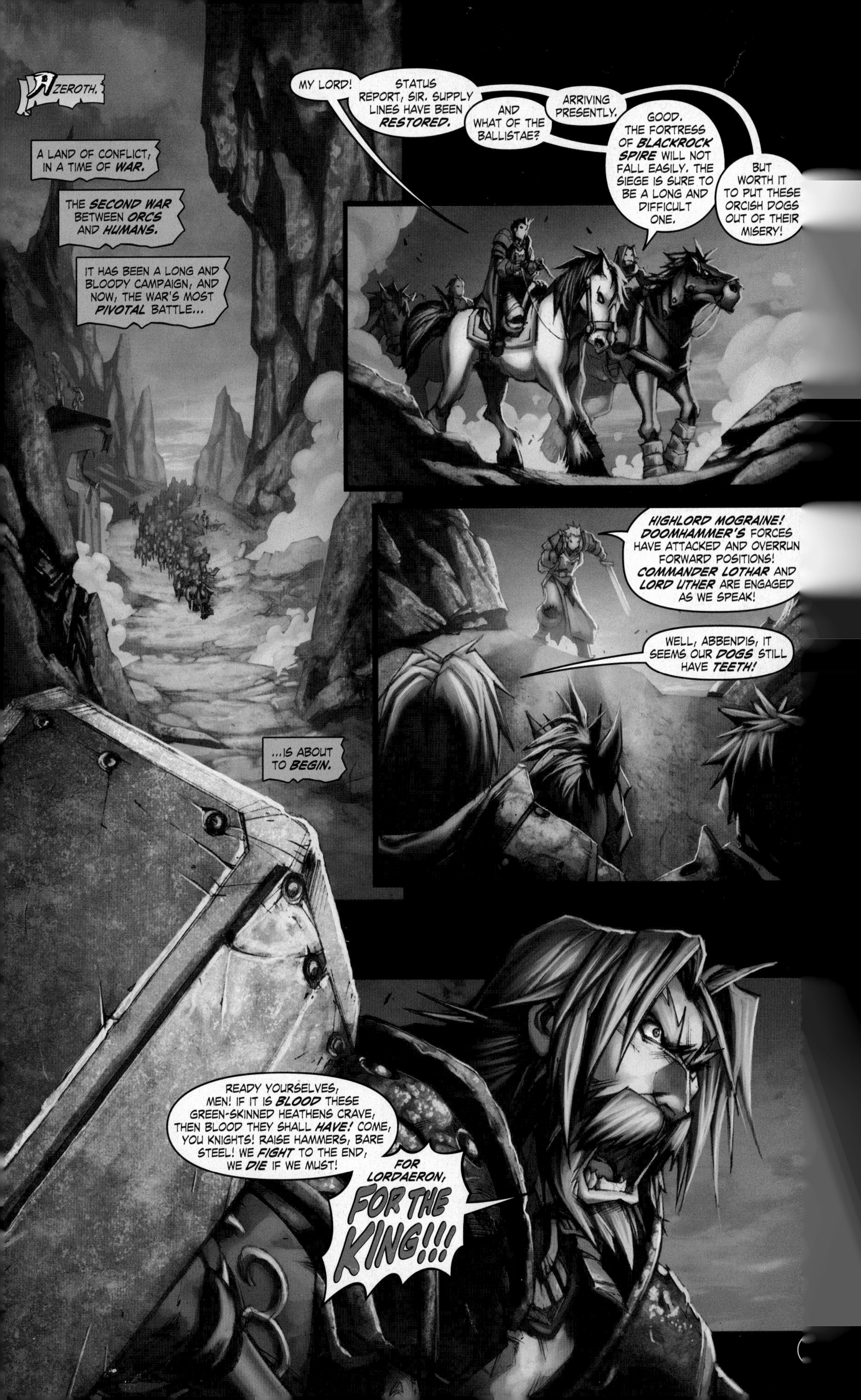
AZEROTH.
A LAND OF CONFLICT, IN A TIME OF WAR.
THE SECOND WAR BETWEEN ORCS AND HUMANS.
IT HAS BEEN A LONG AND BLOODY CAMPAIGN, AND NOW, THE WAR'S MOST PIVOTAL BATTLE...
MY LORD!
STATUS REPORT, SIR. SUPPLY LINES HAVE BEEN RESTORED.
AND WHAT OF THE BALLISTAE?
ARRIVING PRESENTLY.
GOOD. THE FORTRESS OF BLACKROCK SPIRE WILL NOT FALL EASILY. THE SIEGE IS SURE TO BE A LONG AND DIFFICULT ONE.
BUT WORTH IT TO PUT THESE ORCISH DOGS OUT OF THEIR MISERY!
HIGHLORD MOGRAINE! DOOMHAMMER'S FORCES HAVE ATTACKED AND OVERRUN FORWARD POSITIONS! COMMANDER LOTHAR AND LORD UTHER ARE ENGAGED AS WE SPEAK!
WELL, ABBENDIS, IT SEEMS OUR DOGS STILL HAVE TEETH!
...IS ABOUT TO BEGIN.
READY YOURSELVES, MEN! IF IT IS BLOOD THESE GREEN-SKINNED HEATHENS CRAVE, THEN BLOOD THEY SHALL HAVE! COME, YOU KNIGHTS! RAISE HAMMERS, BARE STEEL! WE FIGHT TO THE END, WE DIE IF WE MUST!
FOR LORDAERON, FOR THE KING!!!

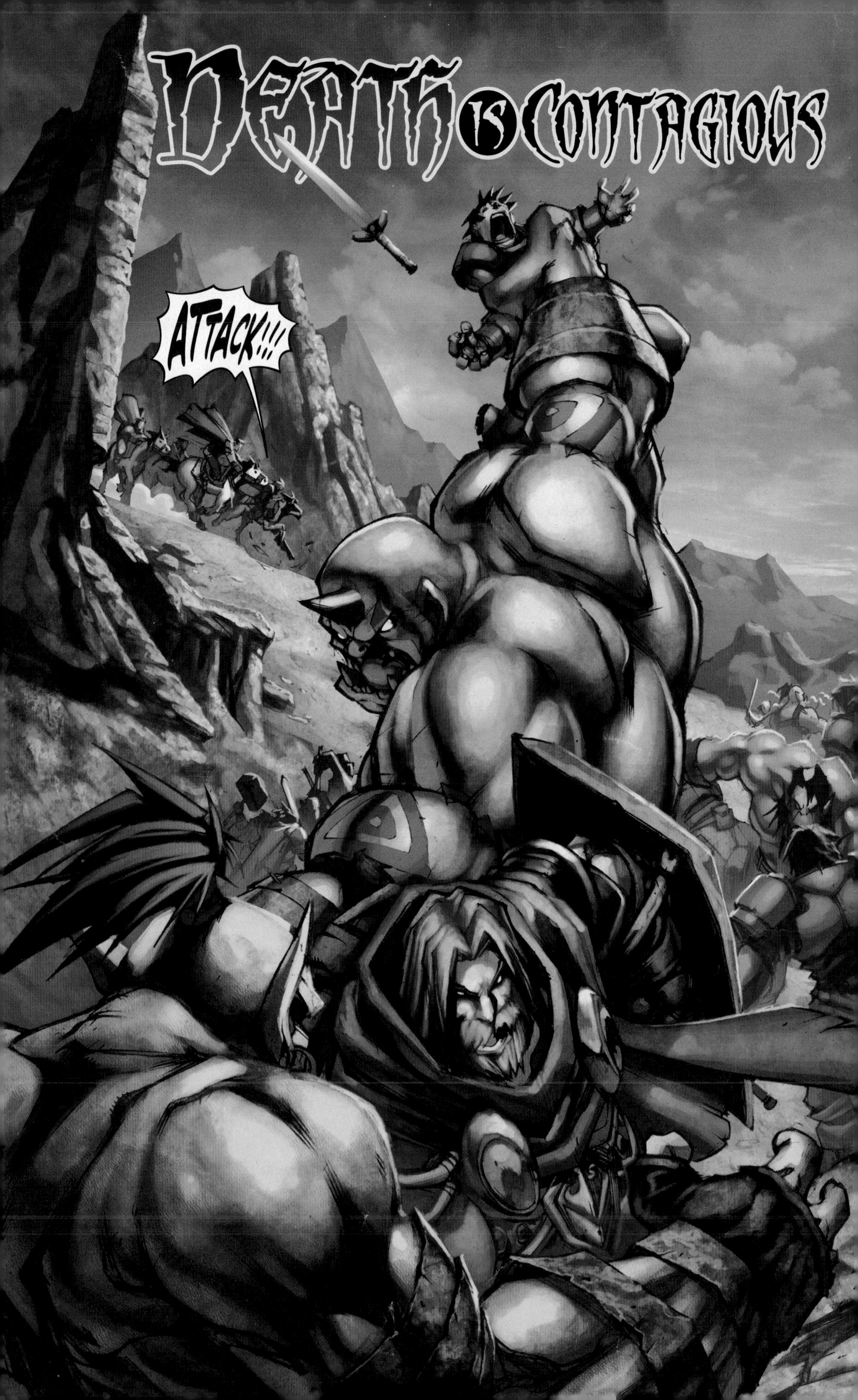
DEATH IS CONTAGIOUS
ATTACK!!!

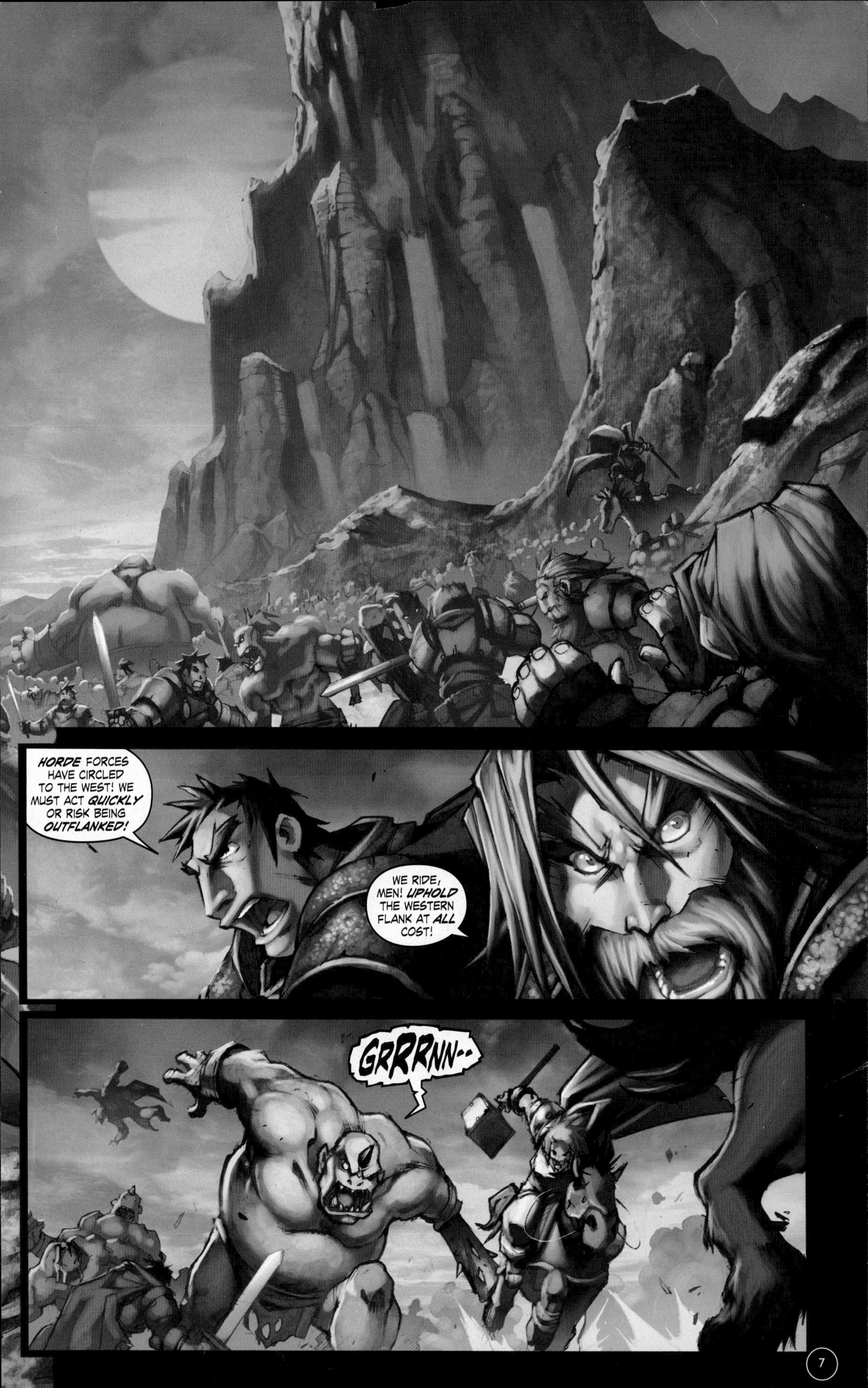
HORDE FORCES HAVE CIRCLED TO THE WEST! WE MUST ACT QUICKLY OR RISK BEING OUTFLANKED!
WE RIDE, MEN! UPHOLD THE WESTERN FLANK AT ALL COST!
GRRRNN--

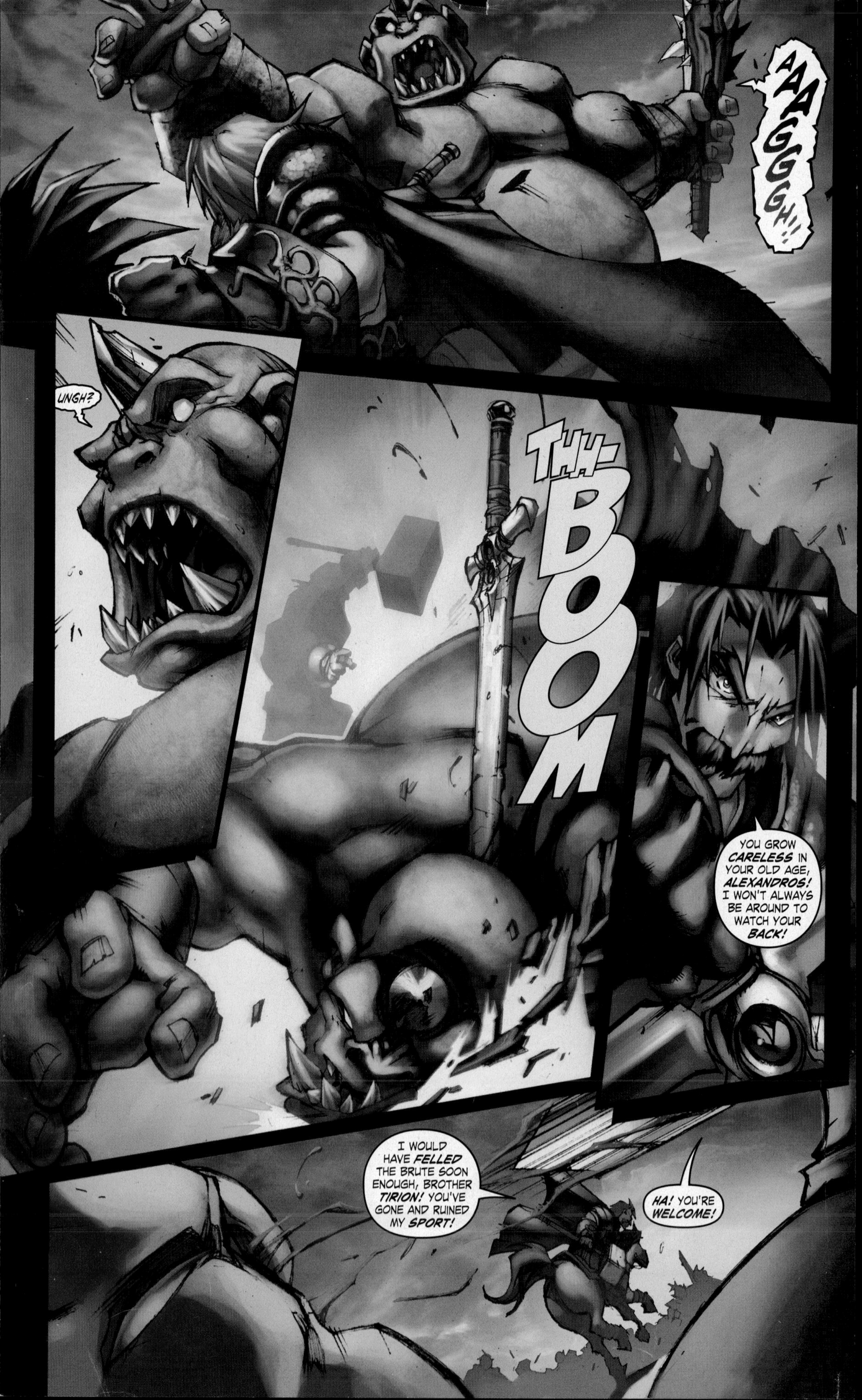
AAAGGGH!!
UNGH?
THH-BOOM
YOU GROW CARELESS IN YOUR OLD AGE, ALEXANDROS! I WON'T ALWAYS BE AROUND TO WATCH YOUR BACK!
I WOULD HAVE FELLED THE BRUTE SOON ENOUGH, BROTHER TIRION! YOU'VE GONE AND RUINED MY SPORT!
HA! YOU'RE WELCOME!

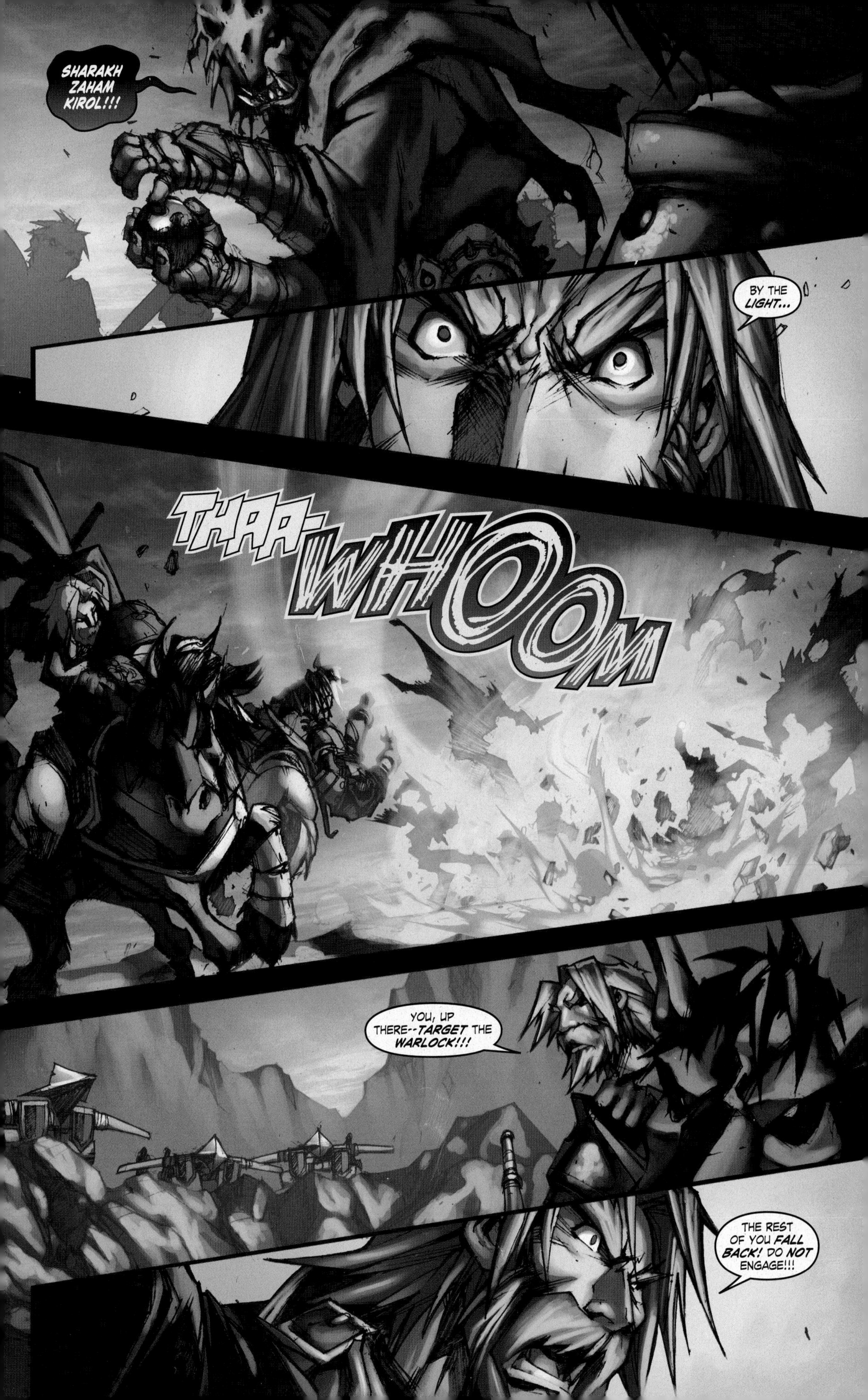
SHARAKH ZAHAM KIROL!!!
BY THE LIGHT...
THAA-WHOOOM
YOU, UP THERE--TARGET THE WARLOCK!!!
THE REST OF YOU FALL BACK! DO NOT ENGAGE!!!

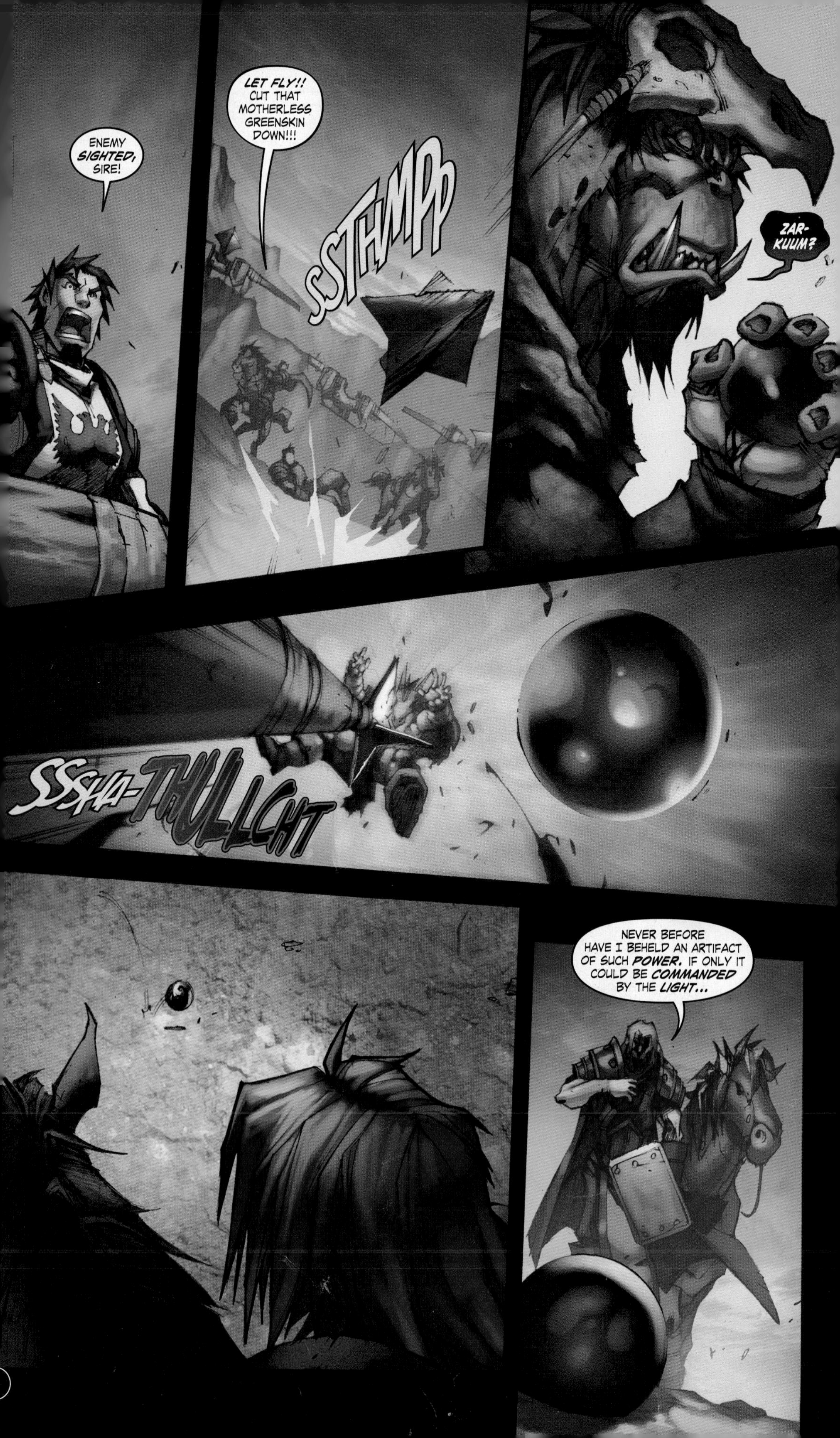
ENEMY SIGHTED, SIRE!
LET FLY!! CUT THAT MOTHERLESS GREENSKIN DOWN!!!
SSTHMPP
ZAR-KUUM?
SSSHA-THULLCHT
NEVER BEFORE HAVE I BEHELD AN ARTIFACT OF SUCH POWER. IF ONLY IT COULD BE COMMANDED BY THE LIGHT...

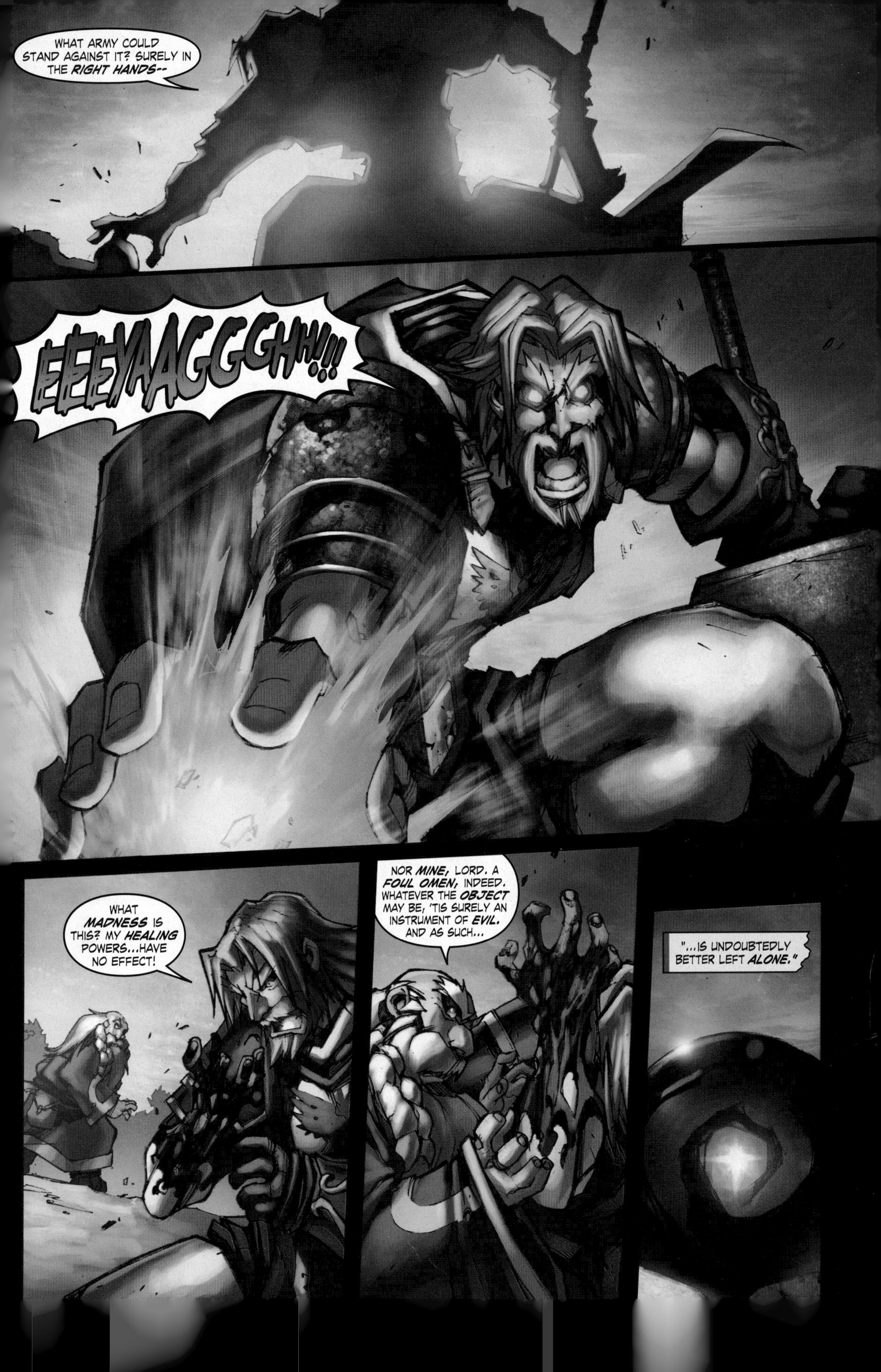
WHAT ARMY COULD STAND AGAINST IT? SURELY IN THE RIGHT HANDS--
EEEYAAGGGHH!!!
WHAT MADNESS IS THIS? MY HEALING POWERS...HAVE NO EFFECT!
NOR MINE, LORD. A FOUL OMEN, INDEED. WHATEVER THE OBJECT MAY BE, 'TIS SURELY AN INSTRUMENT OF EVIL. AND AS SUCH...
"...IS UNDOUBTEDLY BETTER LEFT ALONE."

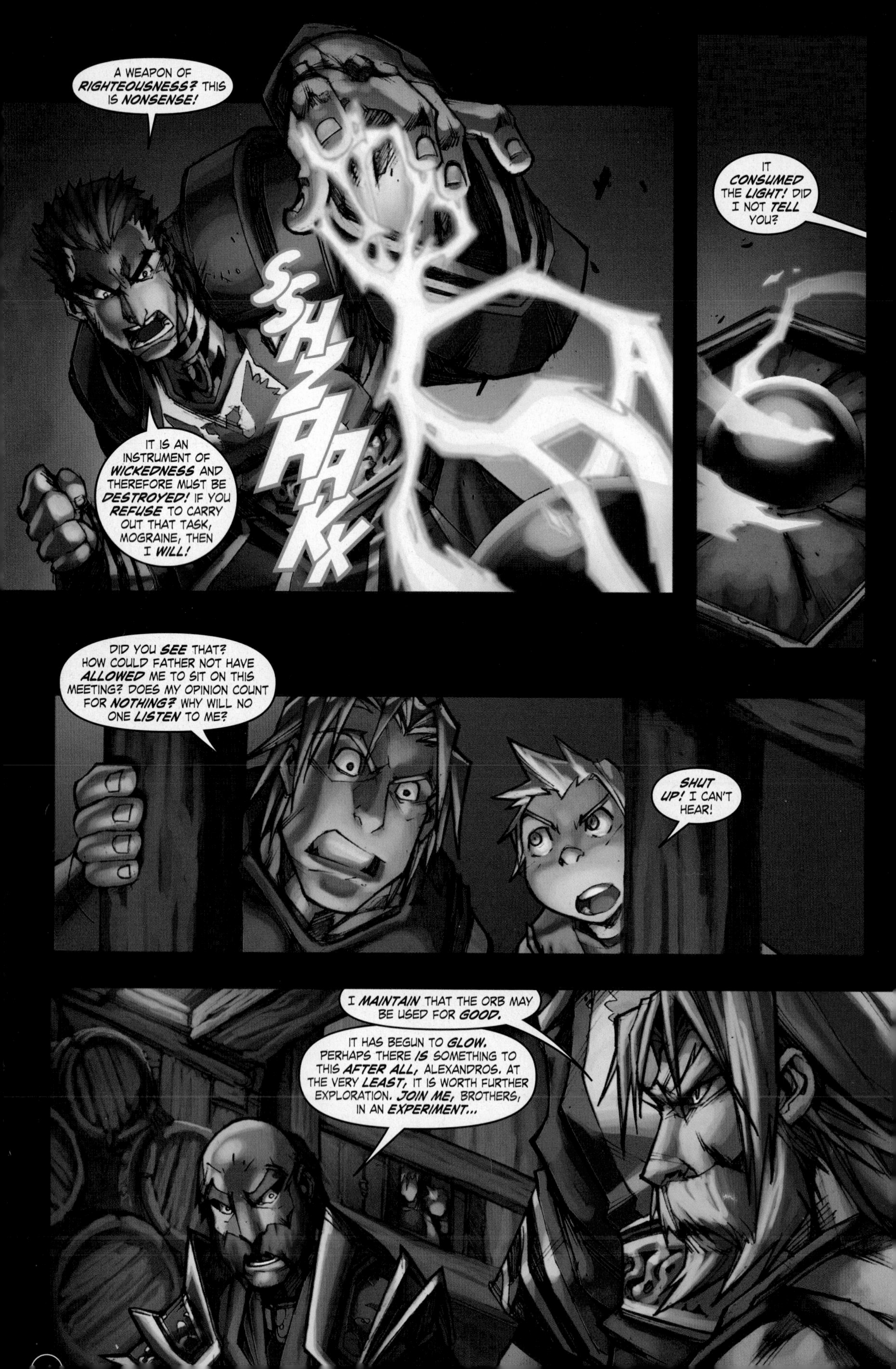
A WEAPON OF RIGHTEOUSNESS? THIS IS NONSENSE!
SSHZAAAKX
IT CONSUMED THE LIGHT! DID I NOT TELL YOU?
IT IS AN INSTRUMENT OF WICKEDNESS AND THEREFORE MUST BE DESTROYED! IF YOU REFUSE TO CARRY OUT THAT TASK, MOGRAINE, THEN I WILL!
DID YOU SEE THAT? HOW COULD FATHER NOT HAVE ALLOWED ME TO SIT ON THIS MEETING? DOES MY OPINION COUNT FOR NOTHING? WHY WILL NO ONE LISTEN TO ME?
SHUT UP! I CAN'T HEAR!
I MAINTAIN THAT THE ORB MAY BE USED FOR GOOD.
IT HAS BEGUN TO GLOW. PERHAPS THERE IS SOMETHING TO THIS AFTER ALL, ALEXANDROS. AT THE VERY LEAST, IT IS WORTH FURTHER EXPLORATION. JOIN ME, BROTHERS, IN AN EXPERIMENT...

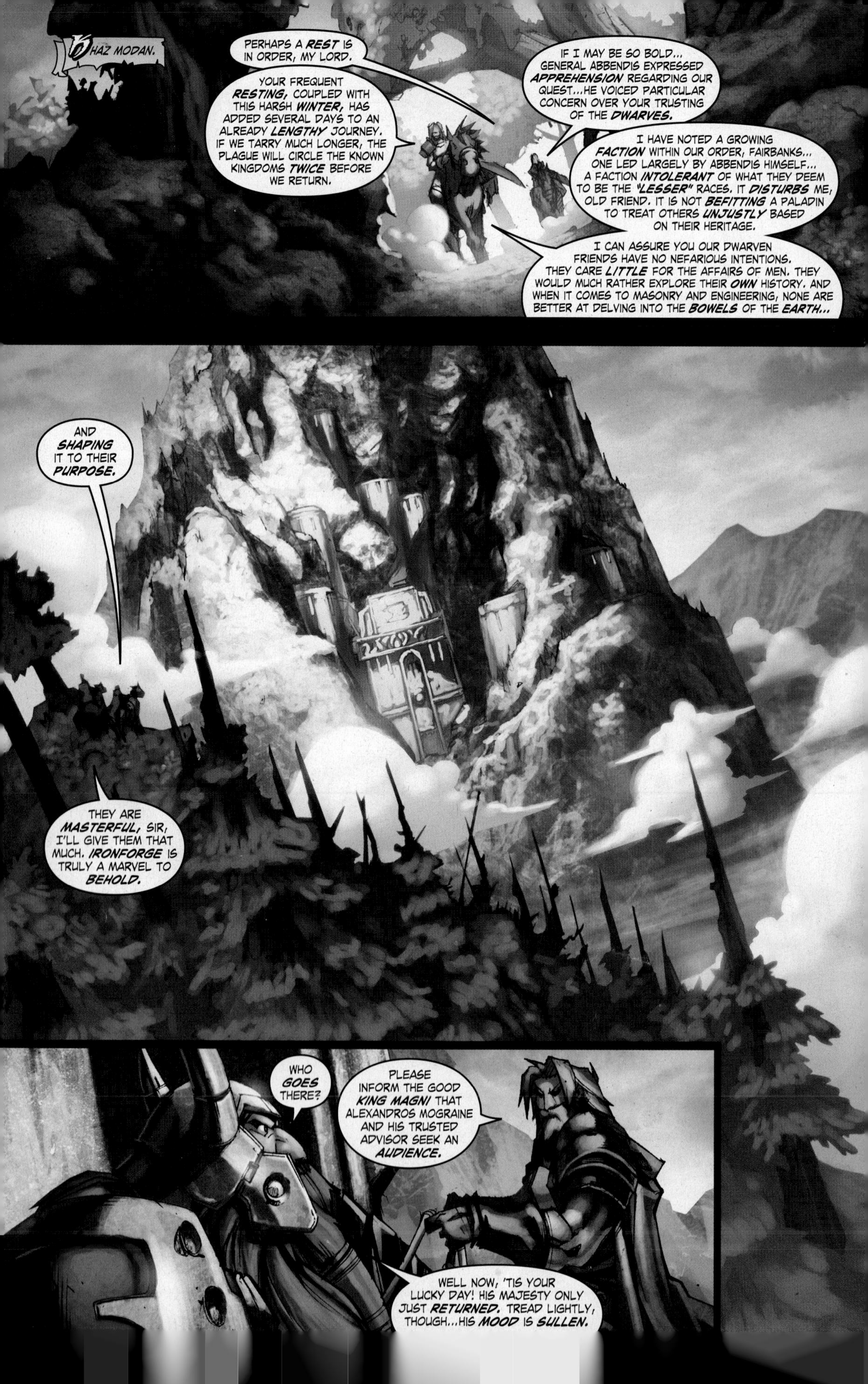
KHAZ MODAN.
PERHAPS A REST IS IN ORDER, MY LORD.
YOUR FREQUENT RESTING, COUPLED WITH THIS HARSH WINTER, HAS ADDED SEVERAL DAYS TO AN ALREADY LENGTHY JOURNEY. IF WE TARRY MUCH LONGER, THE PLAGUE WILL CIRCLE THE KNOWN KINGDOMS TWICE BEFORE WE RETURN.
IF I MAY BE SO BOLD... GENERAL ABBENDIS EXPRESSED APPREHENSION REGARDING OUR QUEST...HE VOICED PARTICULAR CONCERN OVER YOUR TRUSTING OF THE DWARVES.
I HAVE NOTED A GROWING FACTION WITHIN OUR ORDER, FAIRBANKS... ONE LED LARGELY BY ABBENDIS HIMSELF... A FACTION INTOLERANT OF WHAT THEY DEEM TO BE THE "LESSER" RACES. IT DISTURBS ME, OLD FRIEND. IT IS NOT BEFITTING A PALADIN TO TREAT OTHERS UNJUSTLY BASED ON THEIR HERITAGE.
I CAN ASSURE YOU OUR DWARVEN FRIENDS HAVE NO NEFARIOUS INTENTIONS. THEY CARE LITTLE FOR THE AFFAIRS OF MEN. THEY WOULD MUCH RATHER EXPLORE THEIR OWN HISTORY. AND WHEN IT COMES TO MASONRY AND ENGINEERING, NONE ARE BETTER AT DELVING INTO THE BOWELS OF THE EARTH...
AND SHAPING IT TO THEIR PURPOSE.
THEY ARE MASTERFUL, SIR, I'LL GIVE THEM THAT MUCH. IRONFORGE IS TRULY A MARVEL TO BEHOLD.
WHO GOES THERE?
PLEASE INFORM THE GOOD KING MAGNI THAT ALEXANDROS MOGRAINE AND HIS TRUSTED ADVISOR SEEK AN AUDIENCE.
WELL NOW, 'TIS YOUR LUCKY DAY! HIS MAJESTY ONLY JUST RETURNED. TREAD LIGHTLY, THOUGH...HIS MOOD IS SULLEN.

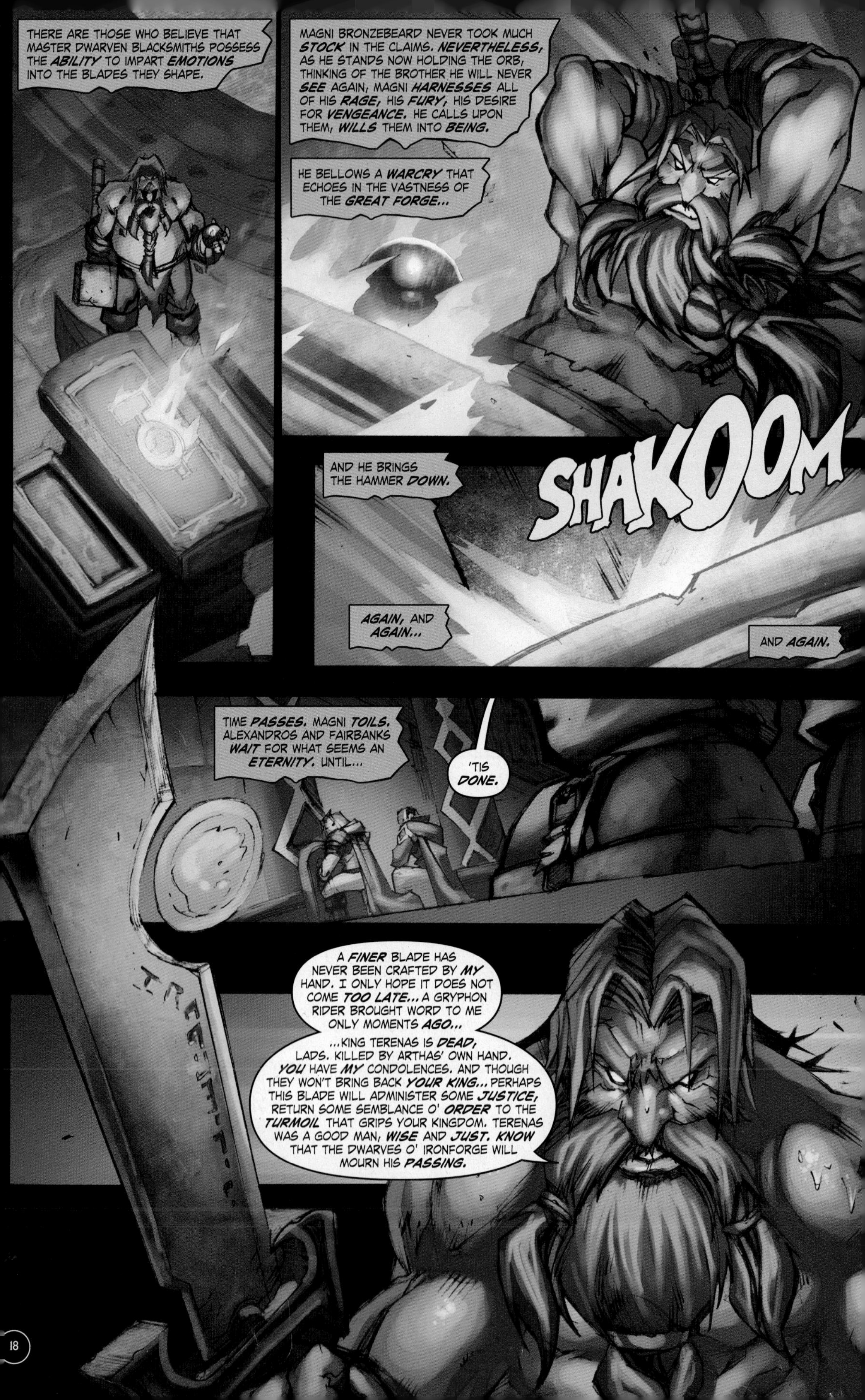
THERE ARE THOSE WHO BELIEVE THAT MASTER DWARVEN BLACKSMITHS POSSESS THE ABILITY TO IMPART EMOTIONS INTO THE BLADES THEY SHAPE.
MAGNI BRONZEBEARD NEVER TOOK MUCH STOCK IN THE CLAIMS. NEVERTHELESS, AS HE STANDS NOW HOLDING THE ORB, THINKING OF THE BROTHER HE WILL NEVER SEE AGAIN, MAGNI HARNESSES ALL OF HIS RAGE, HIS FURY, HIS DESIRE FOR VENGEANCE. HE CALLS UPON THEM, WILLS THEM INTO BEING.
HE BELLOWS A WARCRY THAT ECHOES IN THE VASTNESS OF THE GREAT FORGE...
AND HE BRINGS THE HAMMER DOWN.
SHAKOOM
AGAIN, AND AGAIN...
AND AGAIN.
TIME PASSES. MAGNI TOILS. ALEXANDROS AND FAIRBANKS WAIT FOR WHAT SEEMS AN ETERNITY. UNTIL...
'TIS DONE.
A FINER BLADE HAS NEVER BEEN CRAFTED BY MY HAND. I ONLY HOPE IT DOES NOT COME TOO LATE... A GRYPHON RIDER BROUGHT WORD TO ME ONLY MOMENTS AGO...
...KING TERENAS IS DEAD, LADS. KILLED BY ARTHAS' OWN HAND. YOU HAVE MY CONDOLENCES. AND THOUGH THEY WON'T BRING BACK YOUR KING... PERHAPS THIS BLADE WILL ADMINISTER SOME JUSTICE, RETURN SOME SEMBLANCE O' ORDER TO THE TURMOIL THAT GRIPS YOUR KINGDOM. TERENAS WAS A GOOD MAN, WISE AND JUST. KNOW THAT THE DWARVES O' IRONFORGE WILL MOURN HIS PASSING.

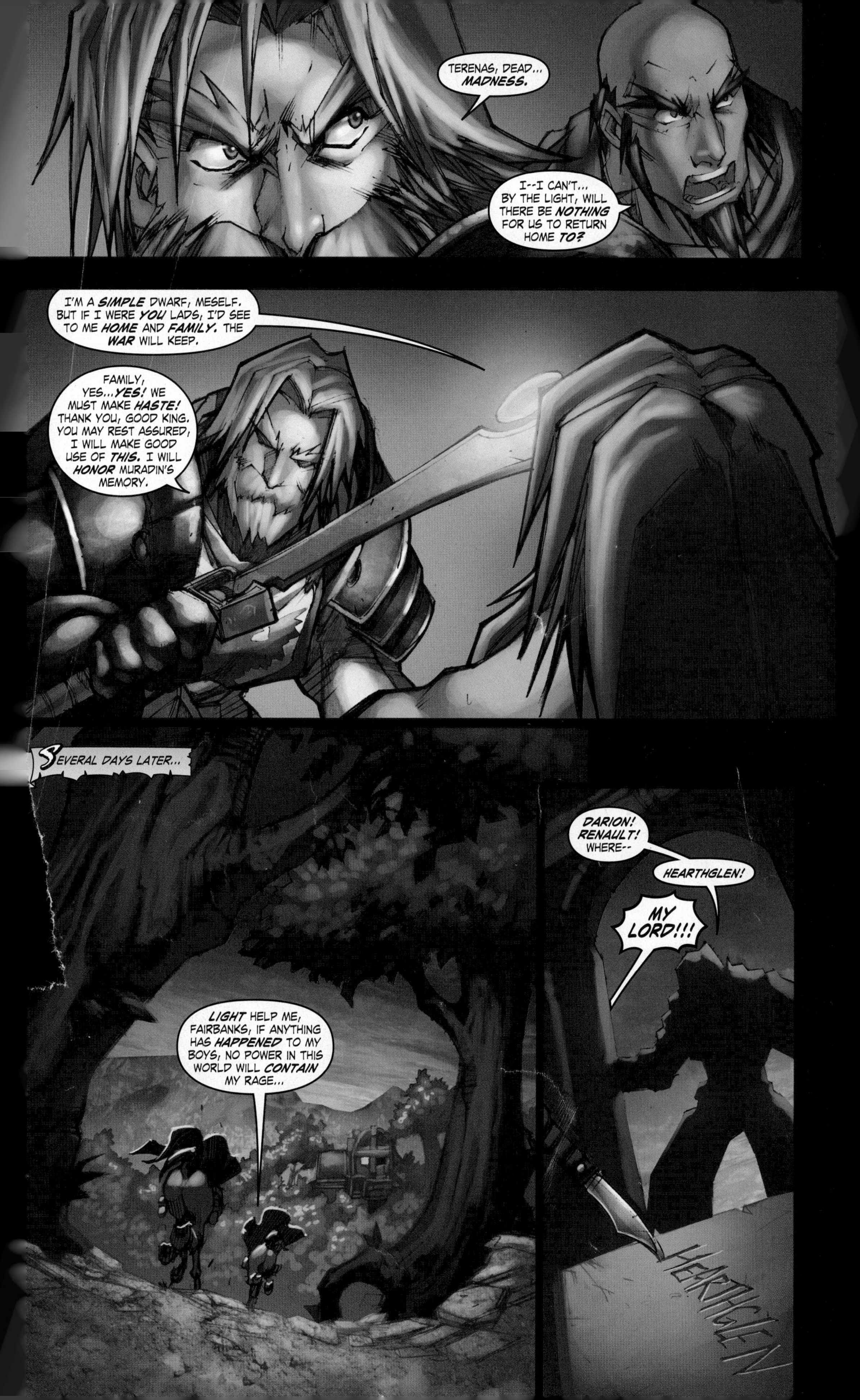
TERENAS, DEAD... MADNESS.
I--I CAN'T... BY THE LIGHT, WILL THERE BE NOTHING FOR US TO RETURN HOME TO?
I'M A SIMPLE DWARF, MESELF. BUT IF I WERE YOU LADS, I'D SEE TO ME HOME AND FAMILY. THE WAR WILL KEEP.
FAMILY, YES...YES! WE MUST MAKE HASTE! THANK YOU, GOOD KING. YOU MAY REST ASSURED, I WILL MAKE GOOD USE OF THIS. I WILL HONOR MURADIN'S MEMORY.
SEVERAL DAYS LATER...
LIGHT HELP ME, FAIRBANKS, IF ANYTHING HAS HAPPENED TO MY BOYS, NO POWER IN THIS WORLD WILL CONTAIN MY RAGE...
DARION! RENAULT! WHERE--
HEARTHGLEN!
MY LORD!!!
HEARTHGLEN

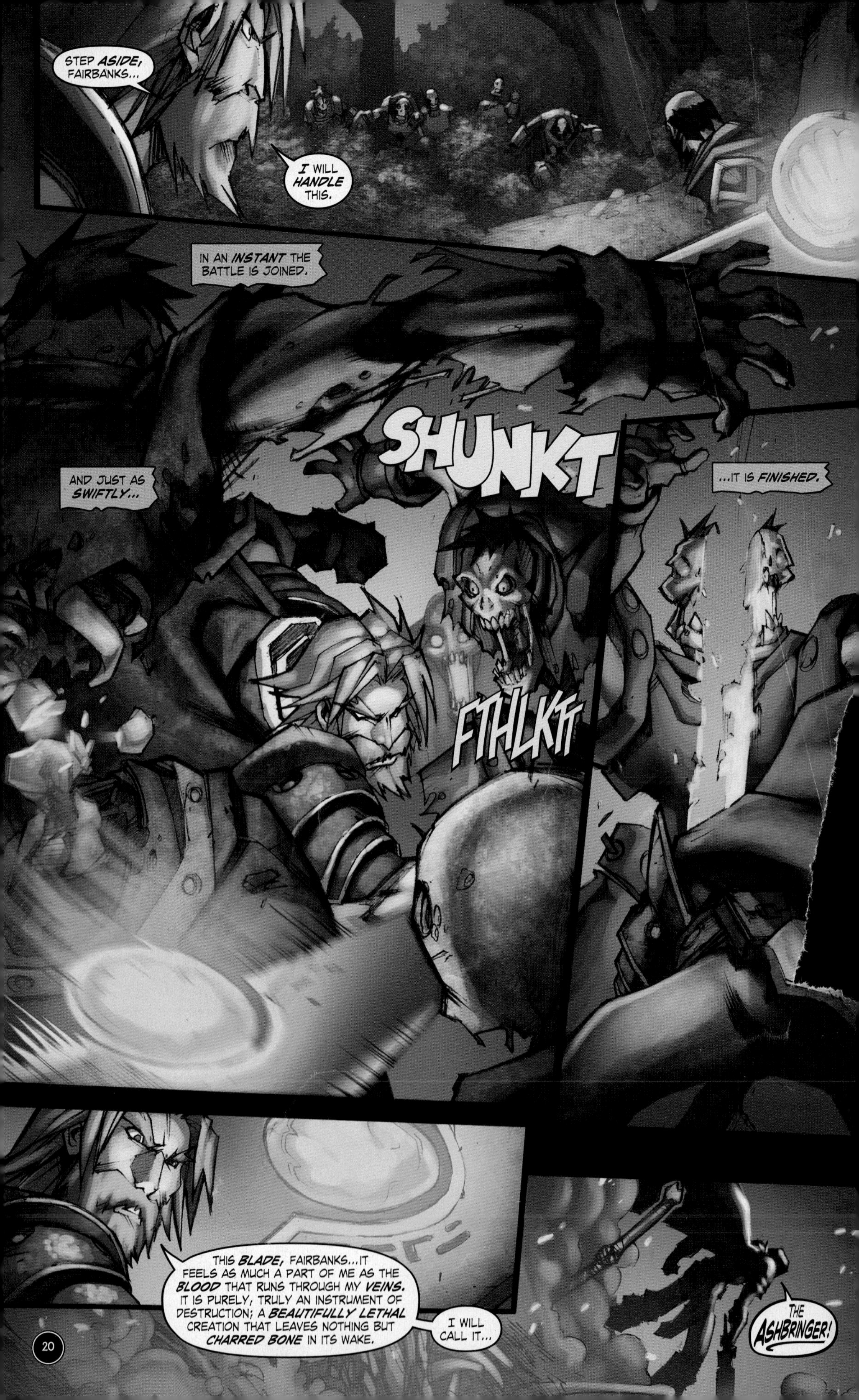
STEP ASIDE, FAIRBANKS...
I WILL HANDLE THIS.
IN AN INSTANT THE BATTLE IS JOINED.
SHUNKT
AND JUST AS SWIFTLY...
FTHLKTT
...IT IS FINISHED.
THIS BLADE, FAIRBANKS...IT FEELS AS MUCH A PART OF ME AS THE BLOOD THAT RUNS THROUGH MY VEINS. IT IS PURELY, TRULY AN INSTRUMENT OF DESTRUCTION; A BEAUTIFULLY LETHAL CREATION THAT LEAVES NOTHING BUT CHARRED BONE IN ITS WAKE.
I WILL CALL IT...
THE ASHBRINGER!

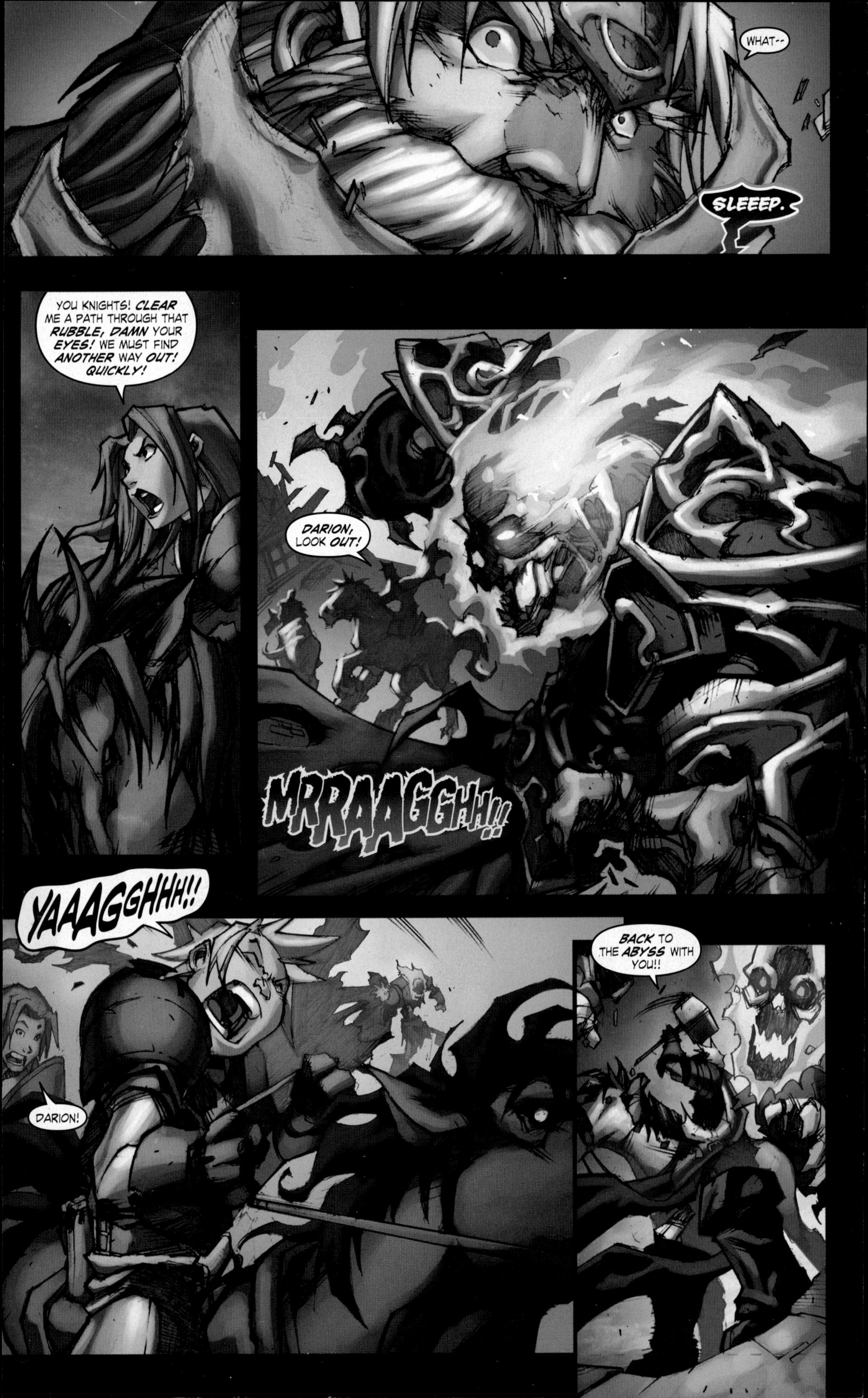
WHAT--
SLEEEP.
YOU KNIGHTS! CLEAR ME A PATH THROUGH THAT RUBBLE, DAMN YOUR EYES! WE MUST FIND ANOTHER WAY OUT! QUICKLY!
DARION, LOOK OUT!
MRRAAGGHH!!
YAAAGGHHH!!
DARION!
BACK TO THE ABYSS WITH YOU!!

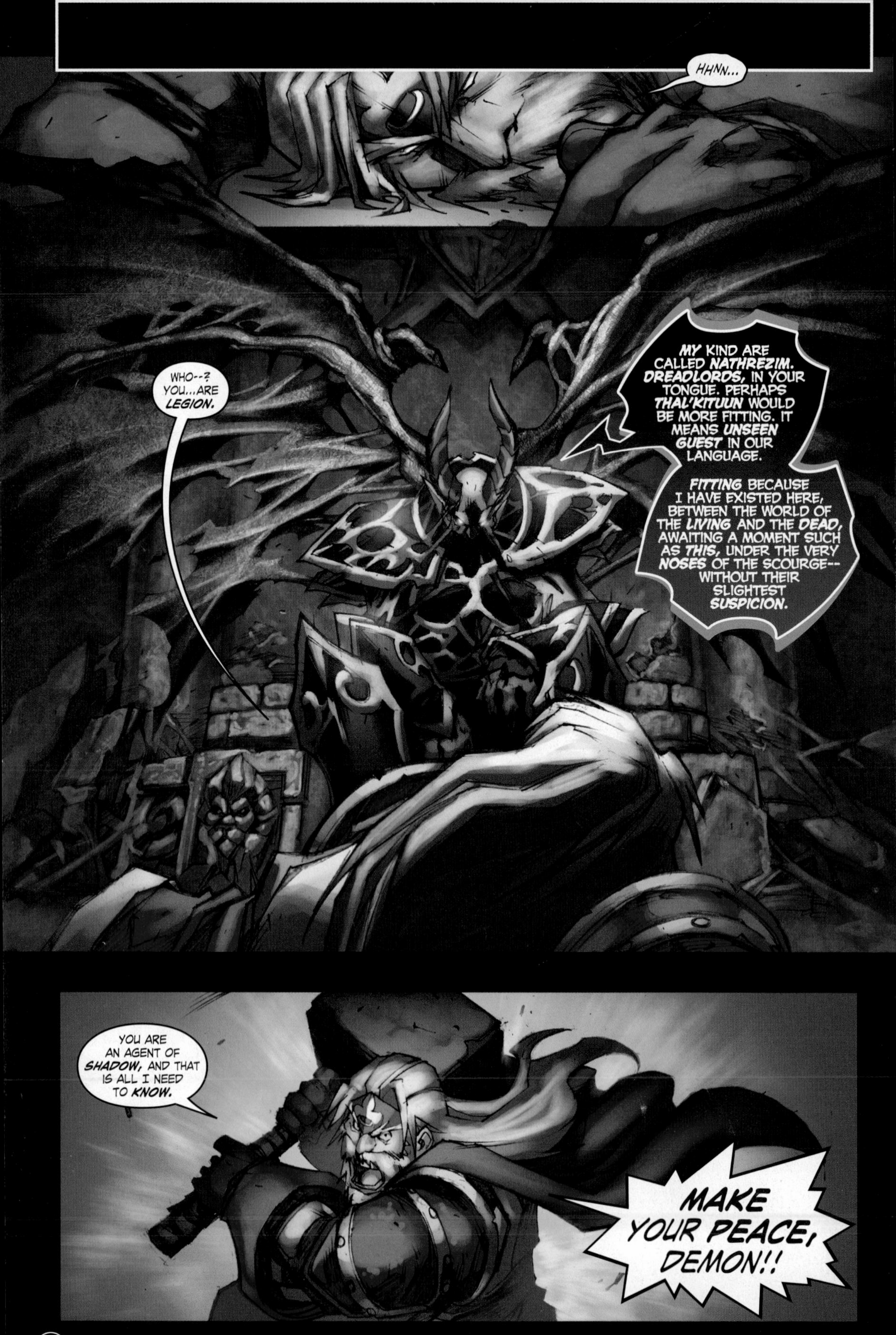
HHNN...
WHO--? YOU...ARE LEGION.
MY KIND ARE CALLED NATHREZIM. DREADLORDS, IN YOUR TONGUE. PERHAPS THAL'KITUUN WOULD BE MORE FITTING. IT MEANS UNSEEN GUEST IN OUR LANGUAGE.
FITTING BECAUSE I HAVE EXISTED HERE, BETWEEN THE WORLD OF THE LIVING AND THE DEAD, AWAITING A MOMENT SUCH AS THIS, UNDER THE VERY NOSES OF THE SCOURGE--WITHOUT THEIR SLIGHTEST SUSPICION.
YOU ARE AN AGENT OF SHADOW, AND THAT IS ALL I NEED TO KNOW.
MAKE YOUR PEACE, DEMON!!

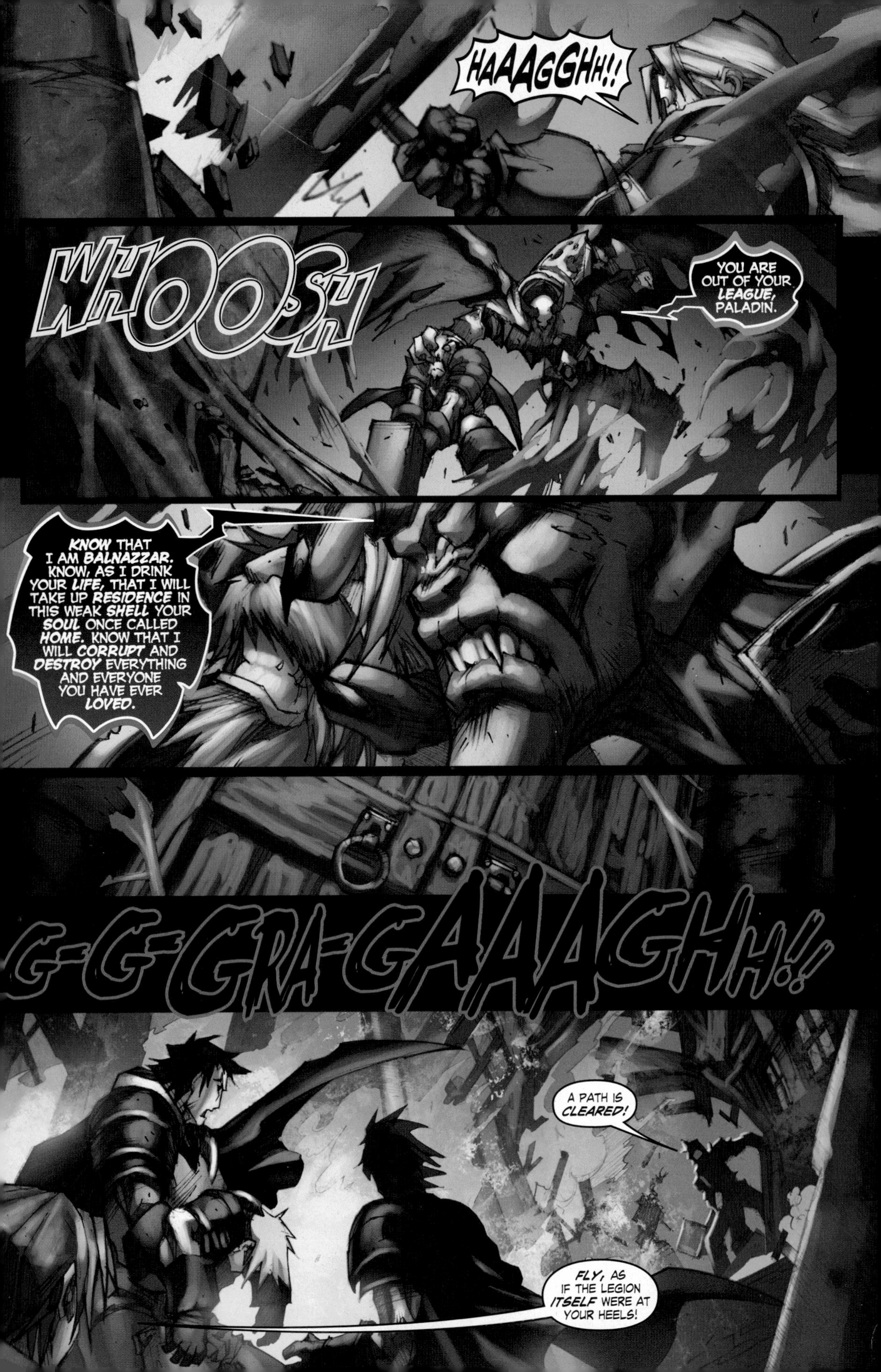
HAAAGGHH!!
WHOOSH
YOU ARE OUT OF YOUR LEAGUE, PALADIN.
KNOW THAT I AM BALNAZZAR. KNOW, AS I DRINK YOUR LIFE, THAT I WILL TAKE UP RESIDENCE IN THIS WEAK SHELL YOUR SOUL ONCE CALLED HOME. KNOW THAT I WILL CORRUPT AND DESTROY EVERYTHING AND EVERYONE YOU HAVE EVER LOVED.
G-G-GRA-GAAAGHH!!
A PATH IS CLEARED!
FLY, AS IF THE LEGION ITSELF WERE AT YOUR HEELS!

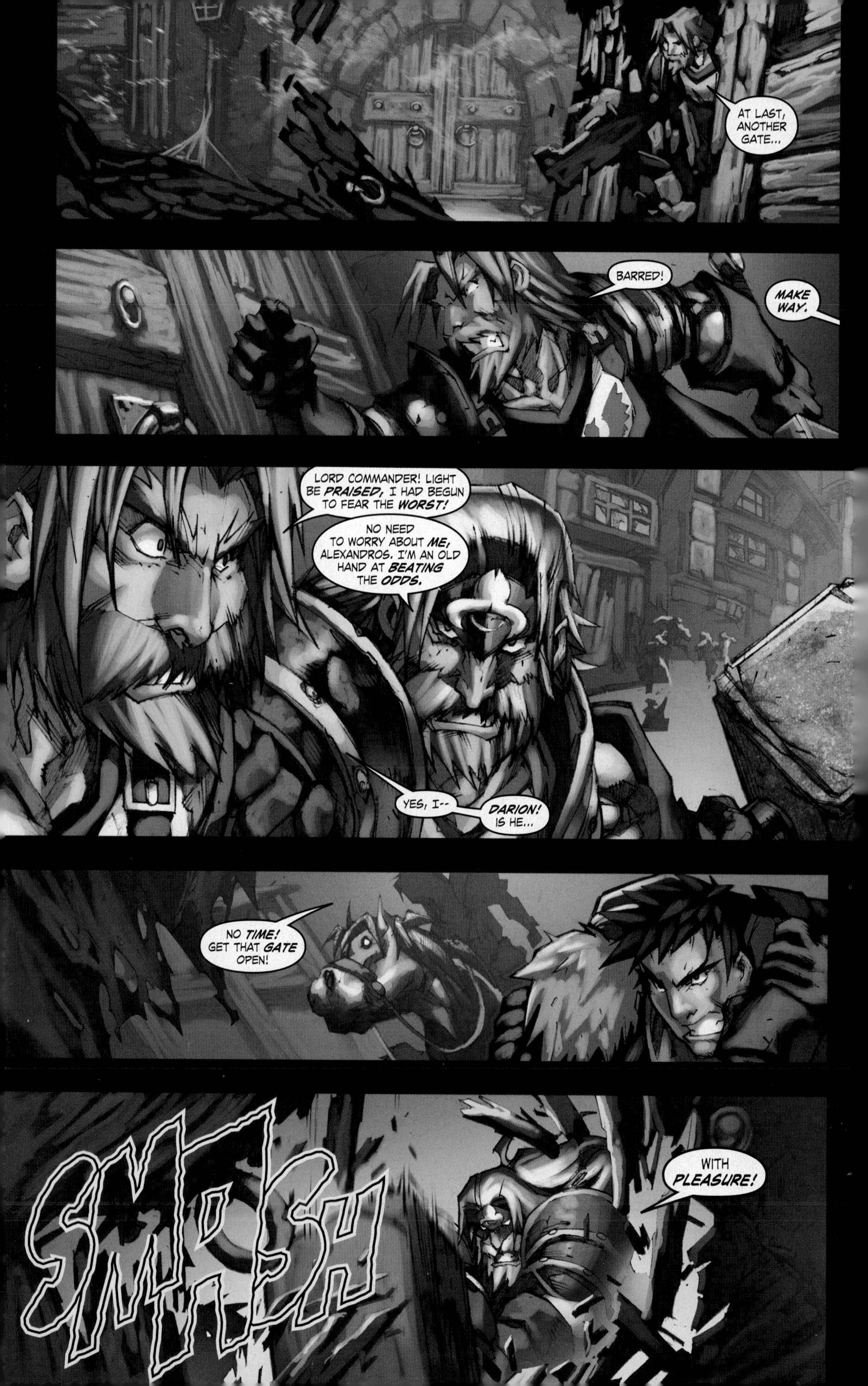
AT LAST, ANOTHER GATE...
BARRED!
MAKE WAY.
LORD COMMANDER! LIGHT BE PRAISED, I HAD BEGUN TO FEAR THE WORST!
NO NEED TO WORRY ABOUT ME, ALEXANDROS. I'M AN OLD HAND AT BEATING THE ODDS.
YES, I--
DARION! IS HE...
NO TIME! GET THAT GATE OPEN!
SMASH
WITH PLEASURE!

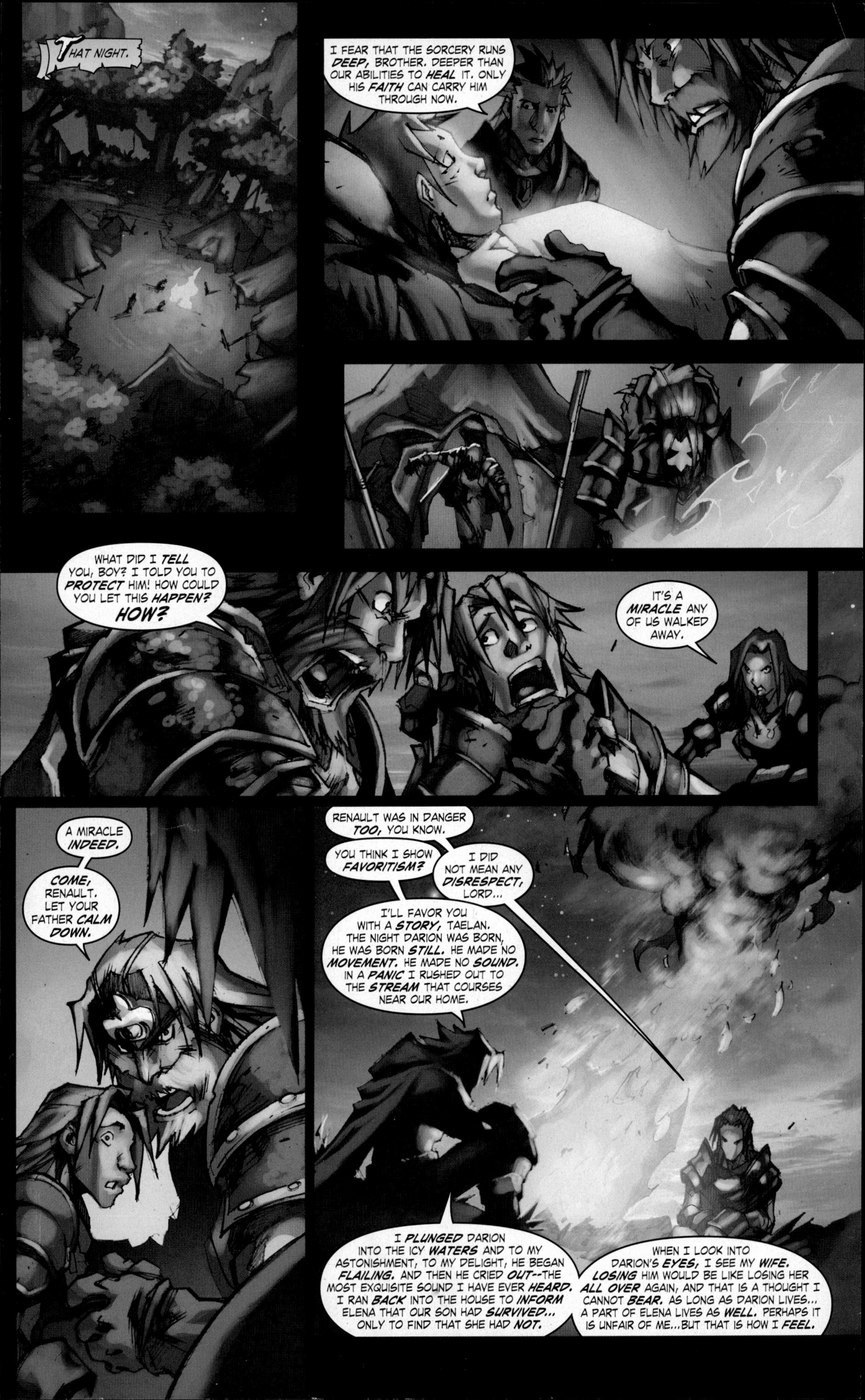
THAT NIGHT.
I FEAR THAT THE SORCERY RUNS DEEP, BROTHER. DEEPER THAN OUR ABILITIES TO HEAL IT. ONLY HIS FAITH CAN CARRY HIM THROUGH NOW.
WHAT DID I TELL YOU, BOY? I TOLD YOU TO PROTECT HIM! HOW COULD YOU LET THIS HAPPEN? HOW?
IT'S A MIRACLE ANY OF US WALKED AWAY.
A MIRACLE INDEED.
COME, RENAULT. LET YOUR FATHER CALM DOWN.
RENAULT WAS IN DANGER TOO, YOU KNOW.
YOU THINK I SHOW FAVORITISM?
I DID NOT MEAN ANY DISRESPECT, LORD...
I'LL FAVOR YOU WITH A STORY, TAELAN. THE NIGHT DARION WAS BORN, HE WAS BORN STILL. HE MADE NO MOVEMENT. HE MADE NO SOUND. IN A PANIC I RUSHED OUT TO THE STREAM THAT COURSES NEAR OUR HOME.
I PLUNGED DARION INTO THE ICY WATERS AND TO MY ASTONISHMENT, TO MY DELIGHT, HE BEGAN FLAILING. AND THEN HE CRIED OUT--THE MOST EXQUISITE SOUND I HAVE EVER HEARD. I RAN BACK INTO THE HOUSE TO INFORM ELENA THAT OUR SON HAD SURVIVED... ONLY TO FIND THAT SHE HAD NOT.
WHEN I LOOK INTO DARION'S EYES, I SEE MY WIFE. LOSING HIM WOULD BE LIKE LOSING HER ALL OVER AGAIN, AND THAT IS A THOUGHT I CANNOT BEAR. AS LONG AS DARION LIVES... A PART OF ELENA LIVES AS WELL. PERHAPS IT IS UNFAIR OF ME...BUT THAT IS HOW I FEEL.

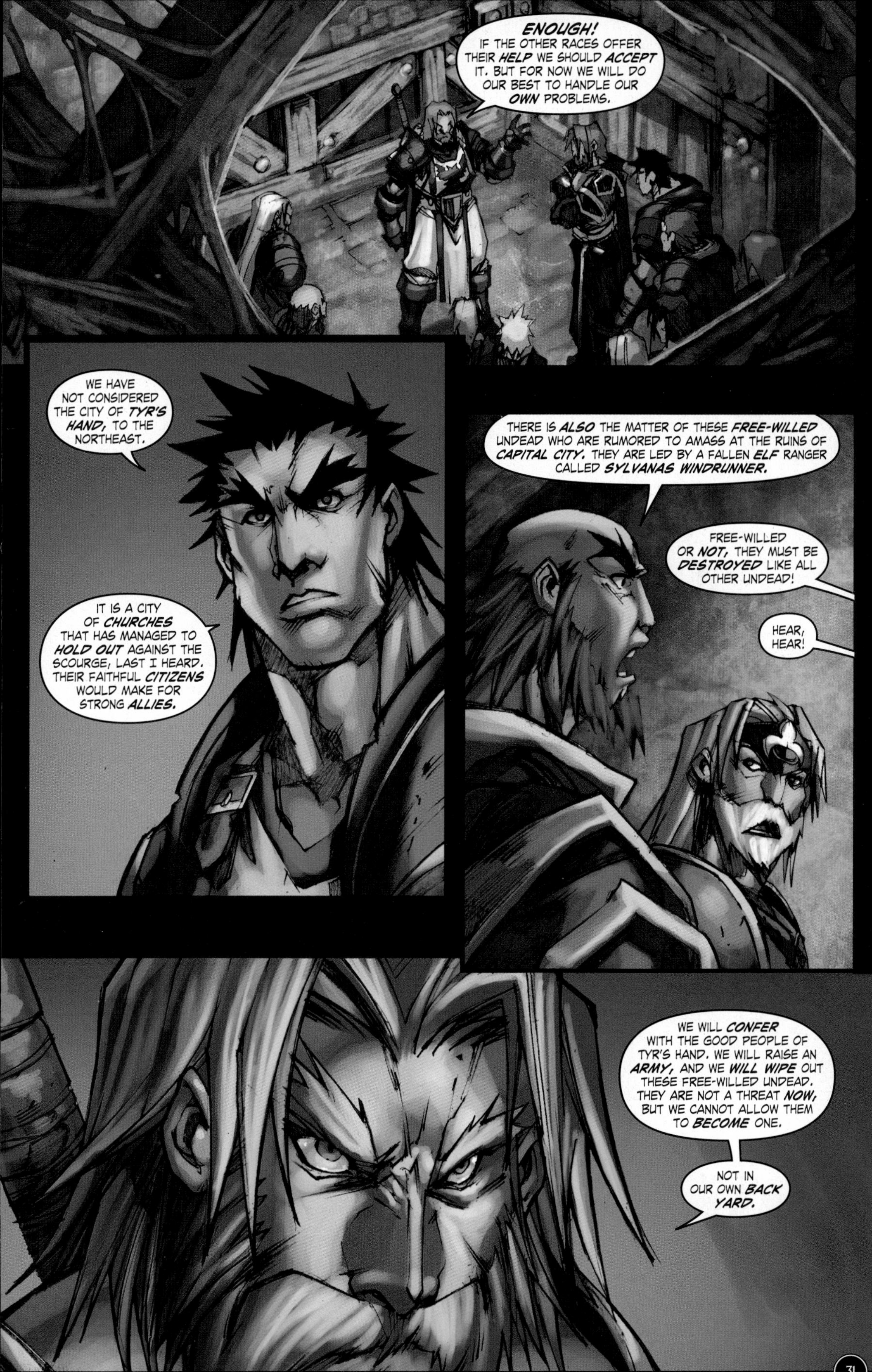
ENOUGH! IF THE OTHER RACES OFFER THEIR HELP WE SHOULD ACCEPT IT. BUT FOR NOW WE WILL DO OUR BEST TO HANDLE OUR OWN PROBLEMS.
WE HAVE NOT CONSIDERED THE CITY OF TYR'S HAND, TO THE NORTHEAST.
IT IS A CITY OF CHURCHES THAT HAS MANAGED TO HOLD OUT AGAINST THE SCOURGE, LAST I HEARD. THEIR FAITHFUL CITIZENS WOULD MAKE FOR STRONG ALLIES.
THERE IS ALSO THE MATTER OF THESE FREE-WILLED UNDEAD WHO ARE RUMORED TO AMASS AT THE RUINS OF CAPITAL CITY. THEY ARE LED BY A FALLEN ELF RANGER CALLED SYLVANAS WINDRUNNER.
FREE-WILLED OR NOT, THEY MUST BE DESTROYED LIKE ALL OTHER UNDEAD!
HEAR, HEAR!
WE WILL CONFER WITH THE GOOD PEOPLE OF TYR'S HAND. WE WILL RAISE AN ARMY, AND WE WILL WIPE OUT THESE FREE-WILLED UNDEAD. THEY ARE NOT A THREAT NOW, BUT WE CANNOT ALLOW THEM TO BECOME ONE.
NOT IN OUR OWN BACK YARD.

CHAPTER 2

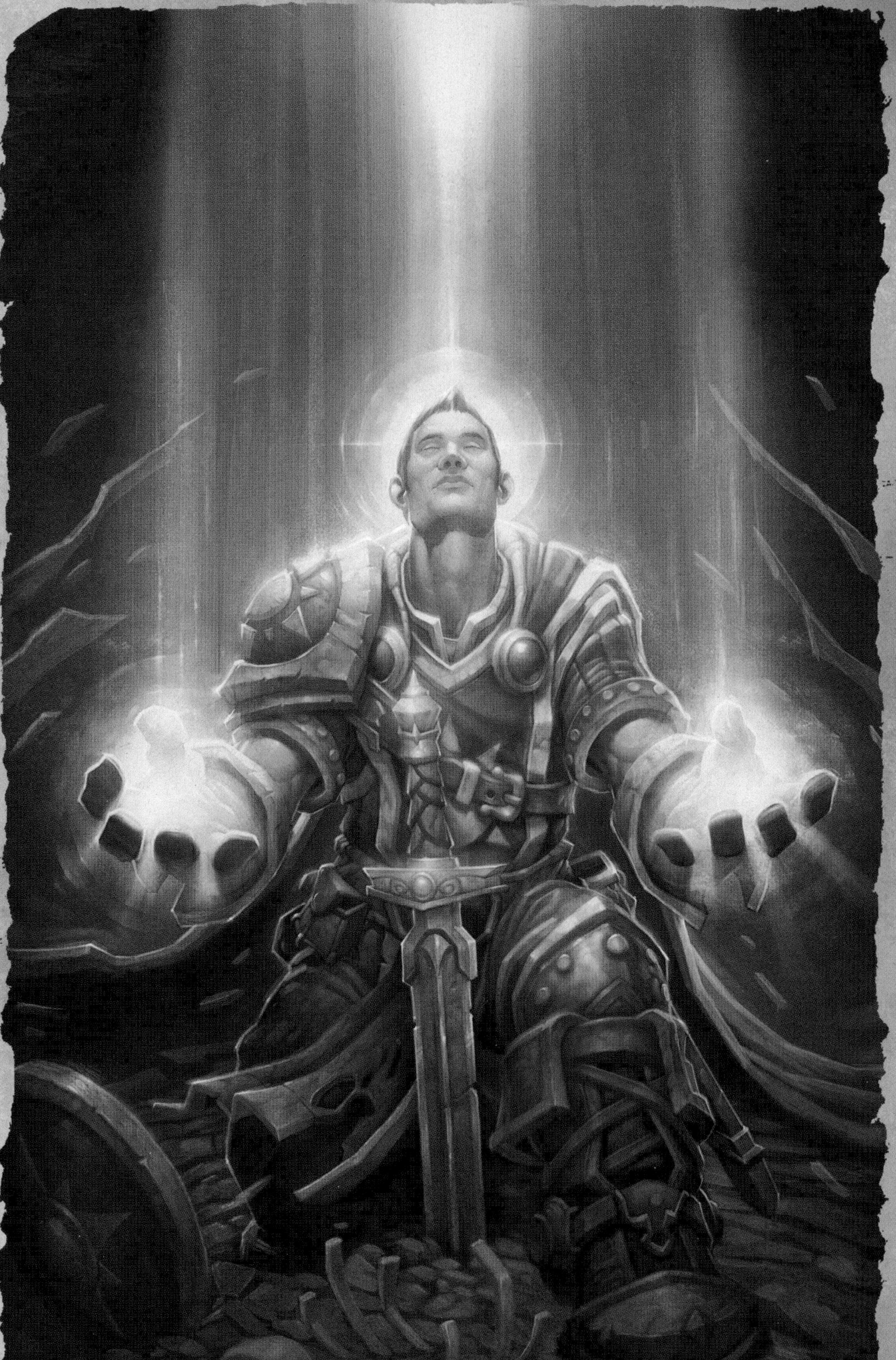

Cover by Chris Robinson

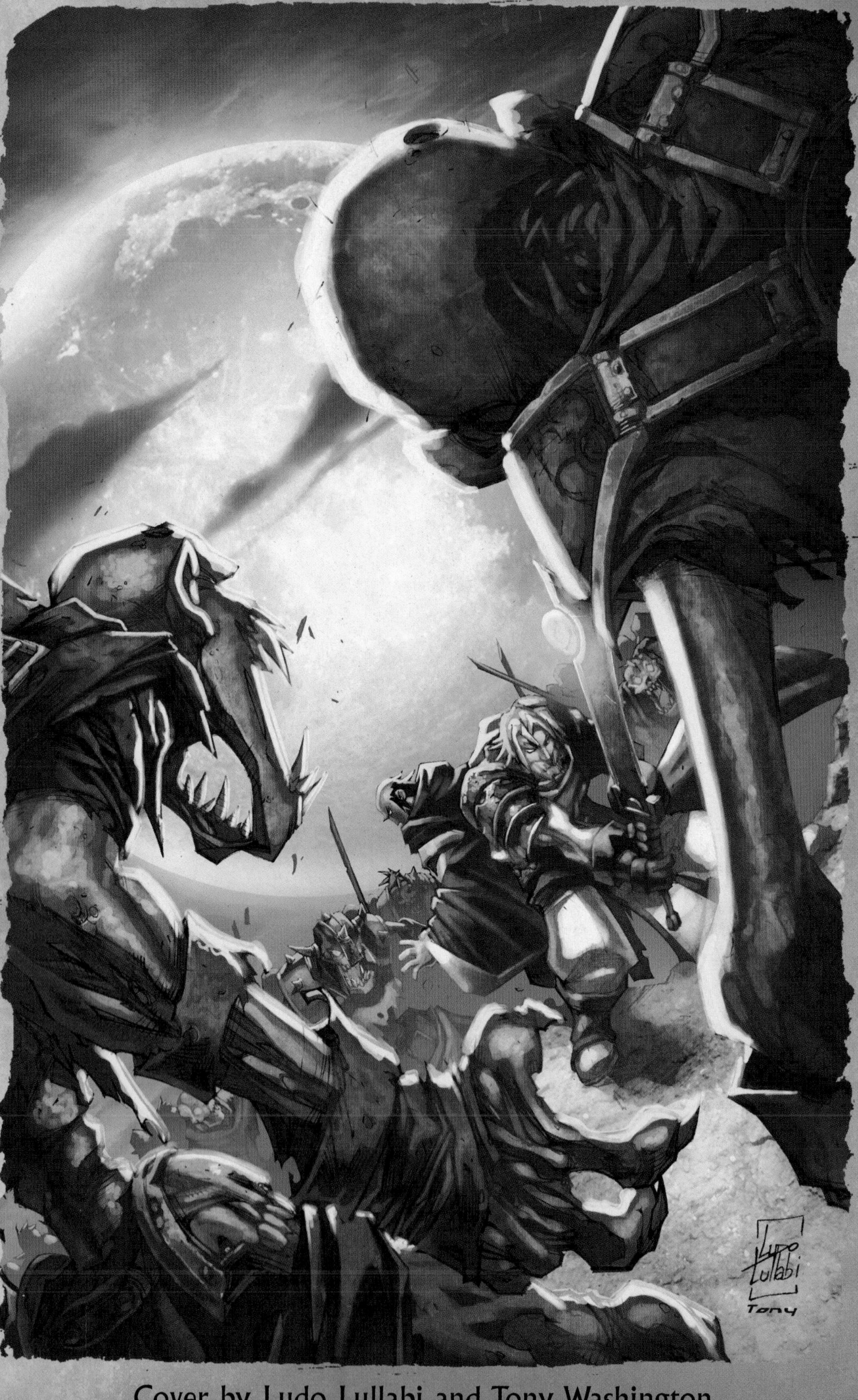
Ludo
Lullabi
Tony

Cover by Ludo Lullabi and Tony Washington

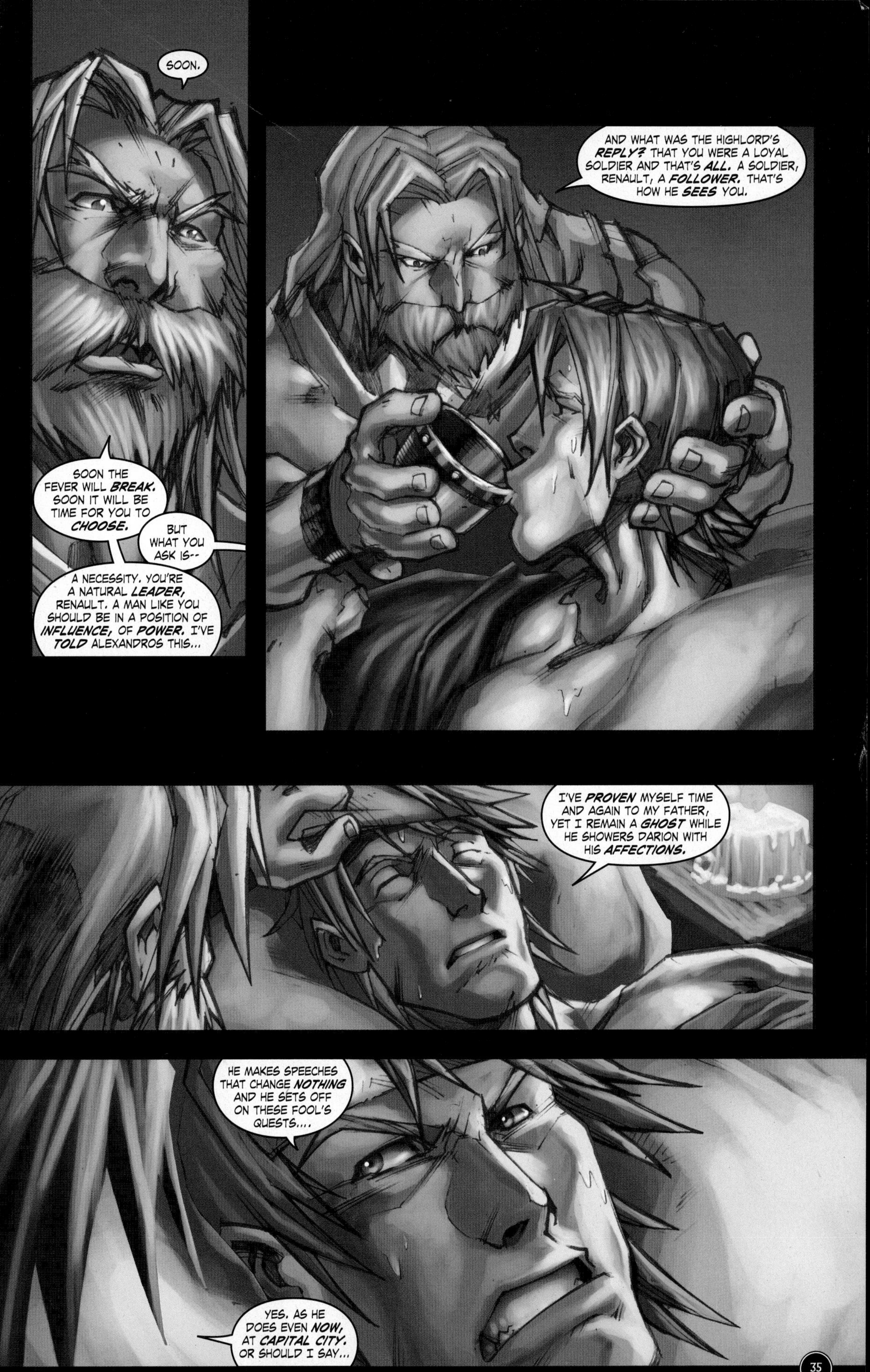
SOON.
SOON THE FEVER WILL BREAK. SOON IT WILL BE TIME FOR YOU TO CHOOSE.
BUT WHAT YOU ASK IS--
A NECESSITY. YOU'RE A NATURAL LEADER, RENAULT. A MAN LIKE YOU SHOULD BE IN A POSITION OF INFLUENCE, OF POWER. I'VE TOLD ALEXANDROS THIS...
AND WHAT WAS THE HIGHLORD'S REPLY? THAT YOU WERE A LOYAL SOLDIER AND THAT'S ALL. A SOLDIER, RENAULT, A FOLLOWER. THAT'S HOW HE SEES YOU.
I'VE PROVEN MYSELF TIME AND AGAIN TO MY FATHER, YET I REMAIN A GHOST WHILE HE SHOWERS DARION WITH HIS AFFECTIONS.
HE MAKES SPEECHES THAT CHANGE NOTHING AND HE SETS OFF ON THESE FOOL'S QUESTS....
YES. AS HE DOES EVEN NOW, AT CAPITAL CITY. OR SHOULD I SAY...

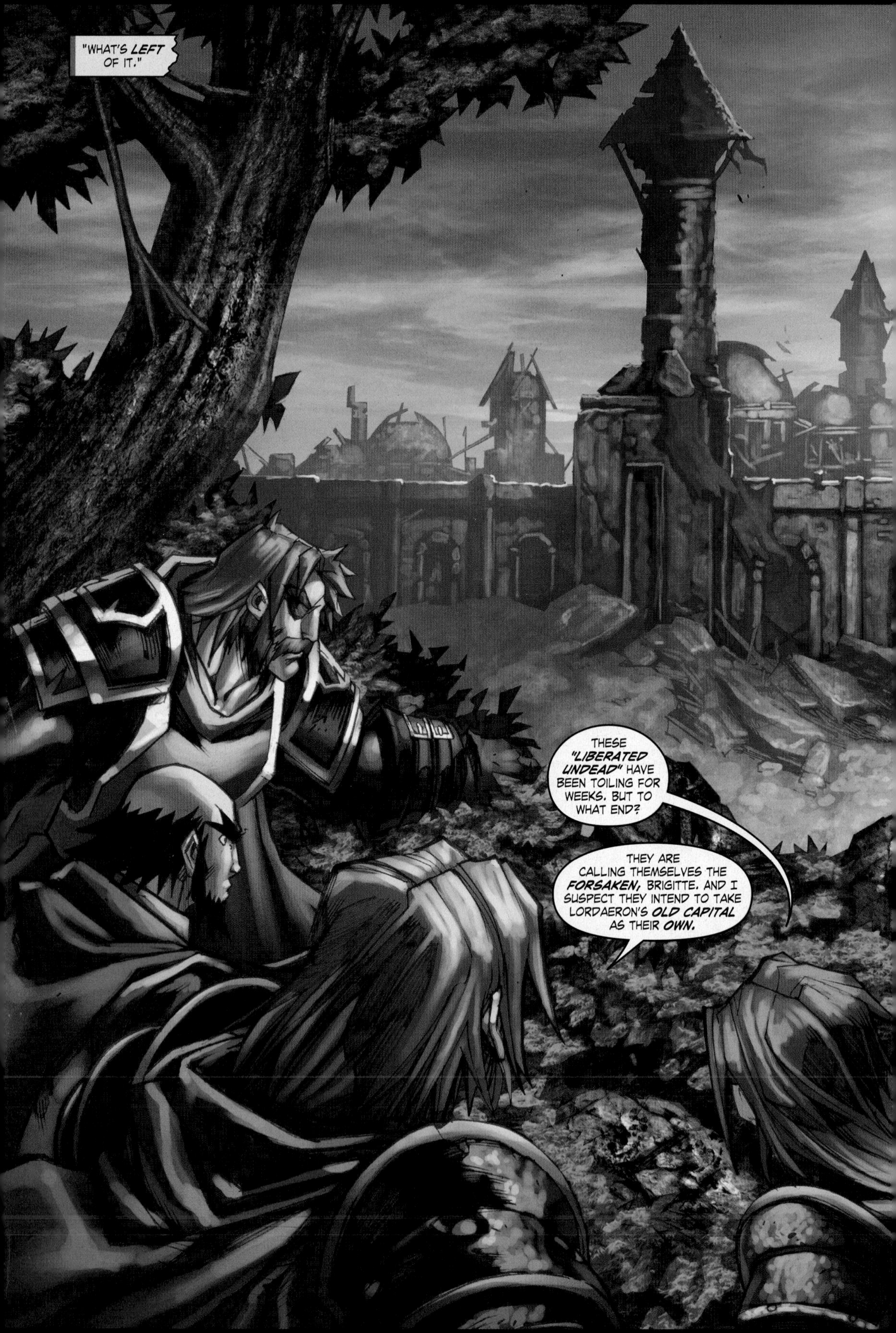
"WHAT'S LEFT OF IT."
THESE "LIBERATED UNDEAD" HAVE BEEN TOILING FOR WEEKS. BUT TO WHAT END?
THEY ARE CALLING THEMSELVES THE FORSAKEN, BRIGITTE. AND I SUSPECT THEY INTEND TO TAKE LORDAERON'S OLD CAPITAL AS THEIR OWN.

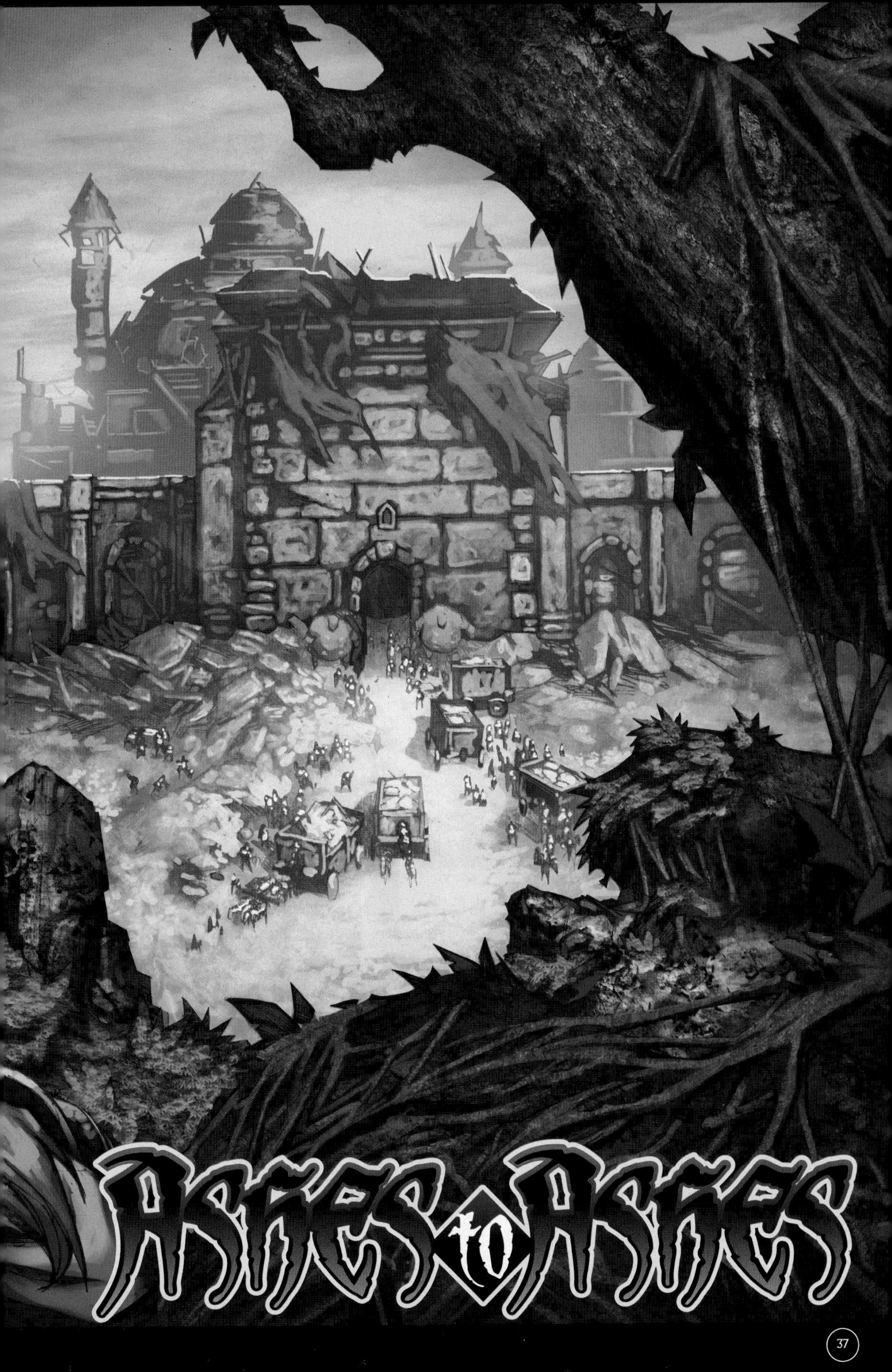
ASHES to ASHES

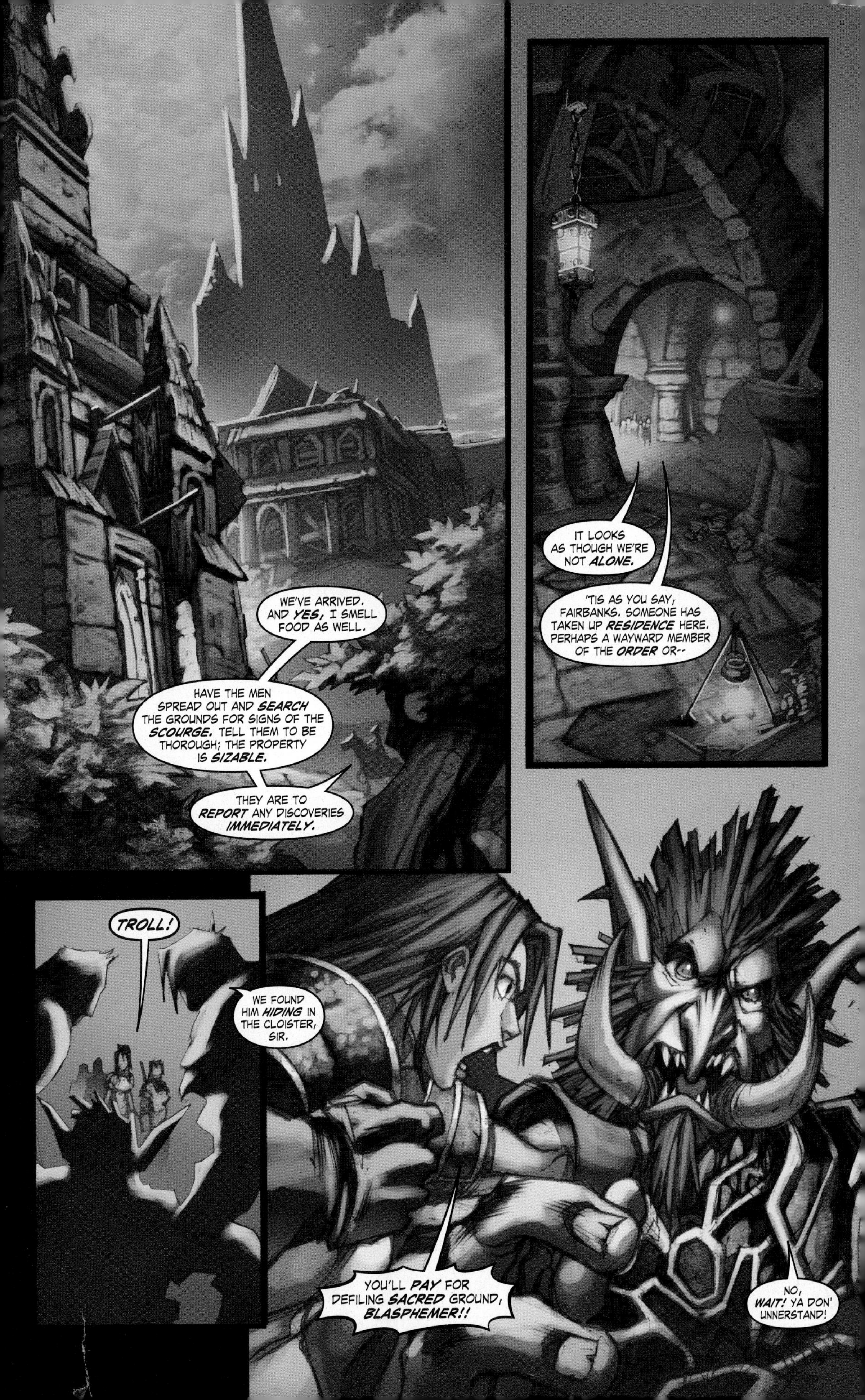

WE'VE ARRIVED. AND YES, I SMELL FOOD AS WELL.
HAVE THE MEN SPREAD OUT AND SEARCH THE GROUNDS FOR SIGNS OF THE SCOURGE. TELL THEM TO BE THOROUGH; THE PROPERTY IS SIZABLE.
THEY ARE TO REPORT ANY DISCOVERIES IMMEDIATELY.
IT LOOKS AS THOUGH WE'RE NOT ALONE.
'TIS AS YOU SAY, FAIRBANKS. SOMEONE HAS TAKEN UP RESIDENCE HERE. PERHAPS A WAYWARD MEMBER OF THE ORDER OR--
TROLL!
WE FOUND HIM HIDING IN THE CLOISTER, SIR.
YOU'LL PAY FOR DEFILING SACRED GROUND, BLASPHEMER!!
NO, WAIT! YA DON' UNNERSTAND!

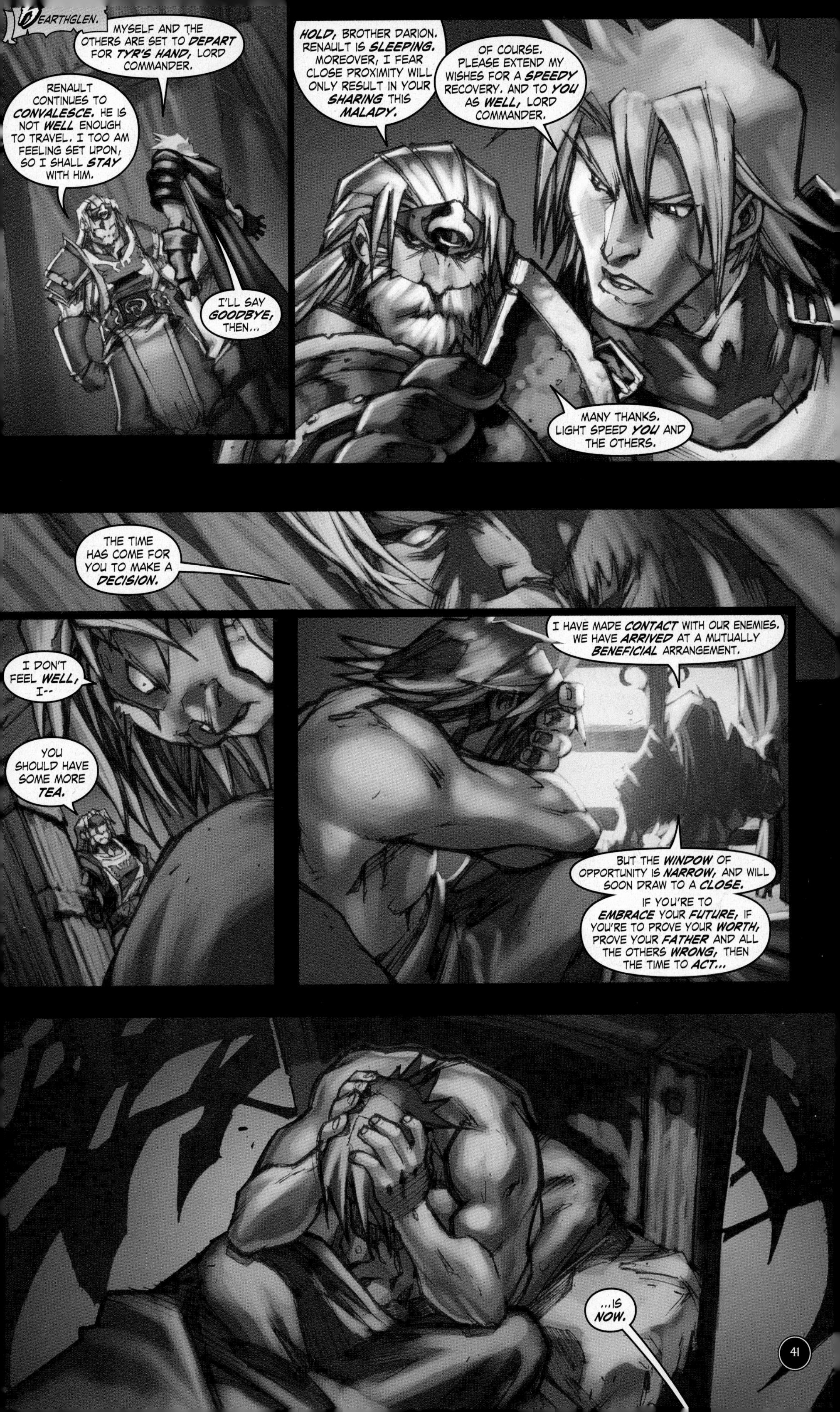
HEARTHGLEN.
MYSELF AND THE OTHERS ARE SET TO DEPART FOR TYR'S HAND, LORD COMMANDER.
RENAULT CONTINUES TO CONVALESCE. HE IS NOT WELL ENOUGH TO TRAVEL. I TOO AM FEELING SET UPON, SO I SHALL STAY WITH HIM.
I'LL SAY GOODBYE, THEN...
HOLD, BROTHER DARION. RENAULT IS SLEEPING. MOREOVER, I FEAR CLOSE PROXIMITY WILL ONLY RESULT IN YOUR SHARING THIS MALADY.
OF COURSE. PLEASE EXTEND MY WISHES FOR A SPEEDY RECOVERY. AND TO YOU AS WELL, LORD COMMANDER.
MANY THANKS. LIGHT SPEED YOU AND THE OTHERS.
THE TIME HAS COME FOR YOU TO MAKE A DECISION.
I DON'T FEEL WELL, I--
YOU SHOULD HAVE SOME MORE TEA.
I HAVE MADE CONTACT WITH OUR ENEMIES. WE HAVE ARRIVED AT A MUTUALLY BENEFICIAL ARRANGEMENT.
BUT THE WINDOW OF OPPORTUNITY IS NARROW, AND WILL SOON DRAW TO A CLOSE.
IF YOU'RE TO EMBRACE YOUR FUTURE, IF YOU'RE TO PROVE YOUR WORTH, PROVE YOUR FATHER AND ALL THE OTHERS WRONG, THEN THE TIME TO ACT...
...IS NOW.

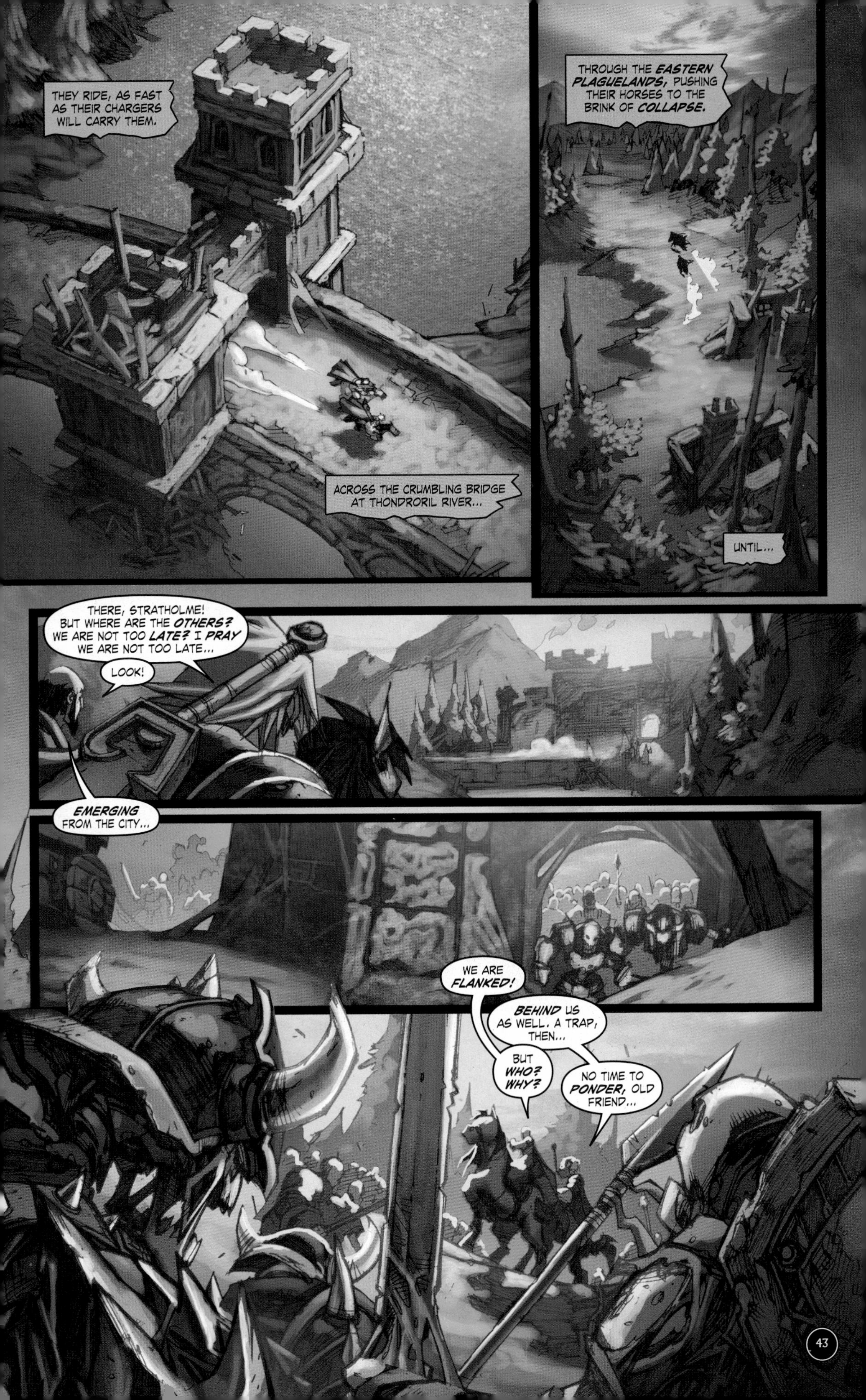

THEY RIDE, AS FAST AS THEIR CHARGERS WILL CARRY THEM.
ACROSS THE CRUMBLING BRIDGE AT THONDRORIL RIVER...
THROUGH THE EASTERN PLAGUELANDS, PUSHING THEIR HORSES TO THE BRINK OF COLLAPSE.
UNTIL...
THERE, STRATHOLME! BUT WHERE ARE THE OTHERS? WE ARE NOT TOO LATE? I PRAY WE ARE NOT TOO LATE...
LOOK!
EMERGING FROM THE CITY...
WE ARE FLANKED!
BEHIND US AS WELL. A TRAP, THEN...
BUT WHO? WHY?
NO TIME TO PONDER, OLD FRIEND...

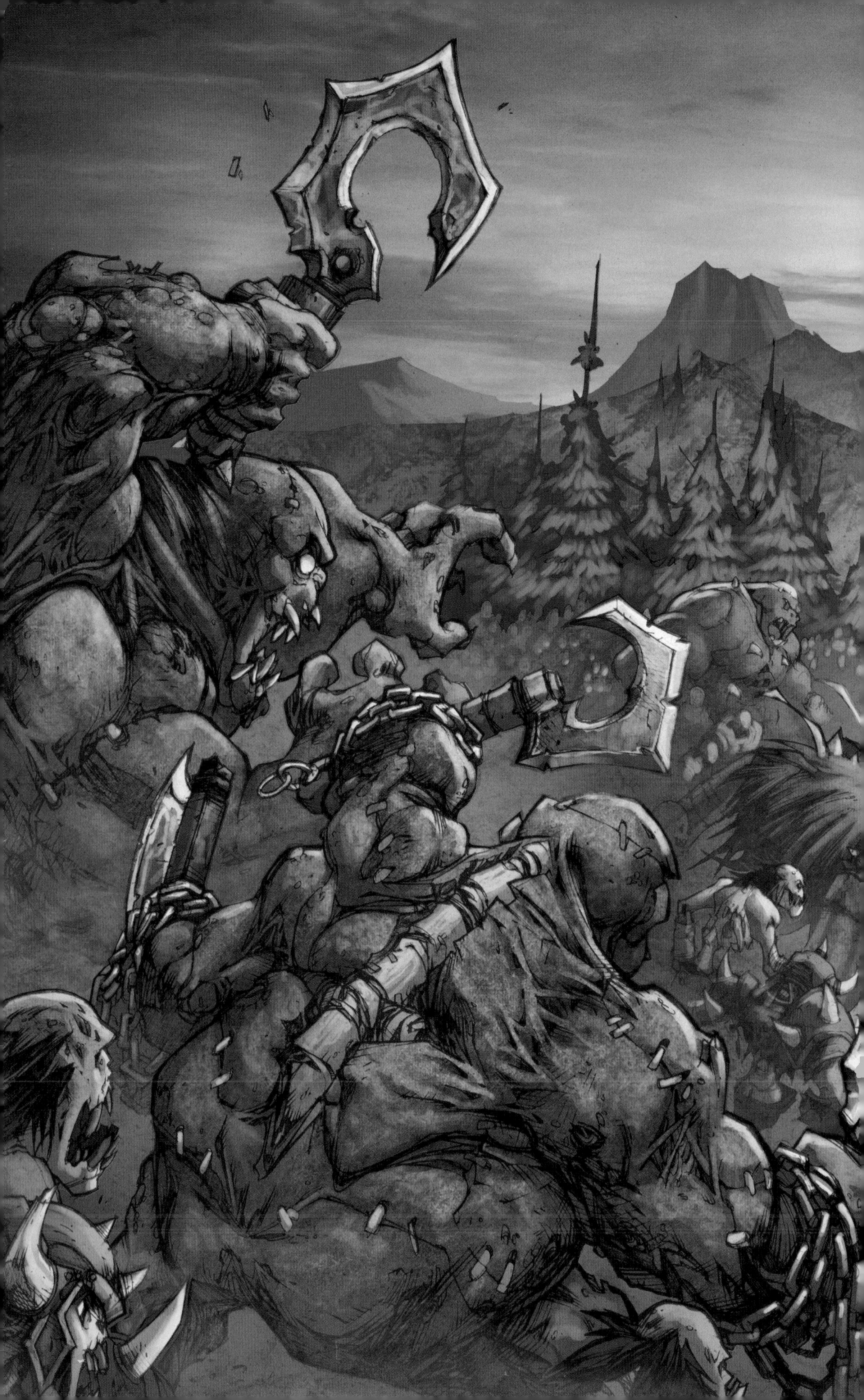

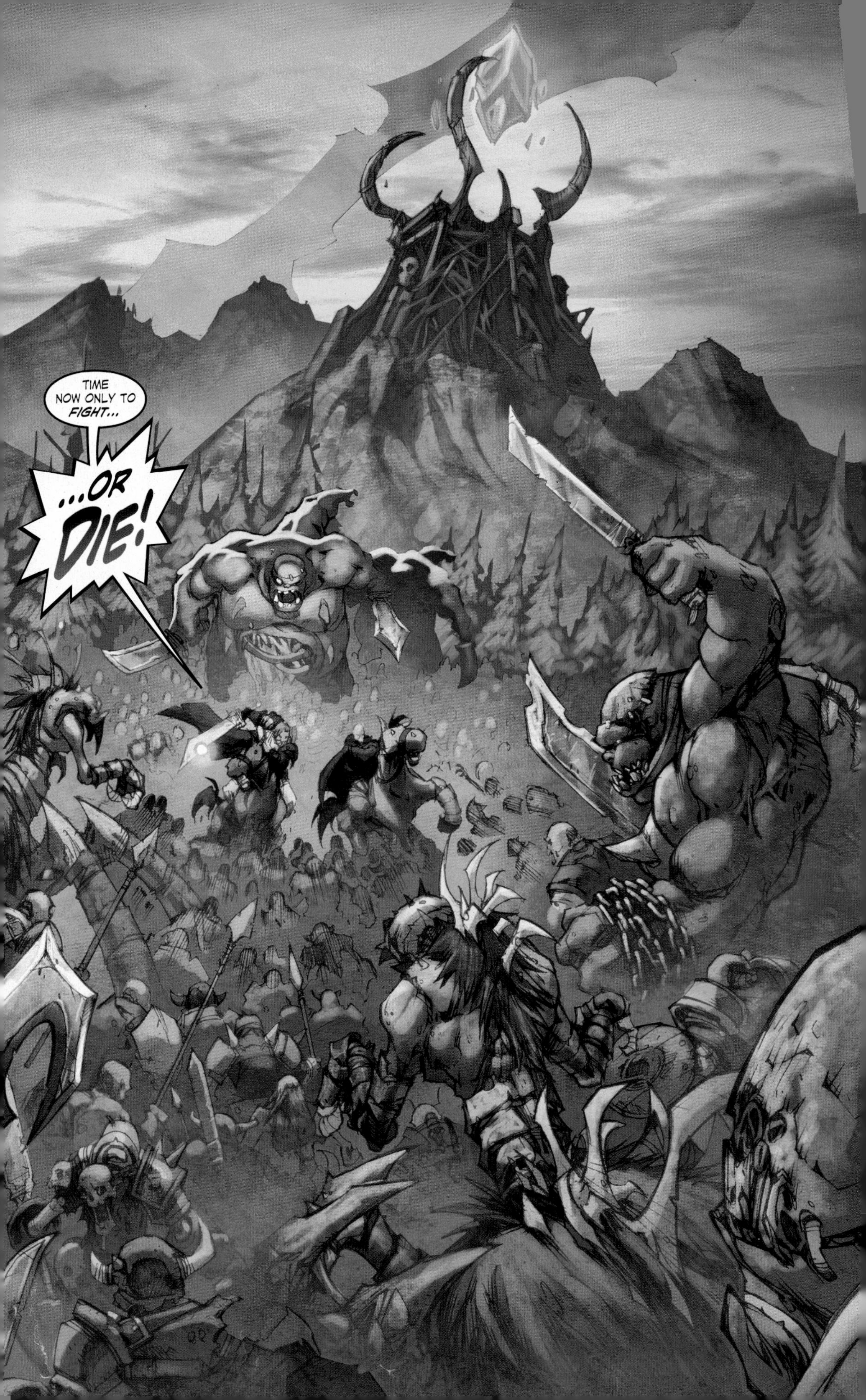
TIME NOW ONLY TO *FIGHT*...
...OR DIE!

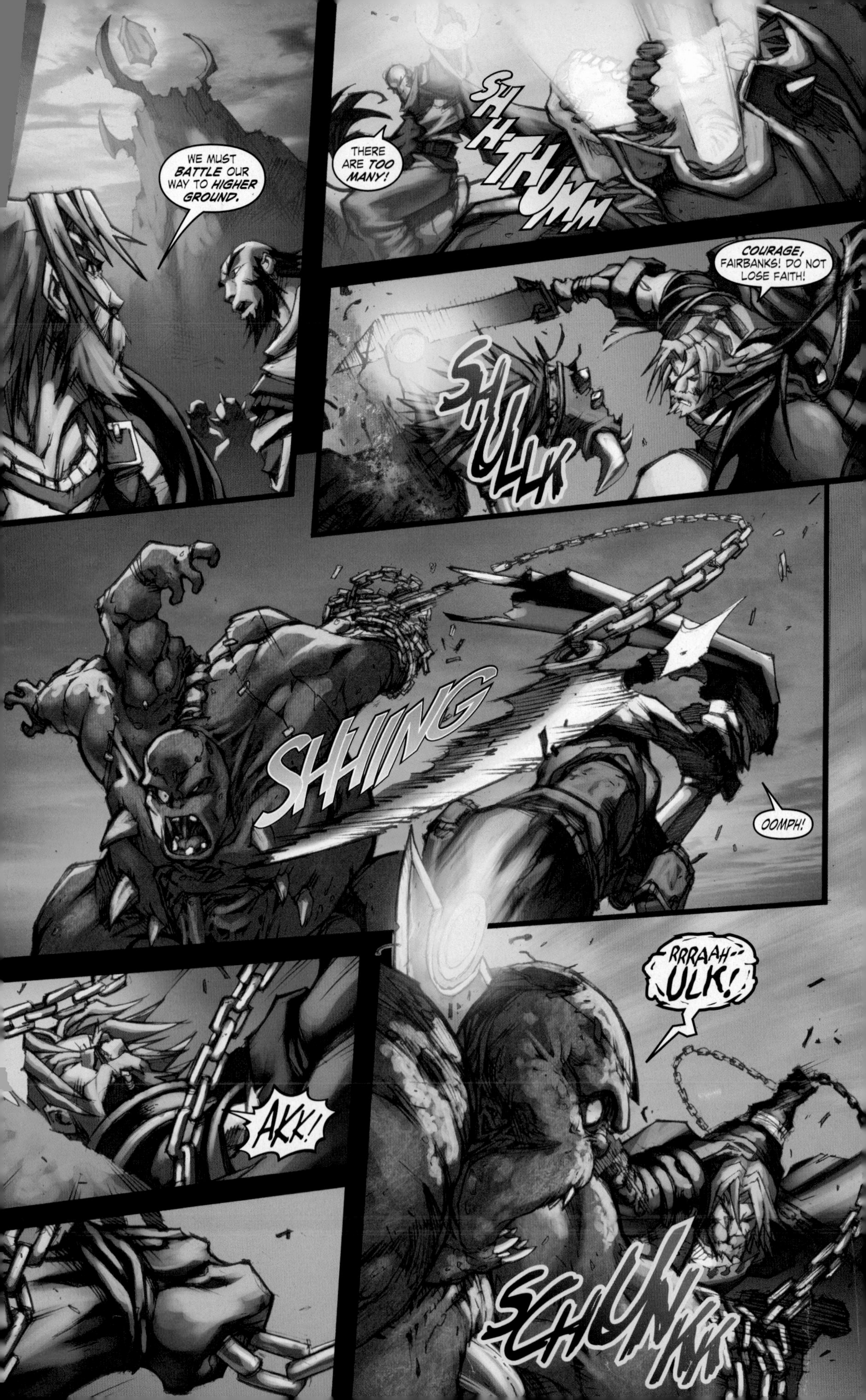
WE MUST BATTLE OUR WAY TO HIGHER GROUND.
THERE ARE TOO MANY!
SHHTHUMM
COURAGE, FAIRBANKS! DO NOT LOSE FAITH!
SHULK
SHING
OOMPH!
RRRAAH--ULK!
AKK!
SCHUNK

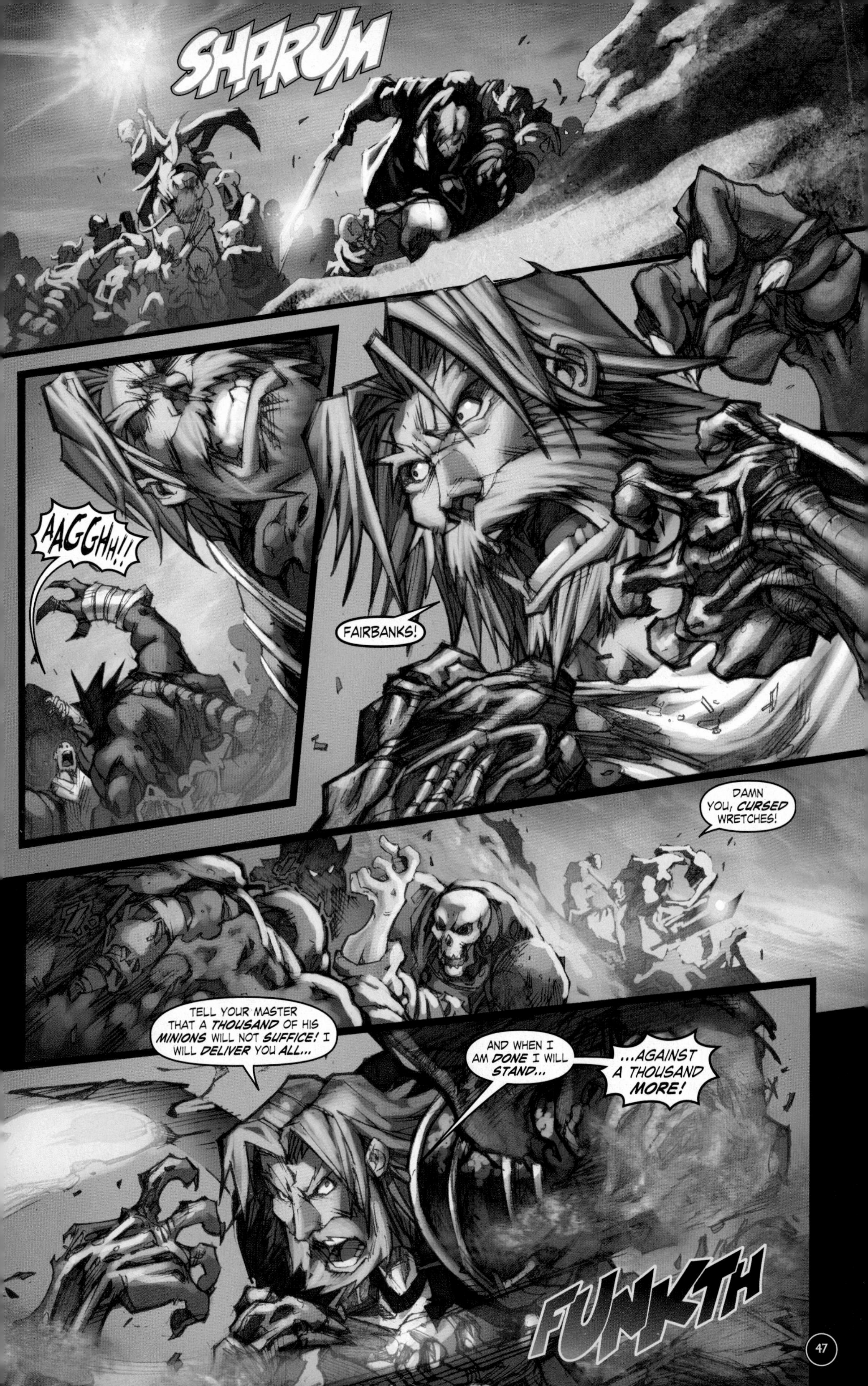

SHARUM
AAGGHH!!
FAIRBANKS!
DAMN YOU, CURSED WRETCHES!
TELL YOUR MASTER THAT A THOUSAND OF HIS MINIONS WILL NOT SUFFICE! I WILL DELIVER YOU ALL...
AND WHEN I AM DONE I WILL STAND...
...AGAINST A THOUSAND MORE!
FUNKTH

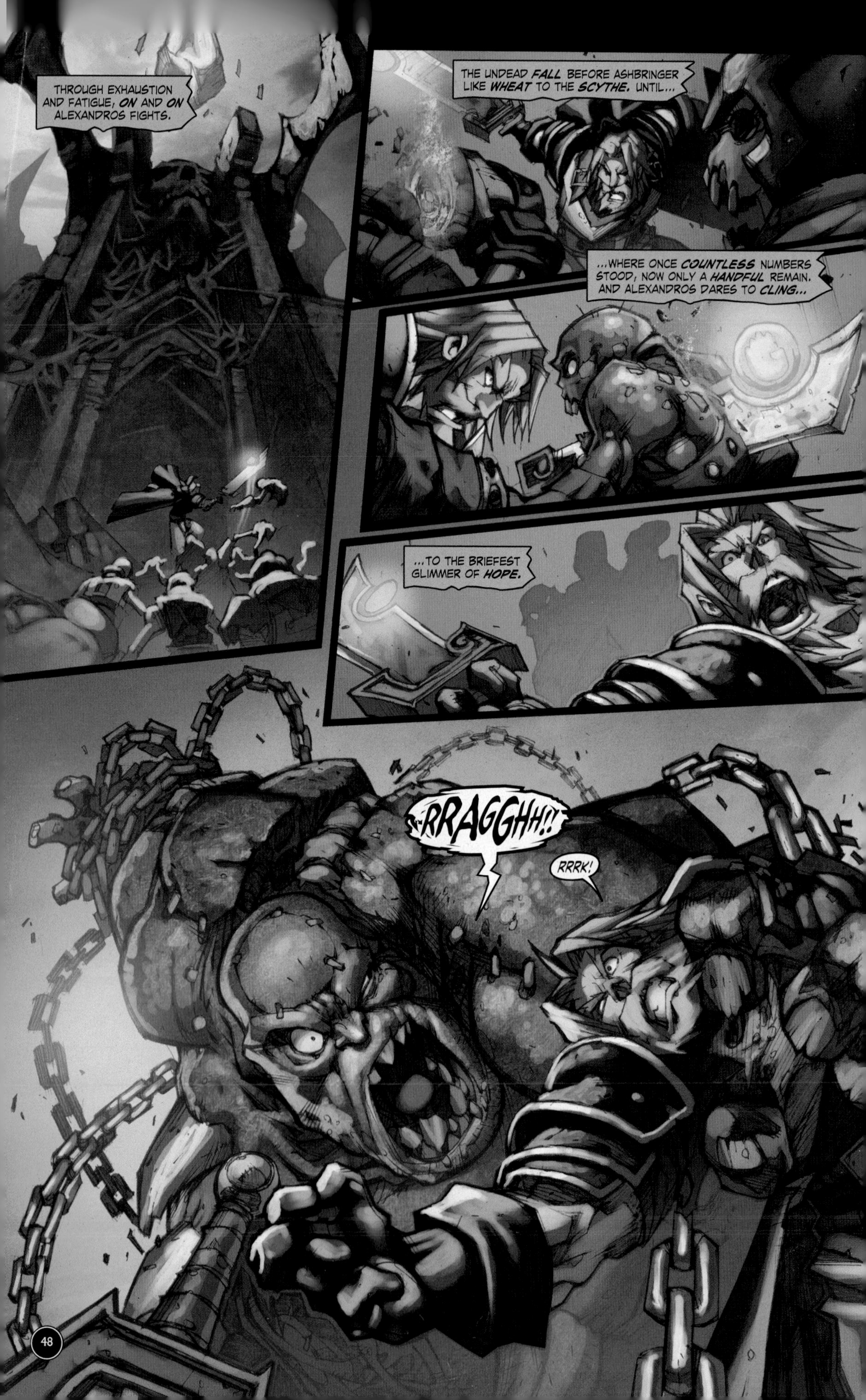
THROUGH EXHAUSTION AND FATIGUE, ON AND ON ALEXANDROS FIGHTS.
THE UNDEAD FALL BEFORE ASHBRINGER LIKE WHEAT TO THE SCYTHE. UNTIL...
...WHERE ONCE COUNTLESS NUMBERS STOOD, NOW ONLY A HANDFUL REMAIN. AND ALEXANDROS DARES TO CLING...
...TO THE BRIEFEST GLIMMER OF HOPE.
RRAGGHH!!
RRRK!

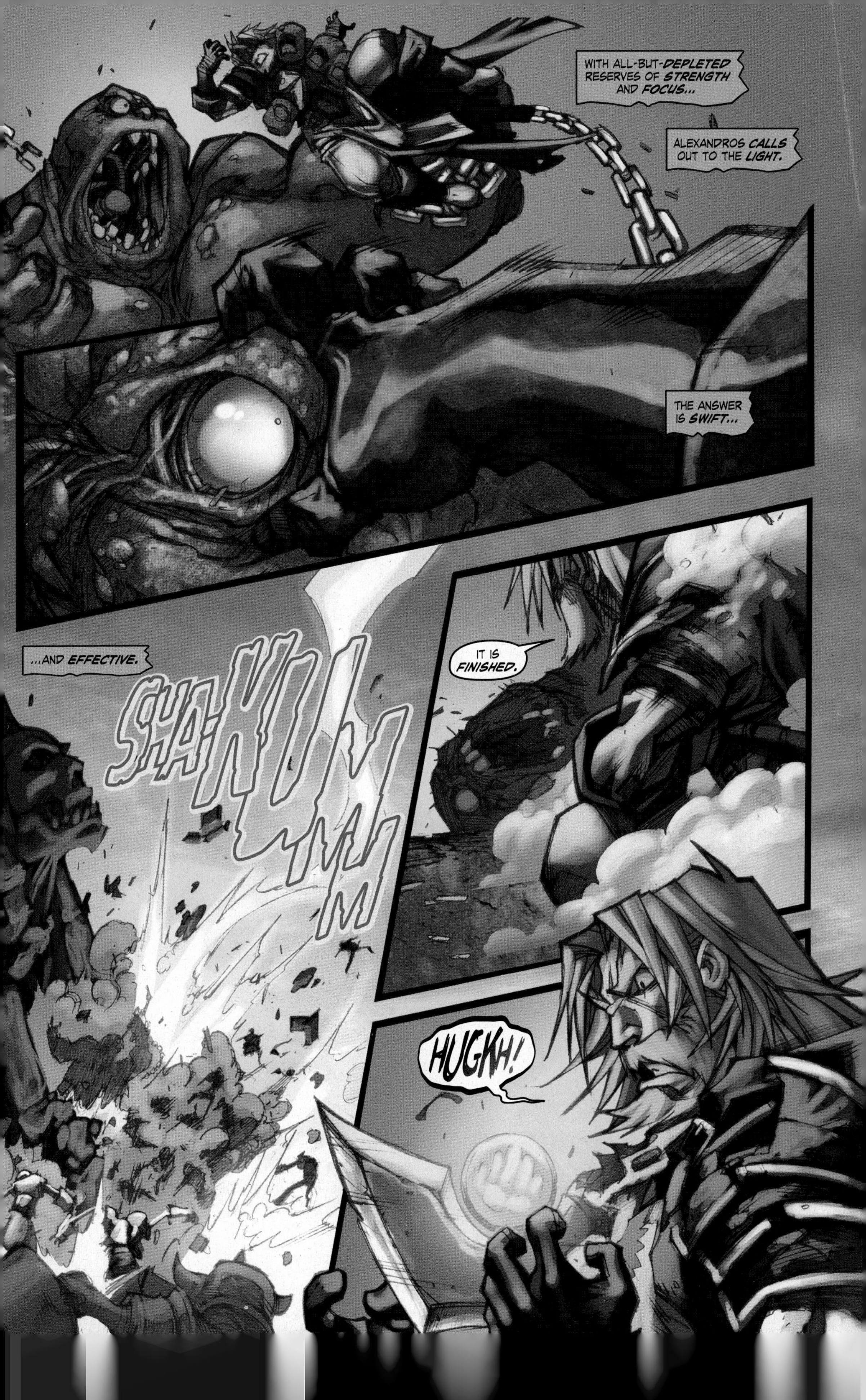

WITH ALL-BUT-DEPLETED RESERVES OF STRENGTH AND FOCUS...
ALEXANDROS CALLS OUT TO THE LIGHT.
THE ANSWER IS SWIFT...
...AND EFFECTIVE.
SHA-KOOMMM
IT IS FINISHED.
HUGKH!

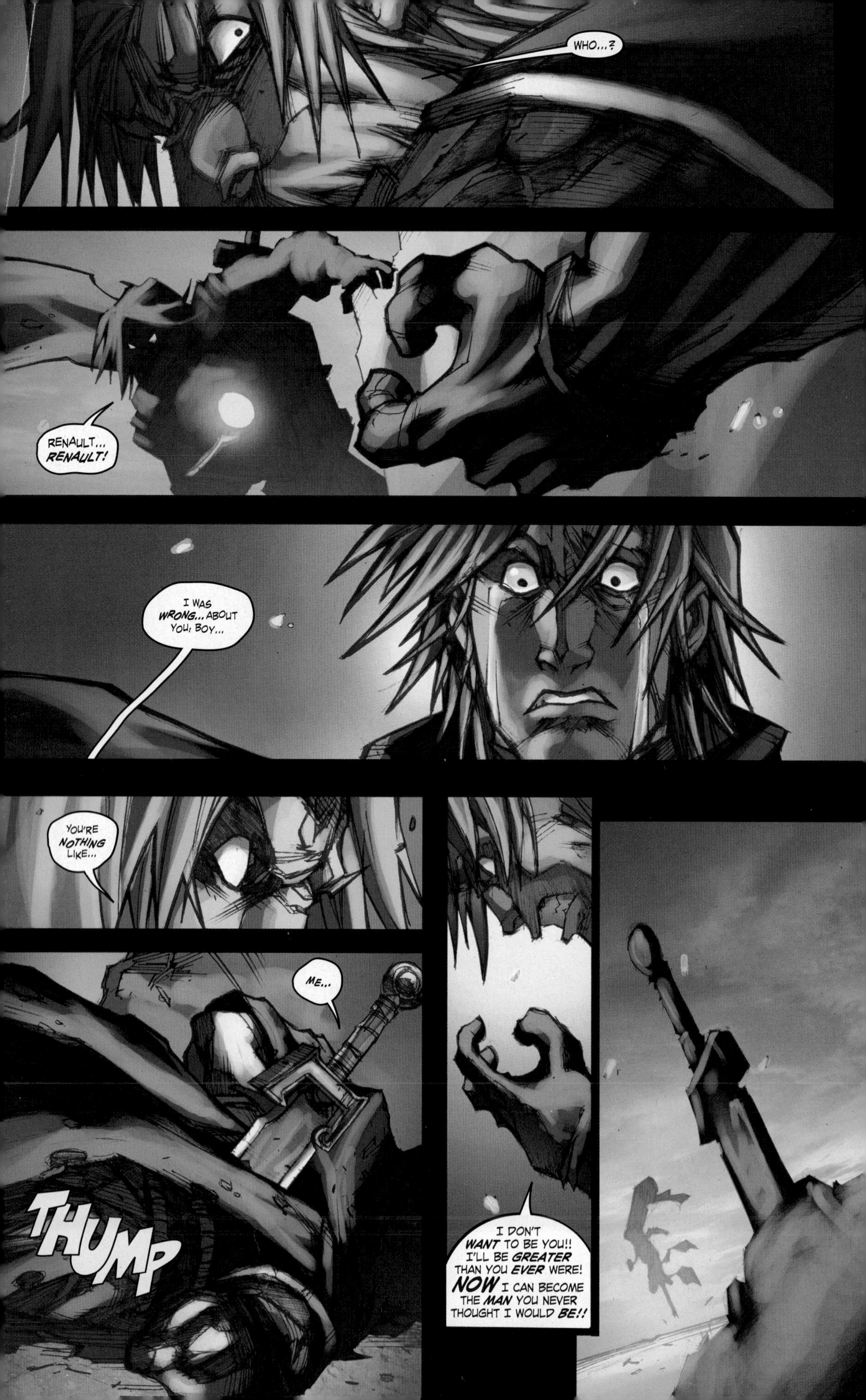
WHO...?
RENAULT... RENAULT!
I WAS WRONG... ABOUT YOU, BOY...
YOU'RE NOTHING LIKE...
ME...
THUMP
I DON'T WANT TO BE YOU!! I'LL BE GREATER THAN YOU EVER WERE! NOW I CAN BECOME THE MAN YOU NEVER THOUGHT I WOULD BE!!

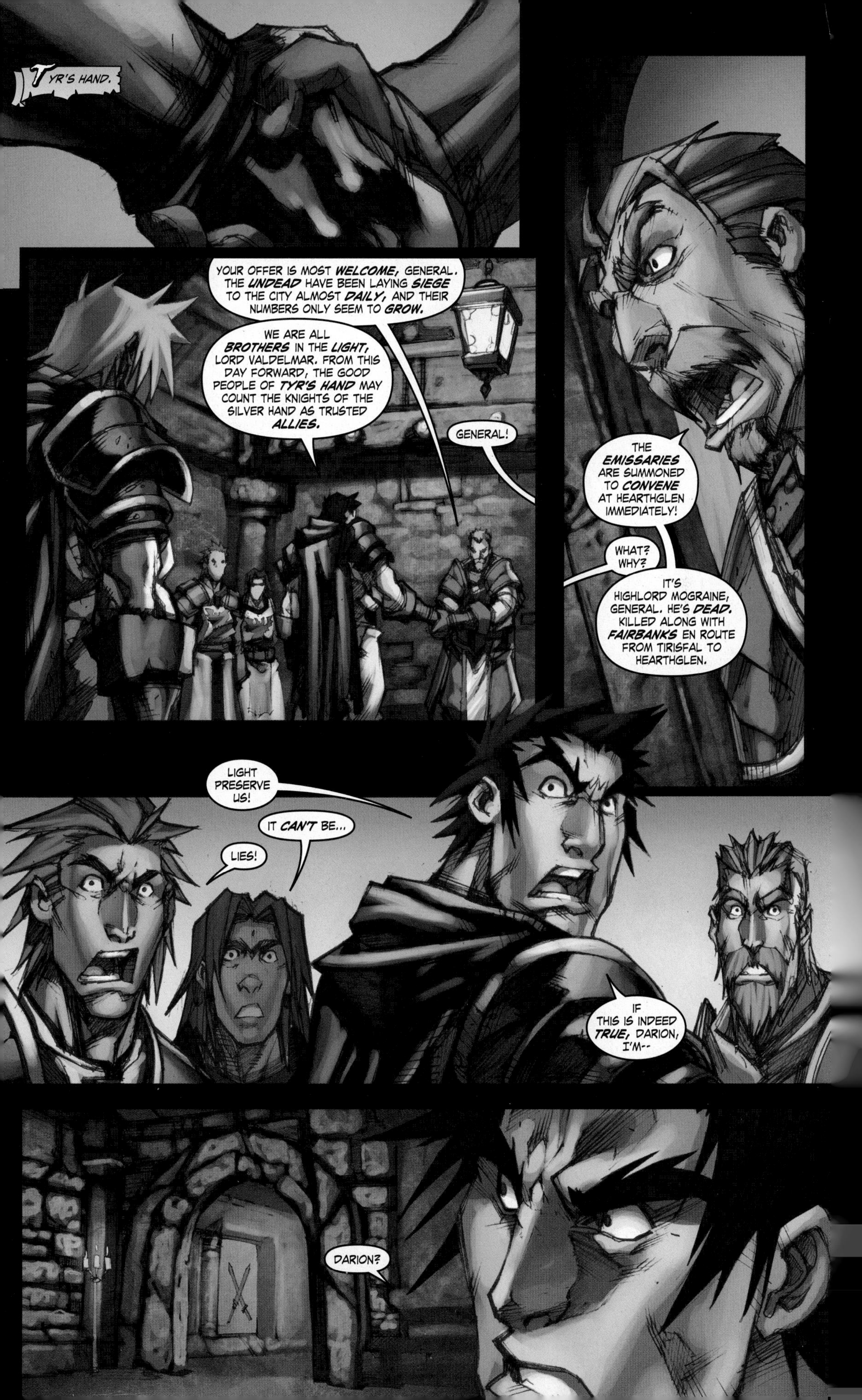
TYR'S HAND.
YOUR OFFER IS MOST WELCOME, GENERAL. THE UNDEAD HAVE BEEN LAYING SIEGE TO THE CITY ALMOST DAILY, AND THEIR NUMBERS ONLY SEEM TO GROW.
WE ARE ALL BROTHERS IN THE LIGHT, LORD VALDELMAR. FROM THIS DAY FORWARD, THE GOOD PEOPLE OF TYR'S HAND MAY COUNT THE KNIGHTS OF THE SILVER HAND AS TRUSTED ALLIES.
GENERAL!
THE EMISSARIES ARE SUMMONED TO CONVENE AT HEARTHGLEN IMMEDIATELY!
WHAT? WHY?
IT'S HIGHLORD MOGRAINE, GENERAL. HE'S DEAD. KILLED ALONG WITH FAIRBANKS EN ROUTE FROM TIRISFAL TO HEARTHGLEN.
LIGHT PRESERVE US!
IT CAN'T BE...
LIES!
IF THIS IS INDEED TRUE, DARION, I'M--
DARION?

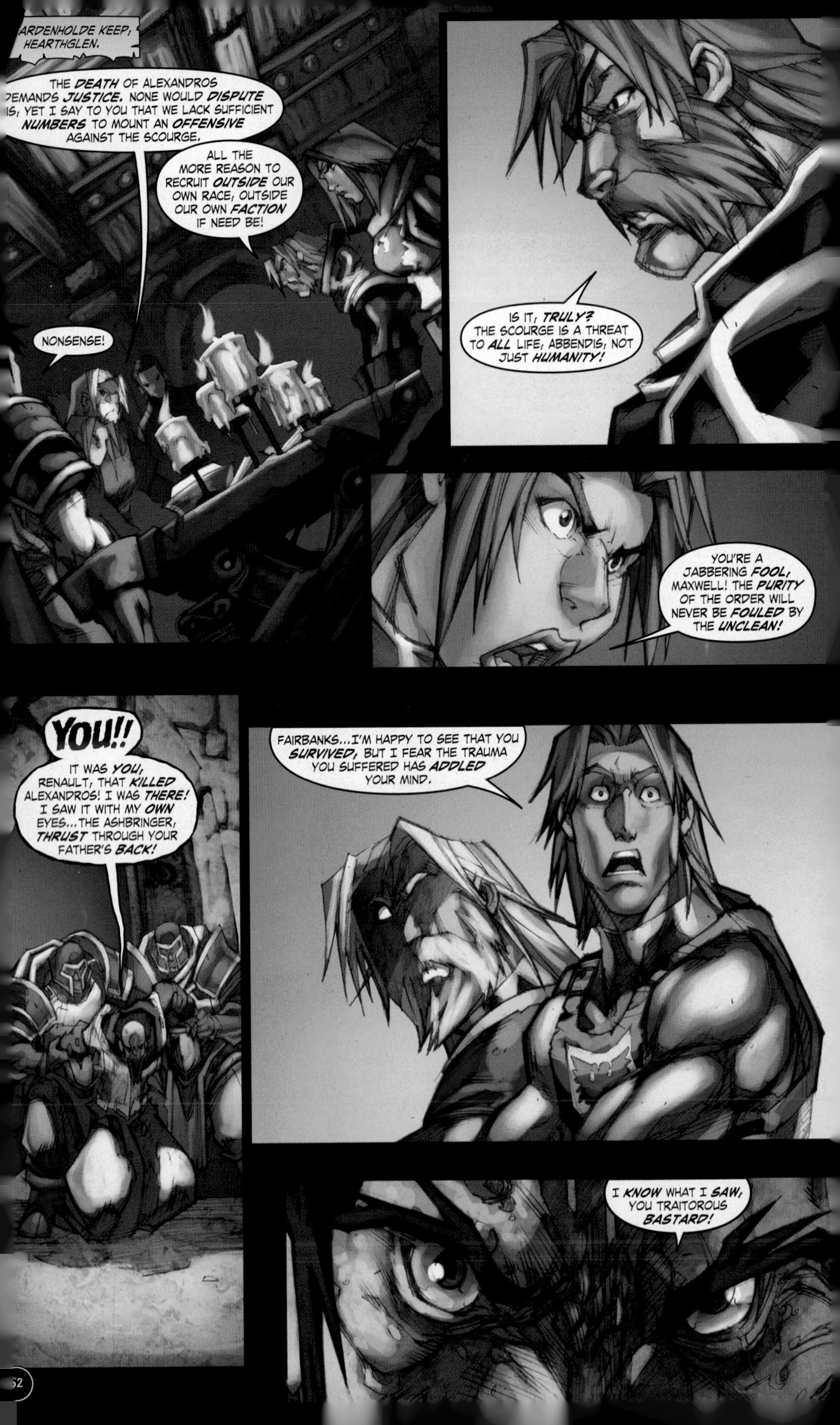
ARDENHOLDE KEEP, HEARTHGLEN.
THE DEATH OF ALEXANDROS DEMANDS JUSTICE. NONE WOULD DISPUTE THIS, YET I SAY TO YOU THAT WE LACK SUFFICIENT NUMBERS TO MOUNT AN OFFENSIVE AGAINST THE SCOURGE.
ALL THE MORE REASON TO RECRUIT OUTSIDE OUR OWN RACE, OUTSIDE OUR OWN FACTION IF NEED BE!
NONSENSE!
IS IT, TRULY? THE SCOURGE IS A THREAT TO ALL LIFE, ABBENDIS, NOT JUST HUMANITY!
YOU'RE A JABBERING FOOL, MAXWELL! THE PURITY OF THE ORDER WILL NEVER BE FOULED BY THE UNCLEAN!
YOU!!
IT WAS YOU, RENAULT, THAT KILLED ALEXANDROS! I WAS THERE! I SAW IT WITH MY OWN EYES...THE ASHBRINGER, THRUST THROUGH YOUR FATHER'S BACK!
FAIRBANKS...I'M HAPPY TO SEE THAT YOU SURVIVED, BUT I FEAR THE TRAUMA YOU SUFFERED HAS ADDLED YOUR MIND.
I KNOW WHAT I SAW, YOU TRAITOROUS BASTARD!

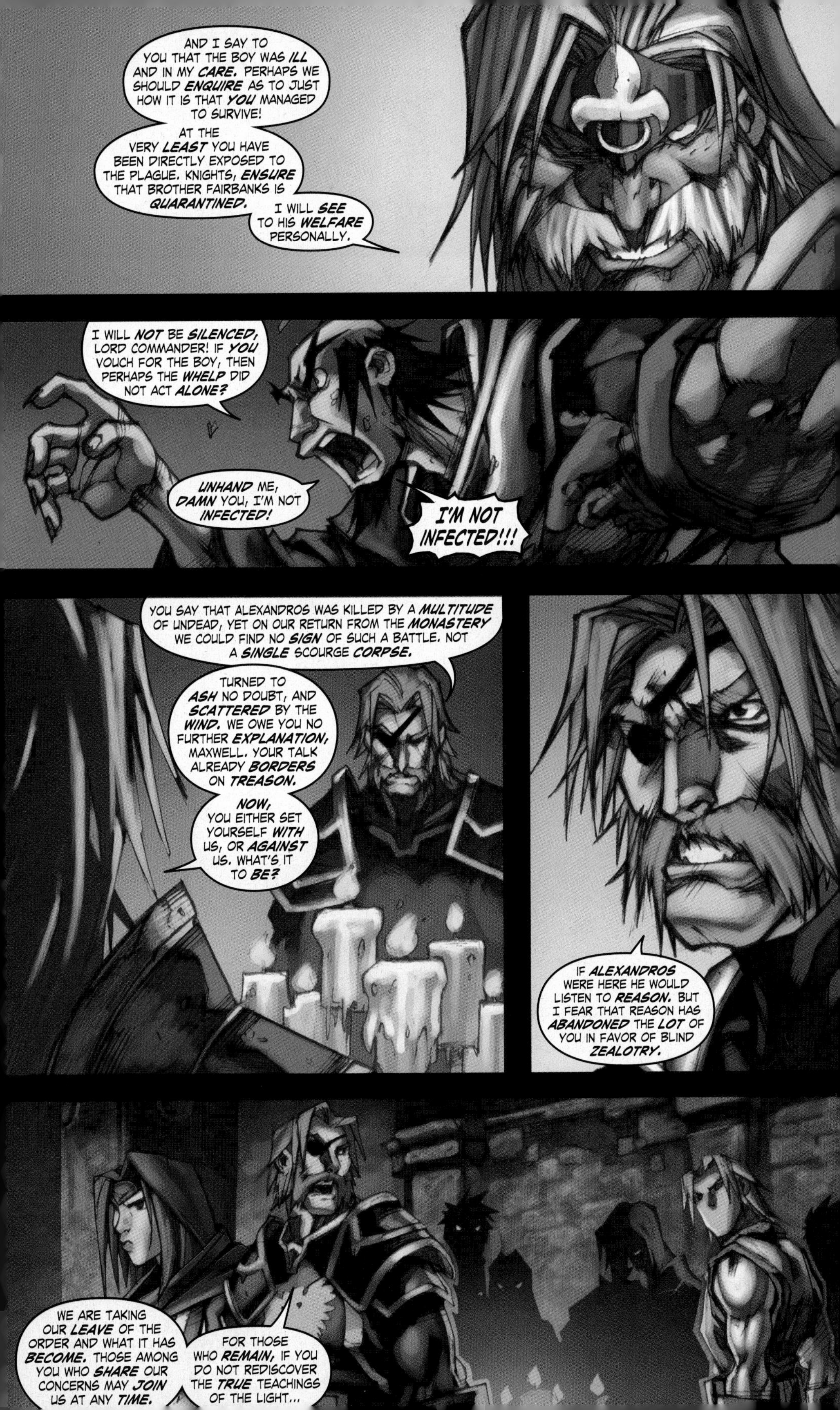
AND I SAY TO YOU THAT THE BOY WAS ILL AND IN MY CARE. PERHAPS WE SHOULD ENQUIRE AS TO JUST HOW IT IS THAT YOU MANAGED TO SURVIVE!
AT THE VERY LEAST YOU HAVE BEEN DIRECTLY EXPOSED TO THE PLAGUE. KNIGHTS, ENSURE THAT BROTHER FAIRBANKS IS QUARANTINED.
I WILL SEE TO HIS WELFARE PERSONALLY.
I WILL NOT BE SILENCED, LORD COMMANDER! IF YOU VOUCH FOR THE BOY, THEN PERHAPS THE WHELP DID NOT ACT ALONE?
UNHAND ME, DAMN YOU, I'M NOT INFECTED!
I'M NOT INFECTED!!!
YOU SAY THAT ALEXANDROS WAS KILLED BY A MULTITUDE OF UNDEAD, YET ON OUR RETURN FROM THE MONASTERY WE COULD FIND NO SIGN OF SUCH A BATTLE. NOT A SINGLE SCOURGE CORPSE.
TURNED TO ASH NO DOUBT, AND SCATTERED BY THE WIND. WE OWE YOU NO FURTHER EXPLANATION, MAXWELL. YOUR TALK ALREADY BORDERS ON TREASON.
NOW, YOU EITHER SET YOURSELF WITH US, OR AGAINST US. WHAT'S IT TO BE?
IF ALEXANDROS WERE HERE HE WOULD LISTEN TO REASON. BUT I FEAR THAT REASON HAS ABANDONED THE LOT OF YOU IN FAVOR OF BLIND ZEALOTRY.
WE ARE TAKING OUR LEAVE OF THE ORDER AND WHAT IT HAS BECOME. THOSE AMONG YOU WHO SHARE OUR CONCERNS MAY JOIN US AT ANY TIME.
FOR THOSE WHO REMAIN, IF YOU DO NOT REDISCOVER THE TRUE TEACHINGS OF THE LIGHT...

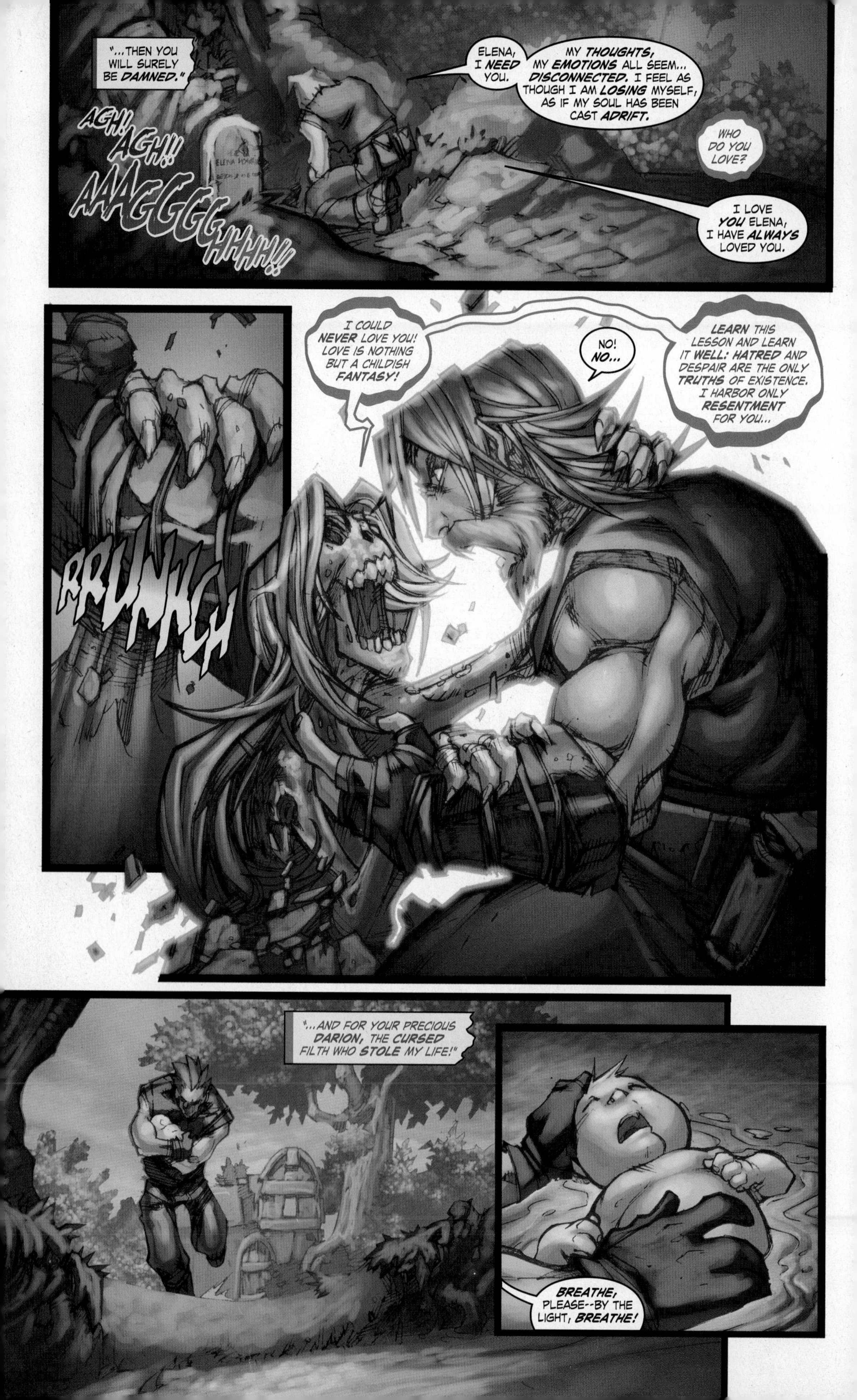
"...THEN YOU WILL SURELY BE DAMNED."
ELENA, I NEED YOU.
MY THOUGHTS, MY EMOTIONS ALL SEEM... DISCONNECTED. I FEEL AS THOUGH I AM LOSING MYSELF, AS IF MY SOUL HAS BEEN CAST ADRIFT.
AGH! AGH!! AAAGGGGHHHH!!
WHO DO YOU LOVE?
I LOVE YOU ELENA, I HAVE ALWAYS LOVED YOU.
I COULD NEVER LOVE YOU! LOVE IS NOTHING BUT A CHILDISH FANTASY!
NO! NO...
LEARN THIS LESSON AND LEARN IT WELL: HATRED AND DESPAIR ARE THE ONLY TRUTHS OF EXISTENCE. I HARBOR ONLY RESENTMENT FOR YOU...
RRUNKCH
"...AND FOR YOUR PRECIOUS DARION, THE CURSED FILTH WHO STOLE MY LIFE!"
BREATHE, PLEASE--BY THE LIGHT, BREATHE!

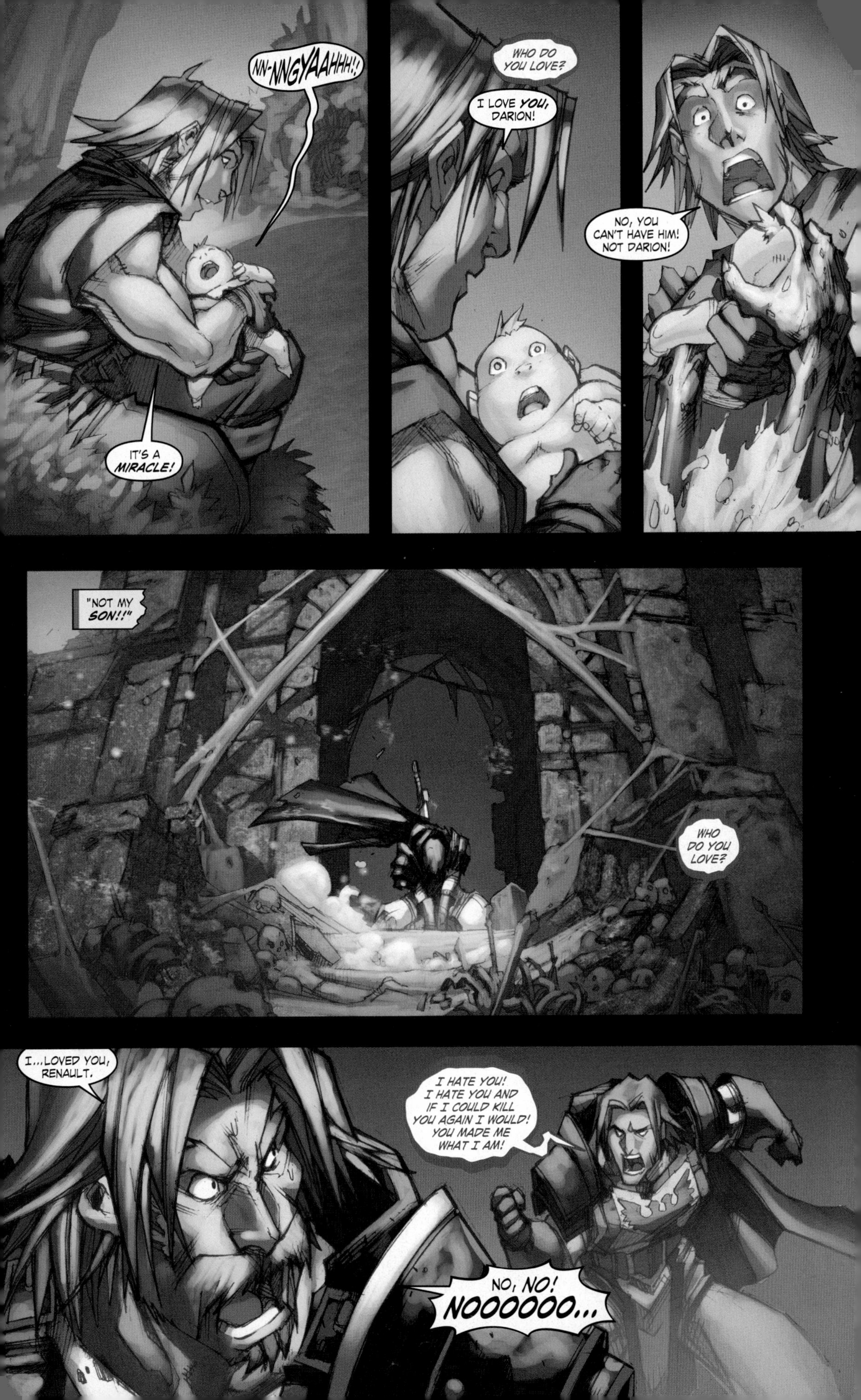
NN-NNGYAAHHH!!
IT'S A MIRACLE!
WHO DO YOU LOVE?
I LOVE YOU, DARION!
NO, YOU CAN'T HAVE HIM! NOT DARION!
"NOT MY SON!!"
WHO DO YOU LOVE?
I...LOVED YOU, RENAULT.
I HATE YOU! I HATE YOU AND IF I COULD KILL YOU AGAIN I WOULD! YOU MADE ME WHAT I AM!
NO, NO! NOOOOOO...

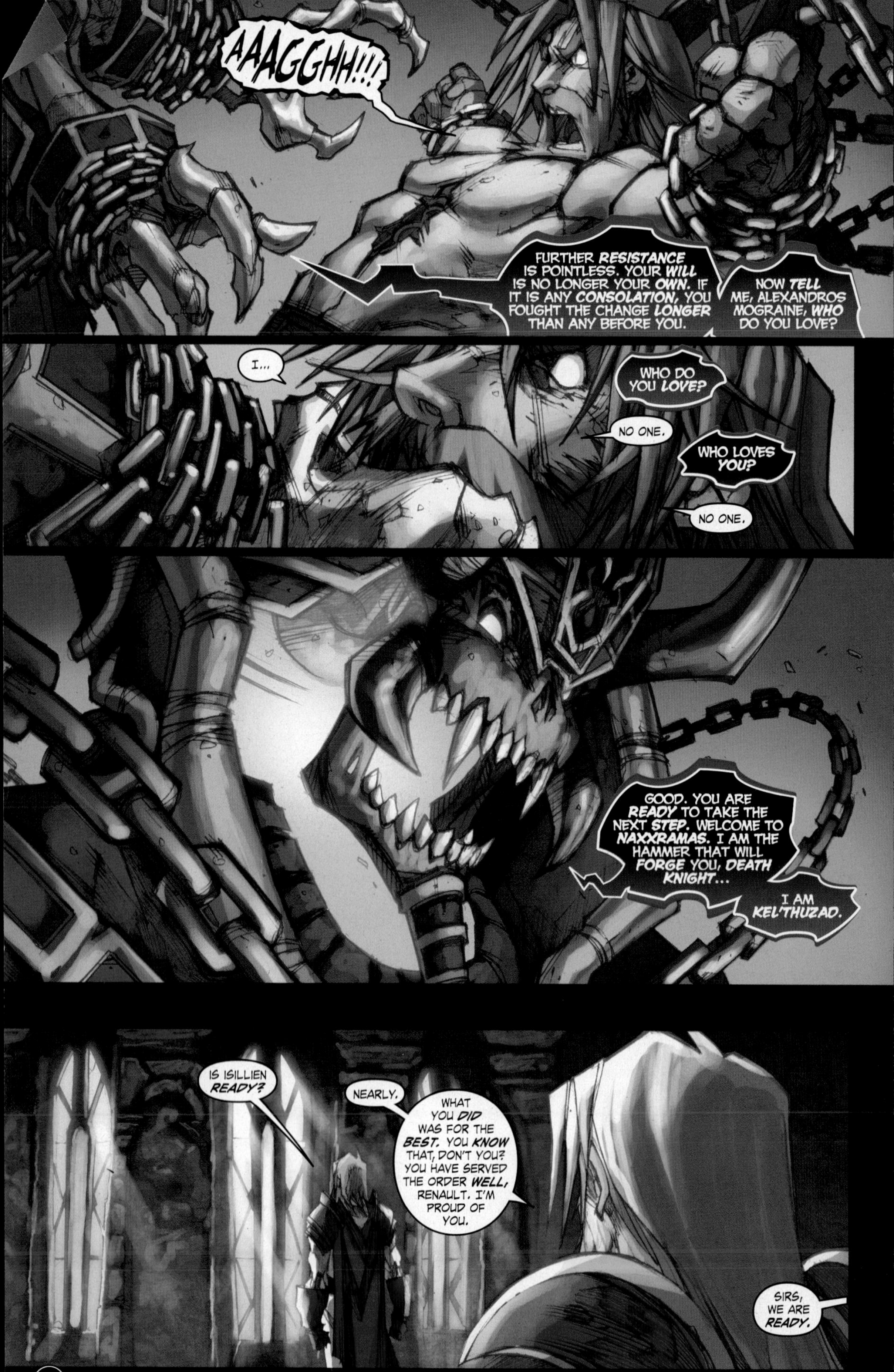
AAAGGHH!!!
FURTHER RESISTANCE IS POINTLESS. YOUR WILL IS NO LONGER YOUR OWN. IF IT IS ANY CONSOLATION, YOU FOUGHT THE CHANGE LONGER THAN ANY BEFORE YOU.
NOW TELL ME, ALEXANDROS MOGRAINE, WHO DO YOU LOVE?
I...
WHO DO YOU LOVE?
NO ONE.
WHO LOVES YOU?
NO ONE.
GOOD. YOU ARE READY TO TAKE THE NEXT STEP. WELCOME TO NAXXRAMAS. I AM THE HAMMER THAT WILL FORGE YOU, DEATH KNIGHT...
I AM KEL'THUZAD.
IS ISILLIEN READY?
NEARLY.
WHAT YOU DID WAS FOR THE BEST. YOU KNOW THAT, DON'T YOU? YOU HAVE SERVED THE ORDER WELL, RENAULT. I'M PROUD OF YOU.
SIRS, WE ARE READY.

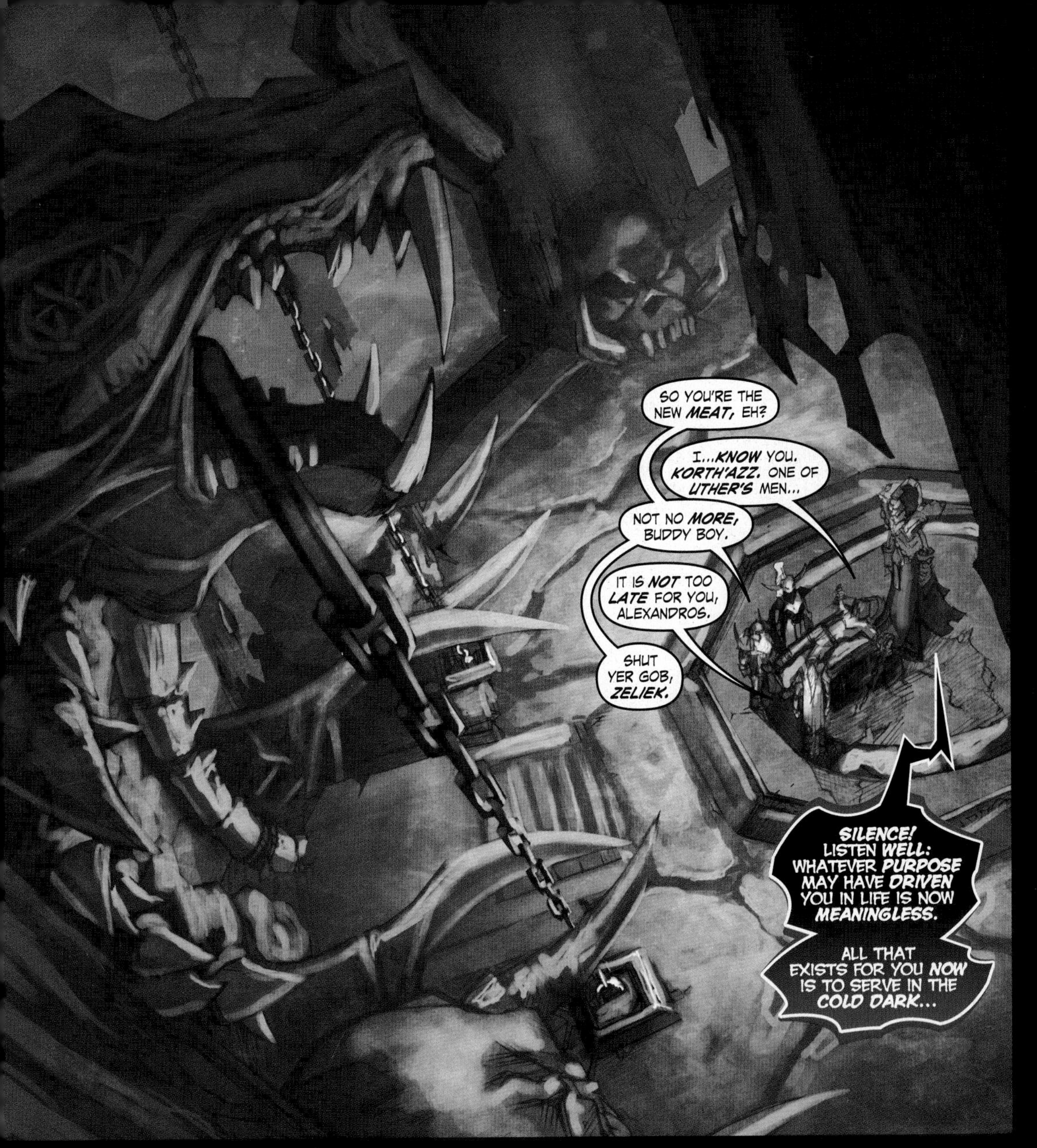
SO YOU'RE THE NEW MEAT, EH?
I...KNOW YOU. KORTH'AZZ. ONE OF UTHER'S MEN...
NOT NO MORE, BUDDY BOY.
IT IS NOT TOO LATE FOR YOU, ALEXANDROS.
SHUT YER GOB, ZELIEK.
SILENCE! LISTEN WELL: WHATEVER PURPOSE MAY HAVE DRIVEN YOU IN LIFE IS NOW MEANINGLESS.
ALL THAT EXISTS FOR YOU NOW IS TO SERVE IN THE COLD DARK...

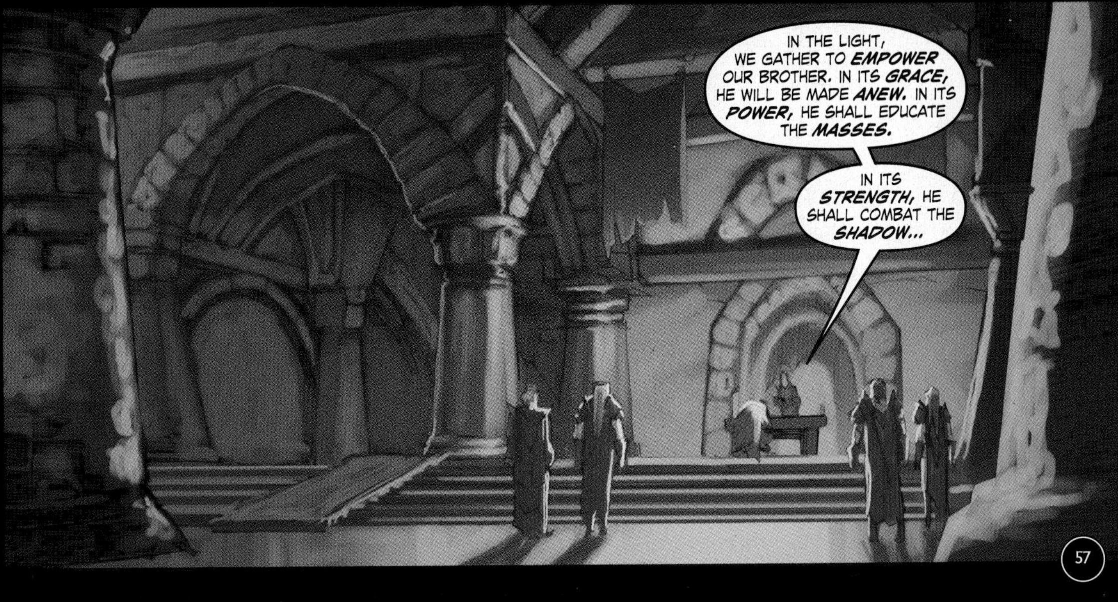
IN THE LIGHT, WE GATHER TO EMPOWER OUR BROTHER. IN ITS GRACE, HE WILL BE MADE ANEW. IN ITS POWER, HE SHALL EDUCATE THE MASSES.
IN ITS STRENGTH, HE SHALL COMBAT THE SHADOW...

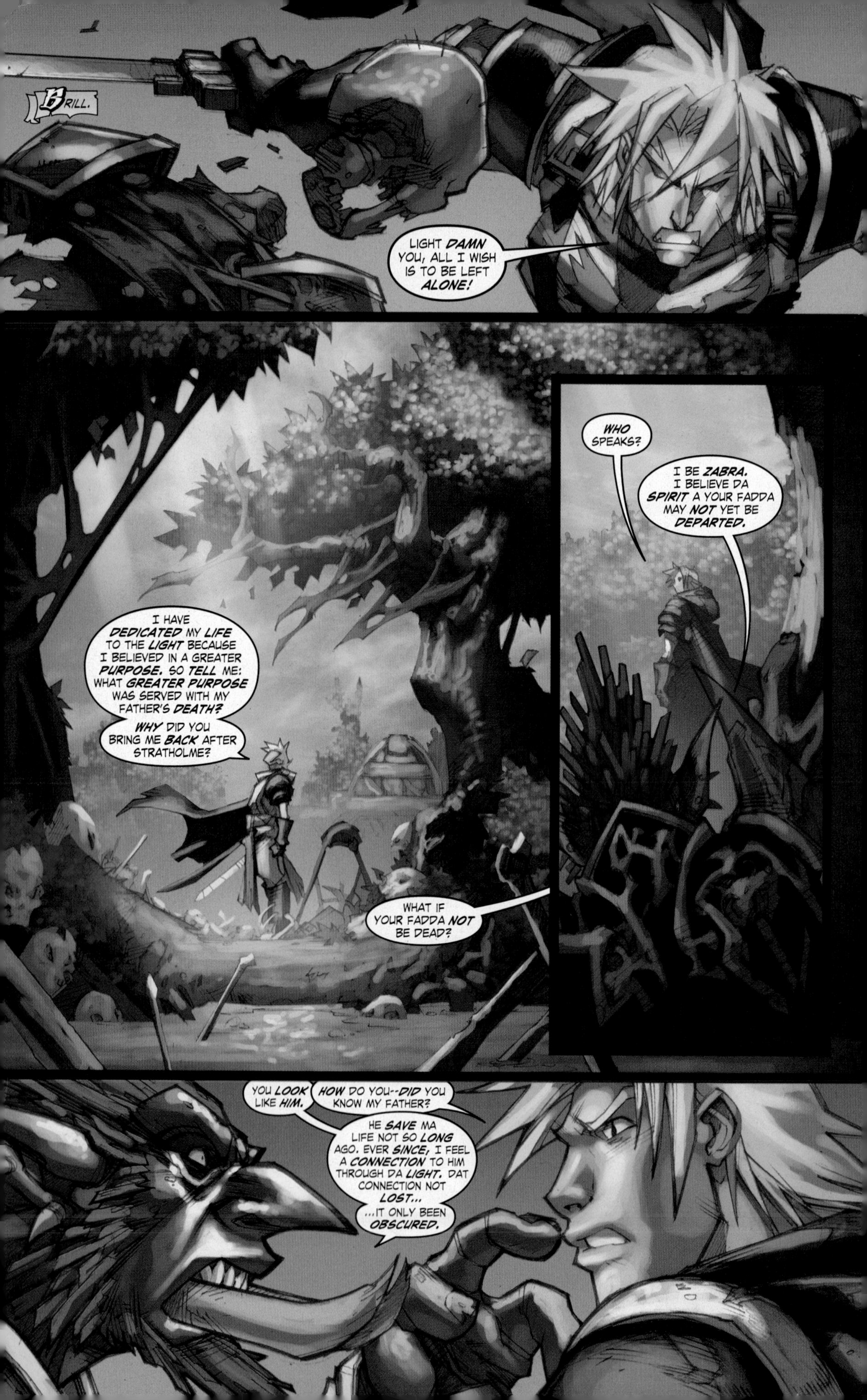
BRILL.
LIGHT DAMN YOU, ALL I WISH IS TO BE LEFT ALONE!
I HAVE DEDICATED MY LIFE TO THE LIGHT BECAUSE I BELIEVED IN A GREATER PURPOSE. SO TELL ME: WHAT GREATER PURPOSE WAS SERVED WITH MY FATHER'S DEATH?
WHY DID YOU BRING ME BACK AFTER STRATHOLME?
WHAT IF YOUR FADDA NOT BE DEAD?
WHO SPEAKS?
I BE ZABRA. I BELIEVE DA SPIRIT A YOUR FADDA MAY NOT YET BE DEPARTED.
YOU LOOK LIKE HIM.
HOW DO YOU--DID YOU KNOW MY FATHER?
HE SAVE MA LIFE NOT SO LONG AGO. EVER SINCE, I FEEL A CONNECTION TO HIM THROUGH DA LIGHT. DAT CONNECTION NOT LOST...
...IT ONLY BEEN OBSCURED.

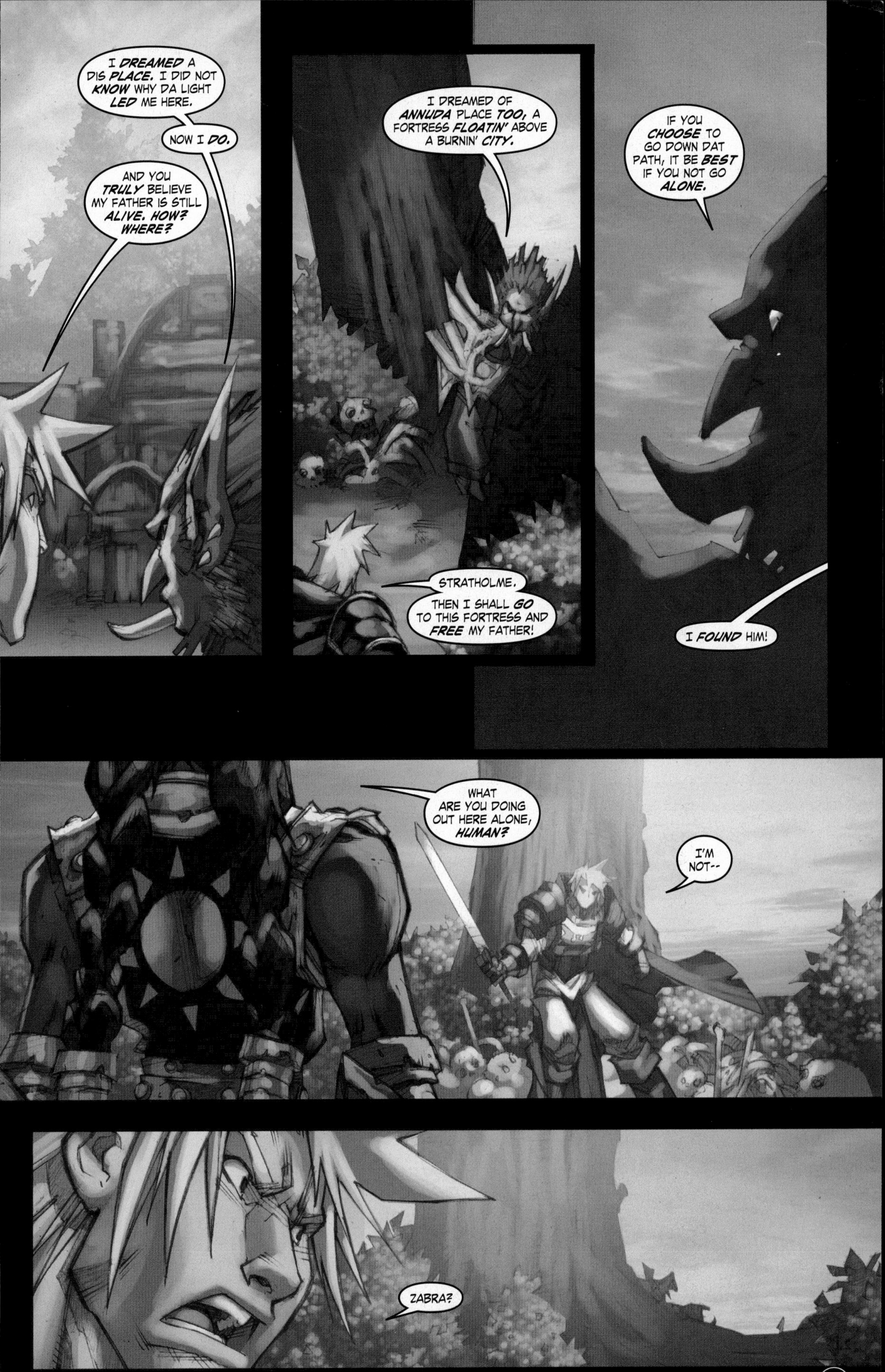
I DREAMED A DIS PLACE. I DID NOT KNOW WHY DA LIGHT LED ME HERE.
NOW I DO.
AND YOU TRULY BELIEVE MY FATHER IS STILL ALIVE. HOW? WHERE?
I DREAMED OF ANNUDA PLACE TOO, A FORTRESS FLOATIN' ABOVE A BURNIN' CITY.
STRATHOLME.
THEN I SHALL GO TO THIS FORTRESS AND FREE MY FATHER!
IF YOU CHOOSE TO GO DOWN DAT PATH, IT BE BEST IF YOU NOT GO ALONE.
I FOUND HIM!
WHAT ARE YOU DOING OUT HERE ALONE, HUMAN?
I'M NOT--
ZABRA?

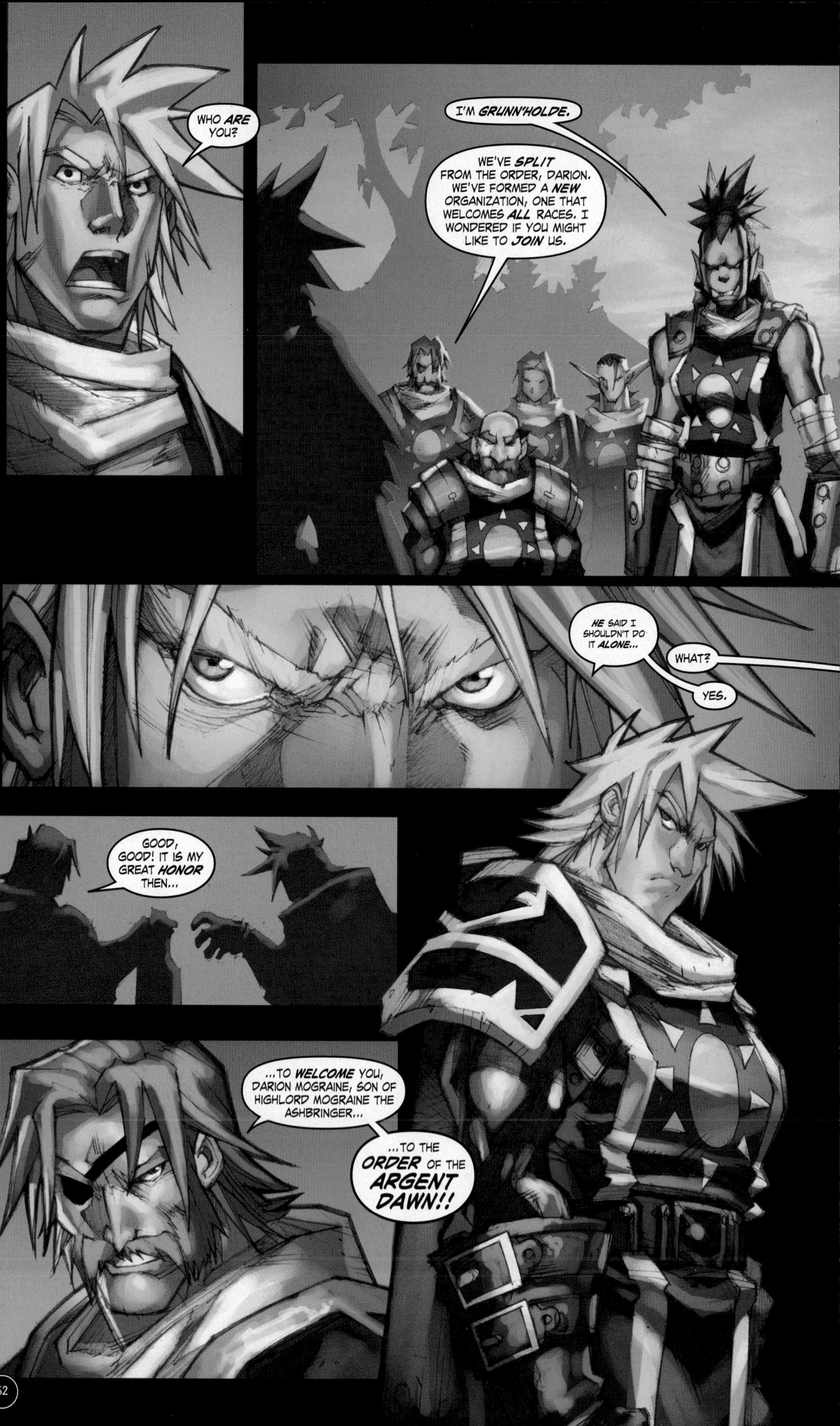

WHO ARE YOU?
I'M GRUNN'HOLDE.
WE'VE SPLIT FROM THE ORDER, DARION. WE'VE FORMED A NEW ORGANIZATION, ONE THAT WELCOMES ALL RACES. I WONDERED IF YOU MIGHT LIKE TO JOIN US.
HE SAID I SHOULDN'T DO IT ALONE...
WHAT?
YES.
GOOD, GOOD! IT IS MY GREAT HONOR THEN...
...TO WELCOME YOU, DARION MOGRAINE, SON OF HIGHLORD MOGRAINE THE ASHBRINGER...
...TO THE ORDER OF THE ARGENT DAWN!!

CHAPTER 3

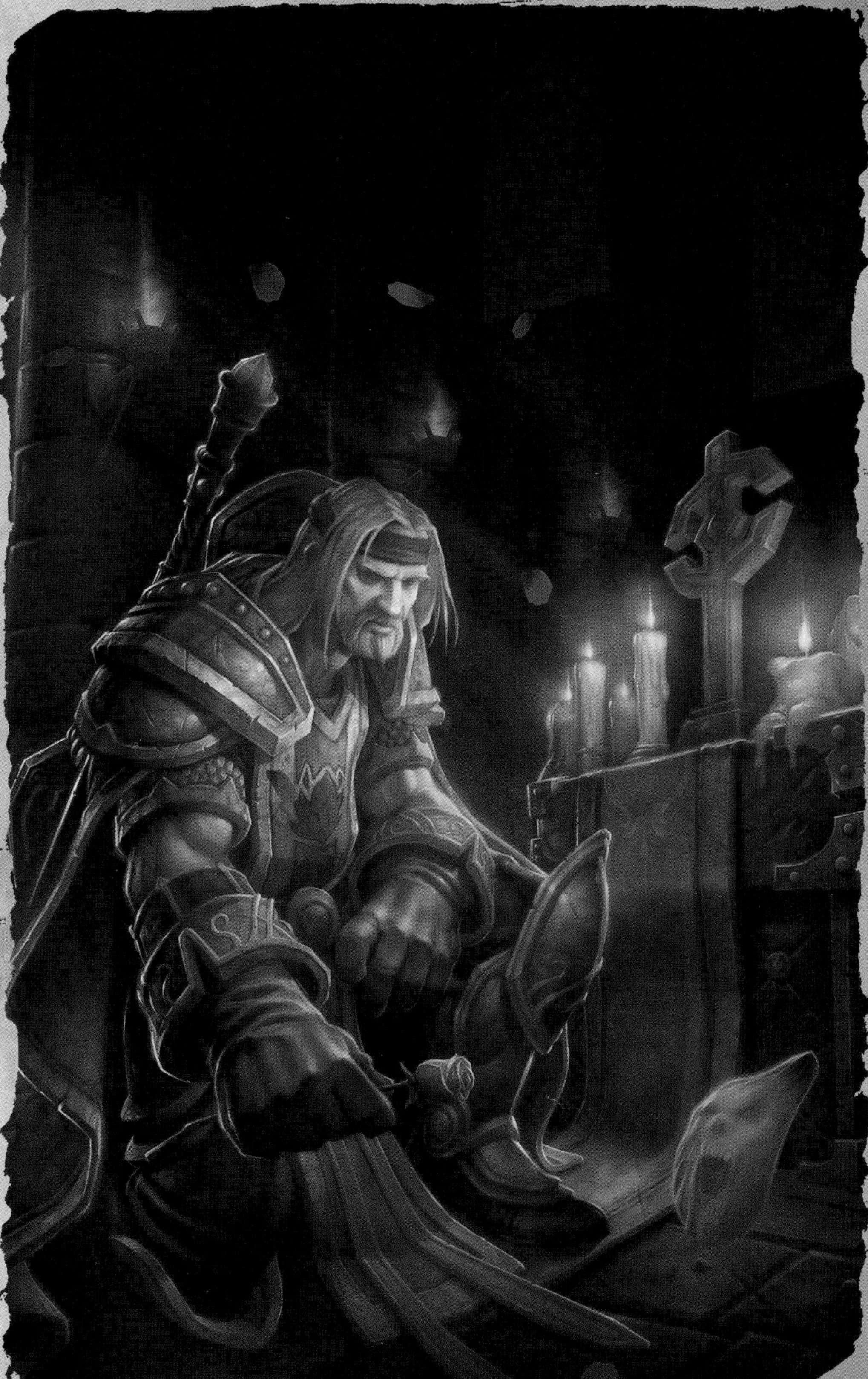

Cover by Chris Robinson

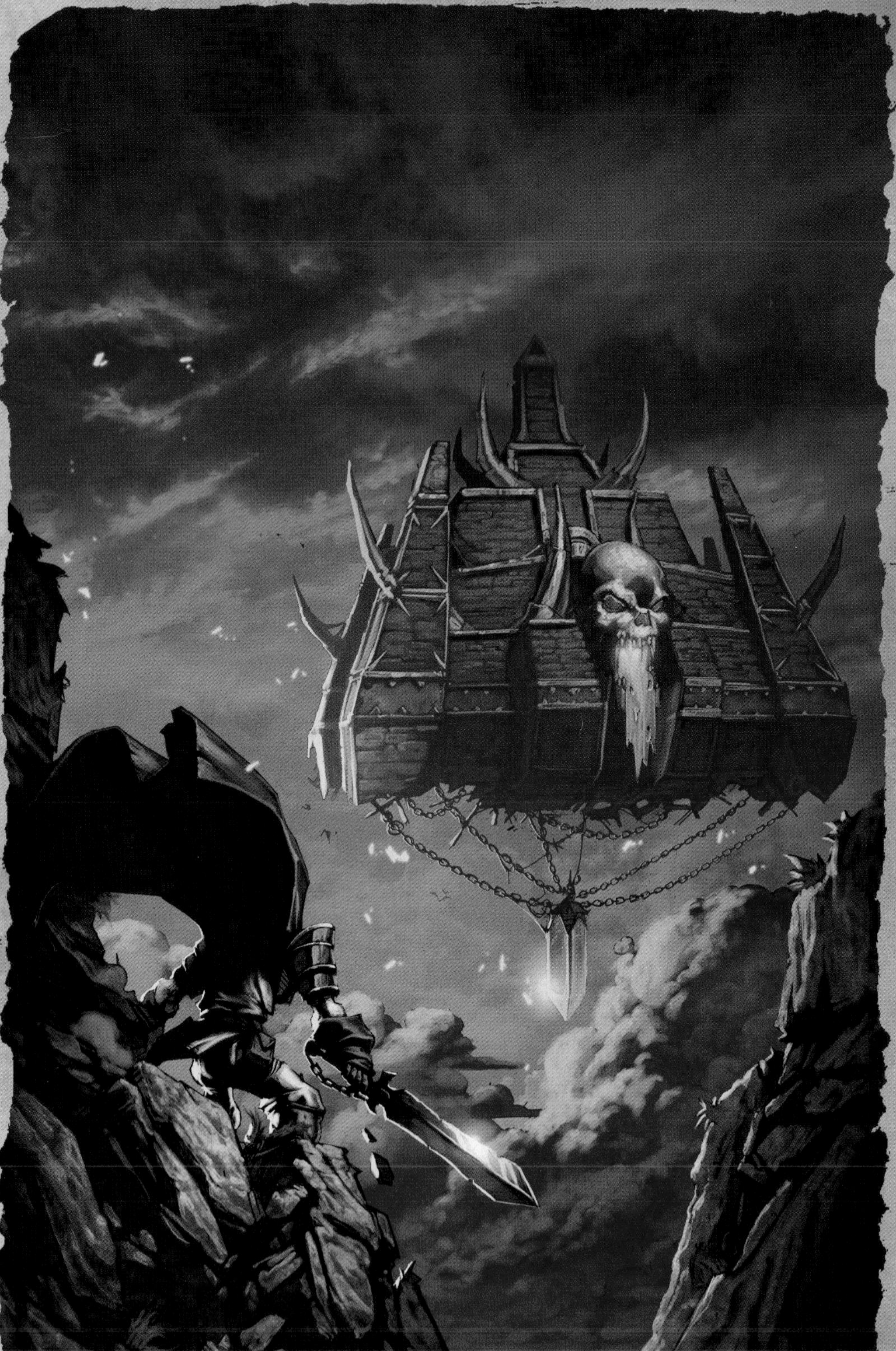

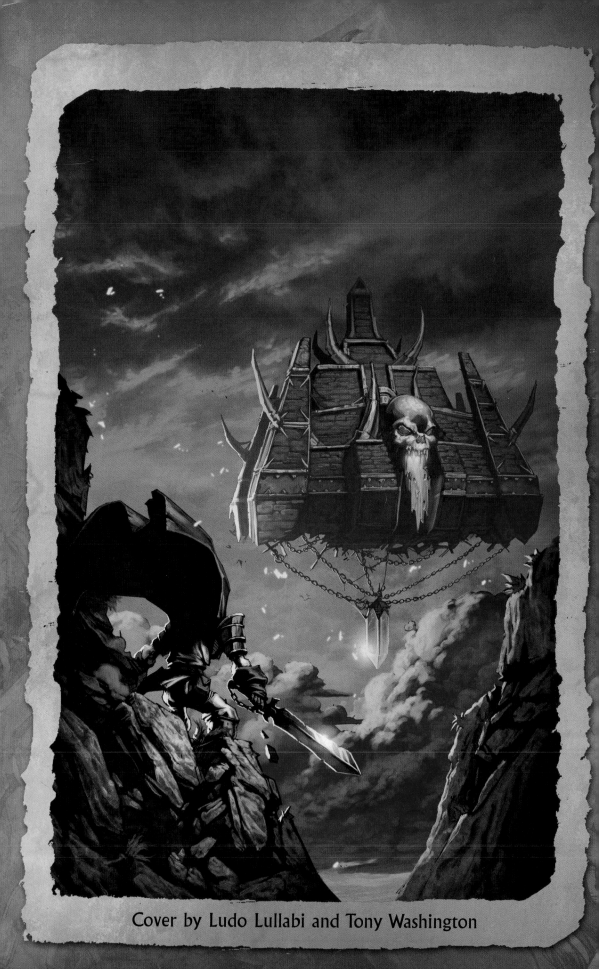

Cover by Ludo Lullabi and Tony Washington

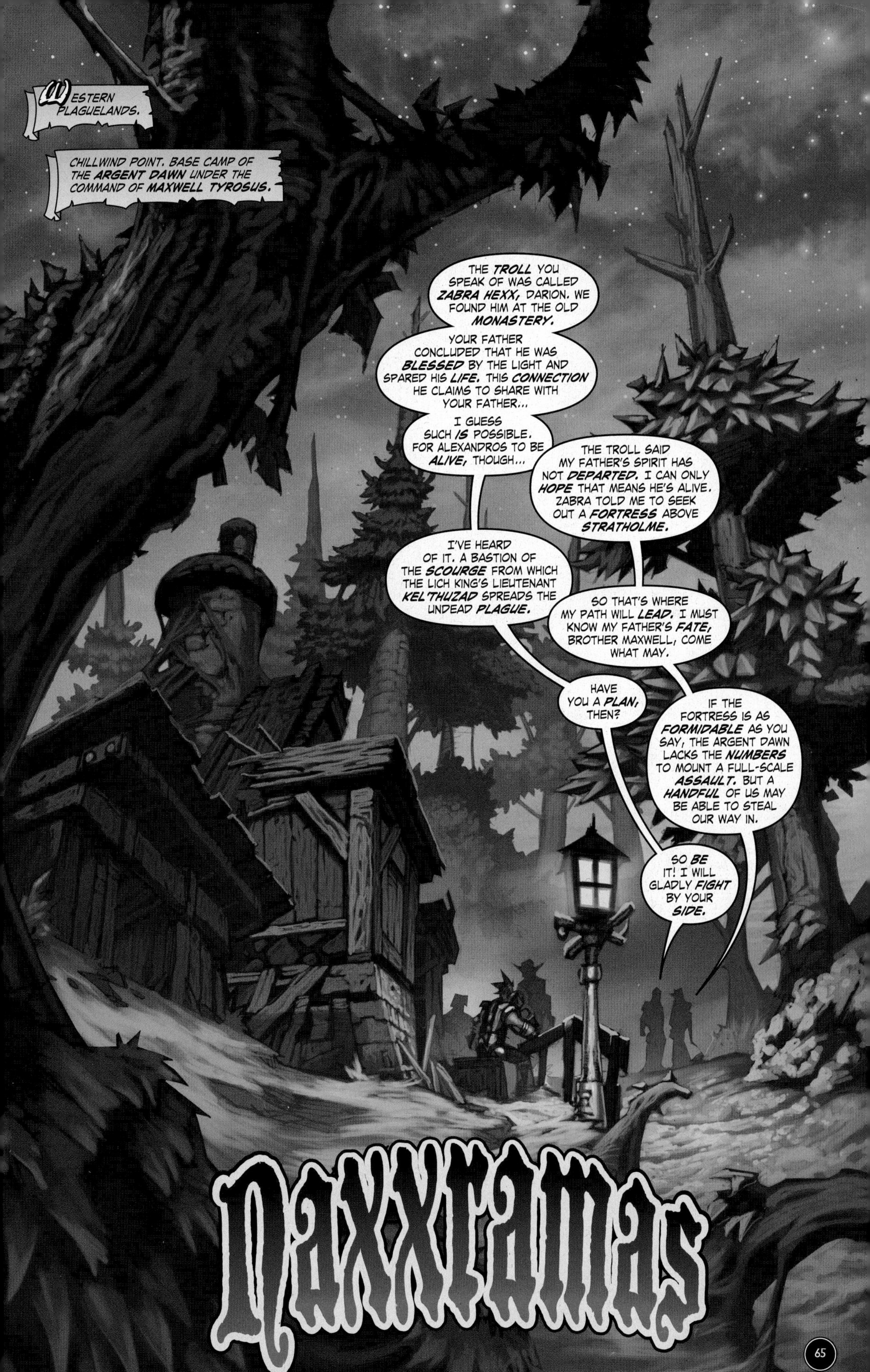
WESTERN PLAGUELANDS.
CHILLWIND POINT. BASE CAMP OF THE ARGENT DAWN UNDER THE COMMAND OF MAXWELL TYROSUS.
THE TROLL YOU SPEAK OF WAS CALLED ZABRA HEXX, DARION. WE FOUND HIM AT THE OLD MONASTERY.
YOUR FATHER CONCLUDED THAT HE WAS BLESSED BY THE LIGHT AND SPARED HIS LIFE. THIS CONNECTION HE CLAIMS TO SHARE WITH YOUR FATHER...
I GUESS SUCH IS POSSIBLE. FOR ALEXANDROS TO BE ALIVE, THOUGH...
THE TROLL SAID MY FATHER'S SPIRIT HAS NOT DEPARTED. I CAN ONLY HOPE THAT MEANS HE'S ALIVE. ZABRA TOLD ME TO SEEK OUT A FORTRESS ABOVE STRATHOLME.
I'VE HEARD OF IT. A BASTION OF THE SCOURGE FROM WHICH THE LICH KING'S LIEUTENANT KEL'THUZAD SPREADS THE UNDEAD PLAGUE.
SO THAT'S WHERE MY PATH WILL LEAD. I MUST KNOW MY FATHER'S FATE, BROTHER MAXWELL, COME WHAT MAY.
HAVE YOU A PLAN, THEN?
IF THE FORTRESS IS AS FORMIDABLE AS YOU SAY, THE ARGENT DAWN LACKS THE NUMBERS TO MOUNT A FULL-SCALE ASSAULT. BUT A HANDFUL OF US MAY BE ABLE TO STEAL OUR WAY IN.
SO BE IT! I WILL GLADLY FIGHT BY YOUR SIDE.
NAXXRAMAS

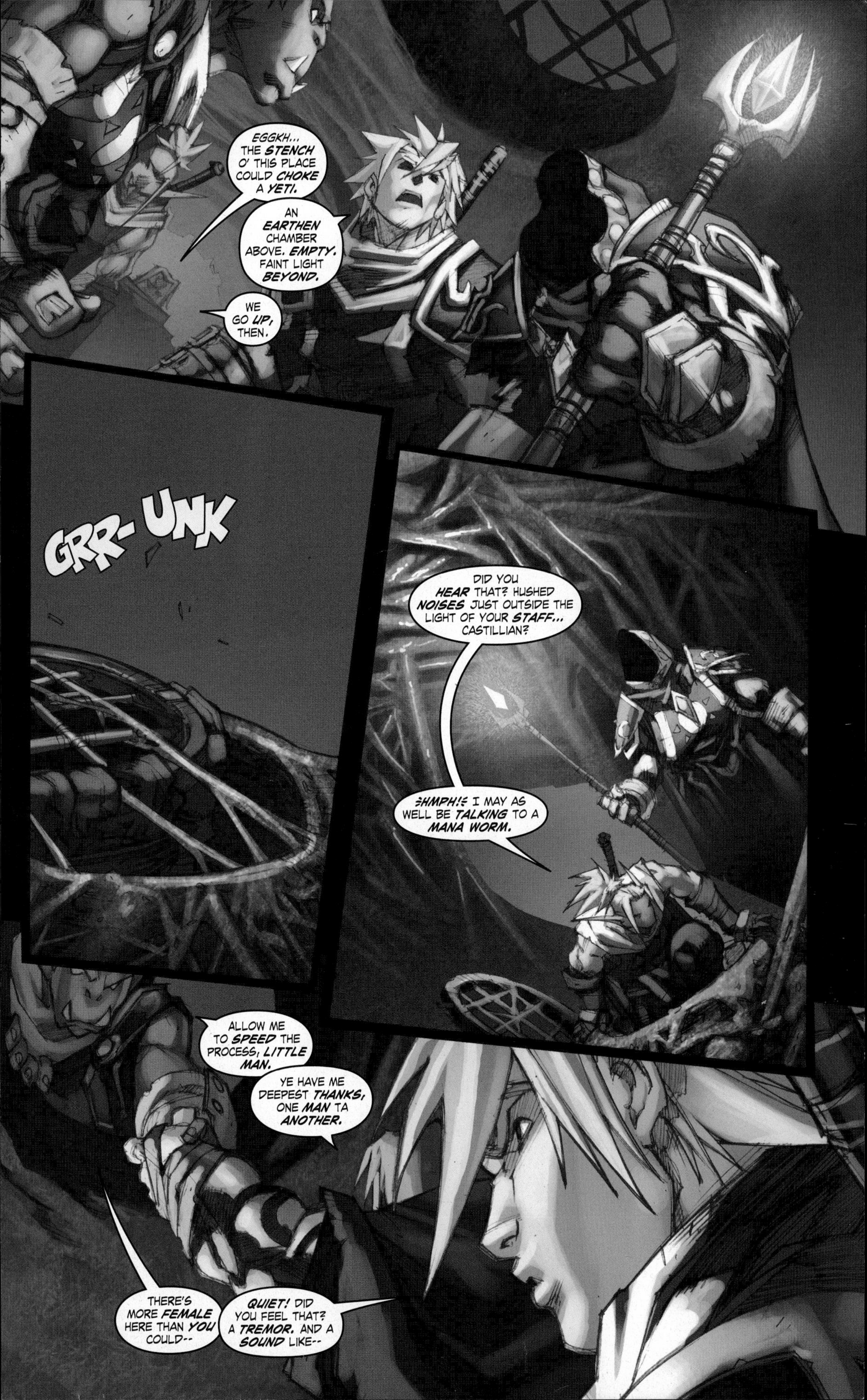
EGGKH... THE STENCH O' THIS PLACE COULD CHOKE A YETI.
AN EARTHEN CHAMBER ABOVE. EMPTY. FAINT LIGHT BEYOND.
WE GO UP, THEN.
GRR- UNK
DID YOU HEAR THAT? HUSHED NOISES JUST OUTSIDE THE LIGHT OF YOUR STAFF... CASTILLIAN?
HMPH! I MAY AS WELL BE TALKING TO A MANA WORM.
ALLOW ME TO SPEED THE PROCESS, LITTLE MAN.
YE HAVE ME DEEPEST THANKS, ONE MAN TA ANOTHER.
THERE'S MORE FEMALE HERE THAN YOU COULD--
QUIET! DID YOU FEEL THAT? A TREMOR. AND A SOUND LIKE--

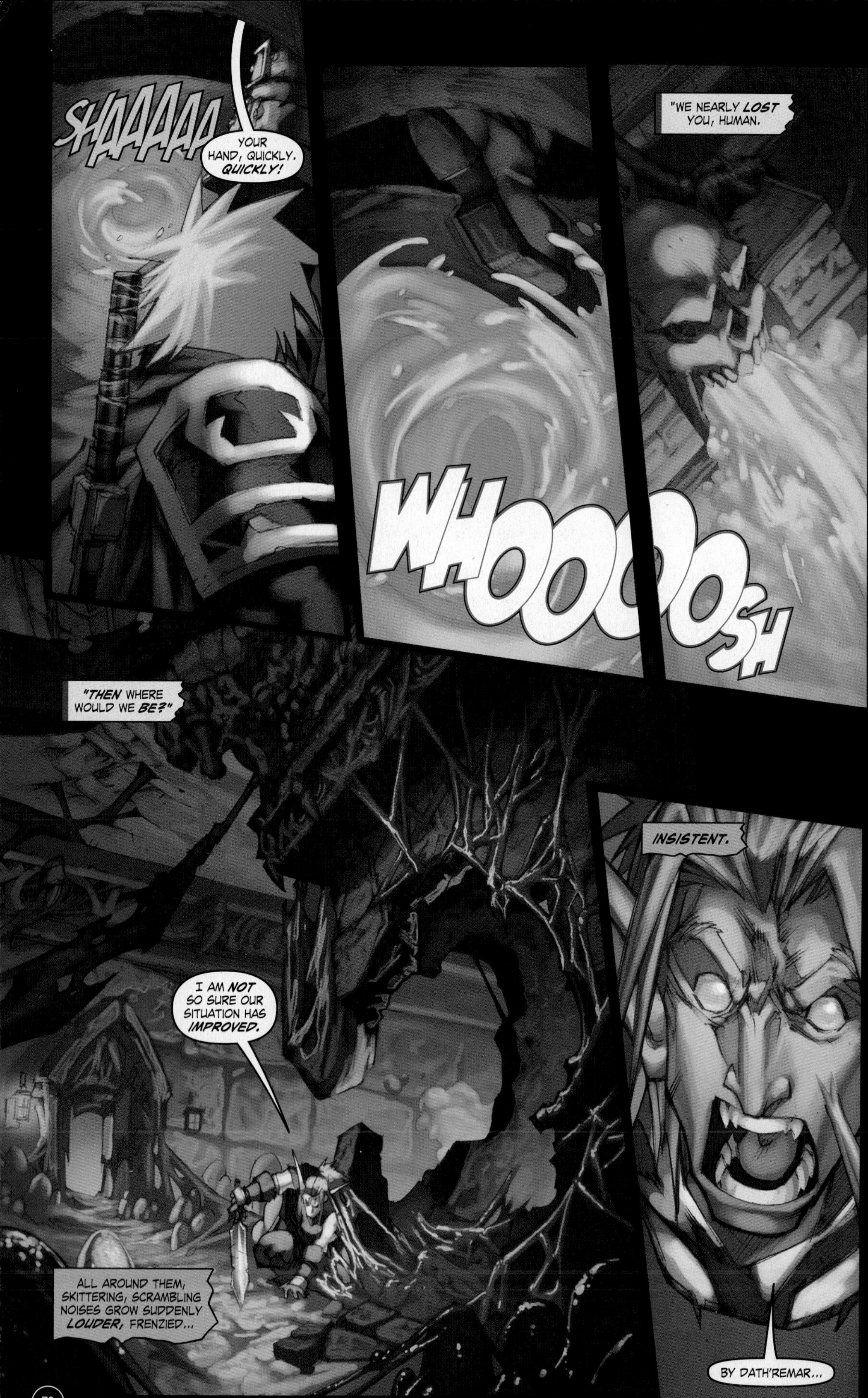
SHAAAAA
YOUR HAND, QUICKLY. QUICKLY!
WHOOOOOOSH
"WE NEARLY LOST YOU, HUMAN.
"THEN WHERE WOULD WE BE?"
I AM NOT SO SURE OUR SITUATION HAS IMPROVED.
INSISTENT.
ALL AROUND THEM, SKITTERING, SCRAMBLING NOISES GROW SUDDENLY LOUDER, FRENZIED...
BY DATH'REMAR...

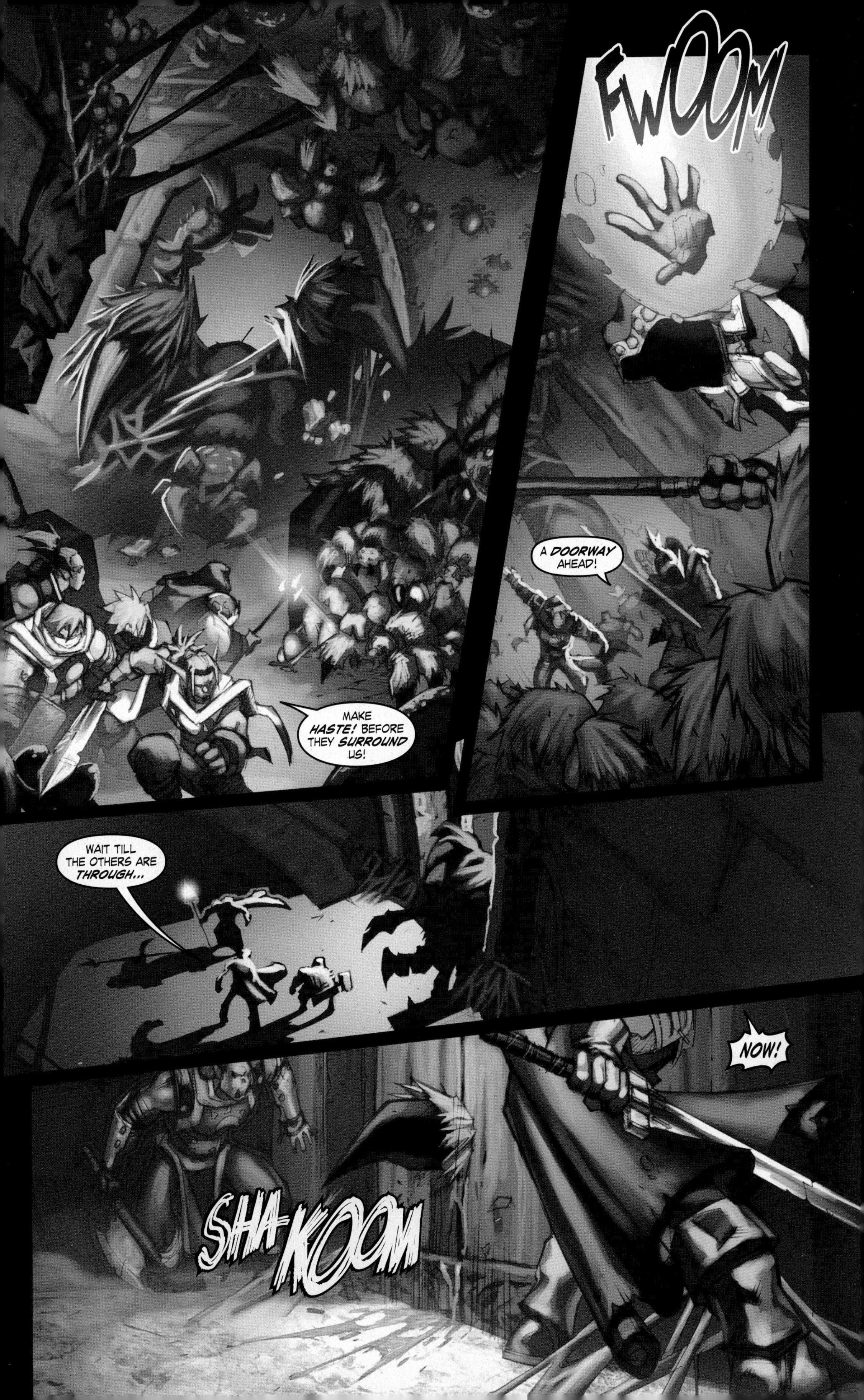
FWOOM
MAKE HASTE! BEFORE THEY SURROUND US!
A DOORWAY AHEAD!
WAIT TILL THE OTHERS ARE THROUGH...
NOW!
SHA-KOOM

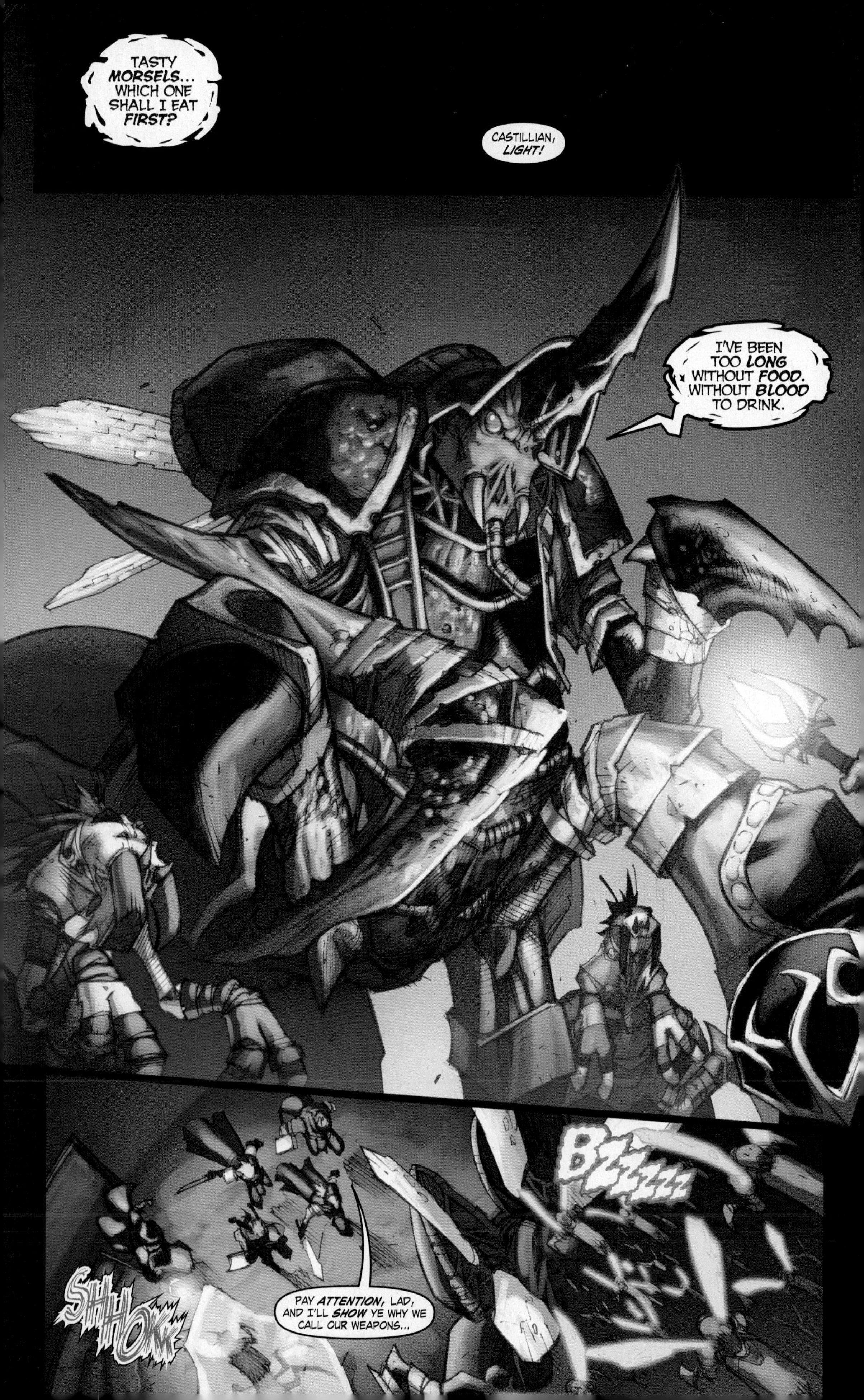
TASTY MORSELS... WHICH ONE SHALL I EAT FIRST?
CASTILLIAN, LIGHT!
I'VE BEEN TOO LONG WITHOUT FOOD. WITHOUT BLOOD TO DRINK.
BZZZZZ
SHHOKK
PAY ATTENTION, LAD, AND I'LL SHOW YE WHY WE CALL OUR WEAPONS...

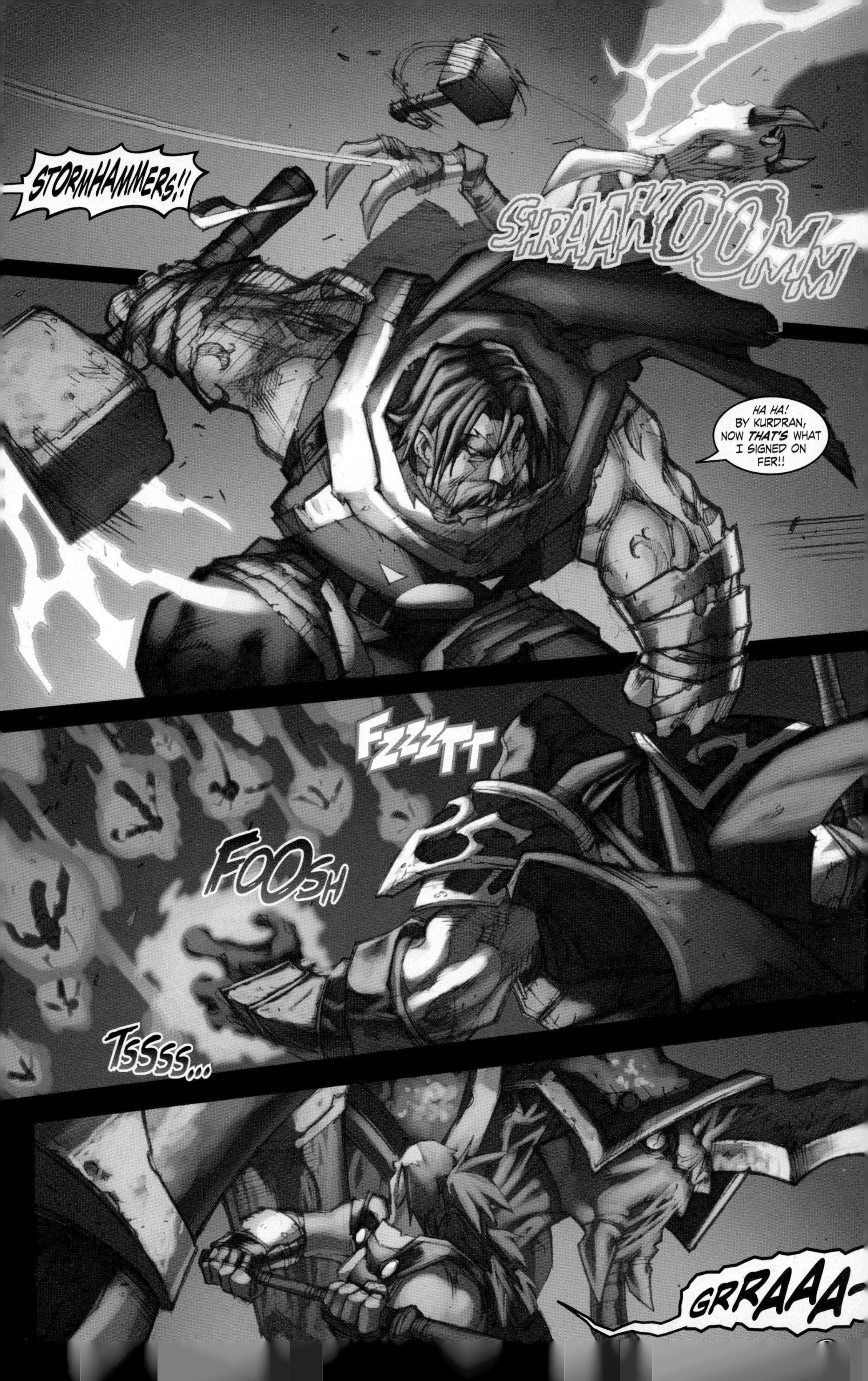
STORMHAMMERS!!
SHRAAKOOMM
HA HA! BY KURDRAN, NOW *THAT'S* WHAT I SIGNED ON FER!!
FZZZTT
FOOSH
TSSSS...
GRRAAA-

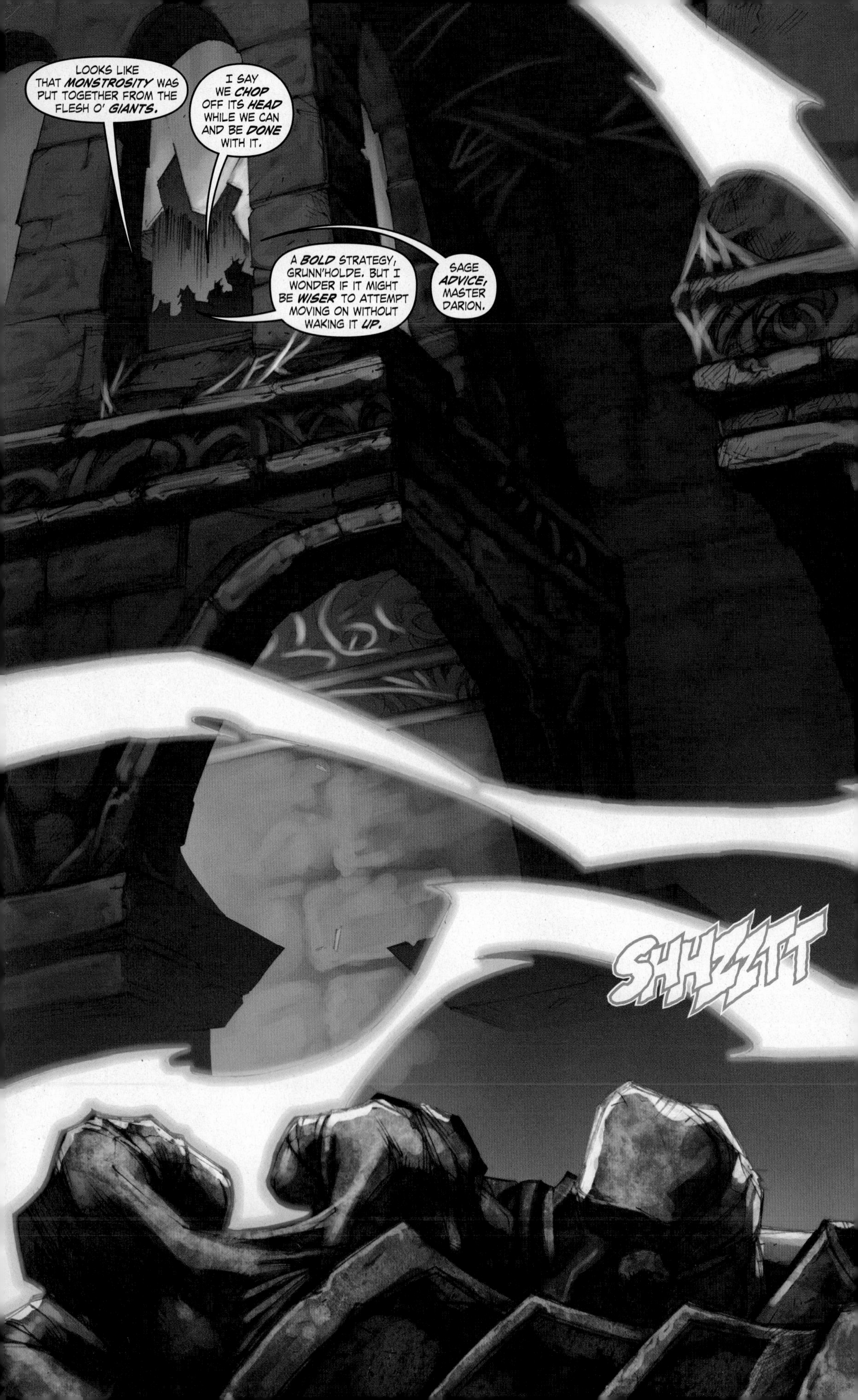
LOOKS LIKE THAT MONSTROSITY WAS PUT TOGETHER FROM THE FLESH O' GIANTS.
I SAY WE CHOP OFF ITS HEAD WHILE WE CAN AND BE DONE WITH IT.
A BOLD STRATEGY, GRUNN'HOLDE. BUT I WONDER IF IT MIGHT BE WISER TO ATTEMPT MOVING ON WITHOUT WAKING IT UP.
SAGE ADVICE, MASTER DARION.
SHZZTT

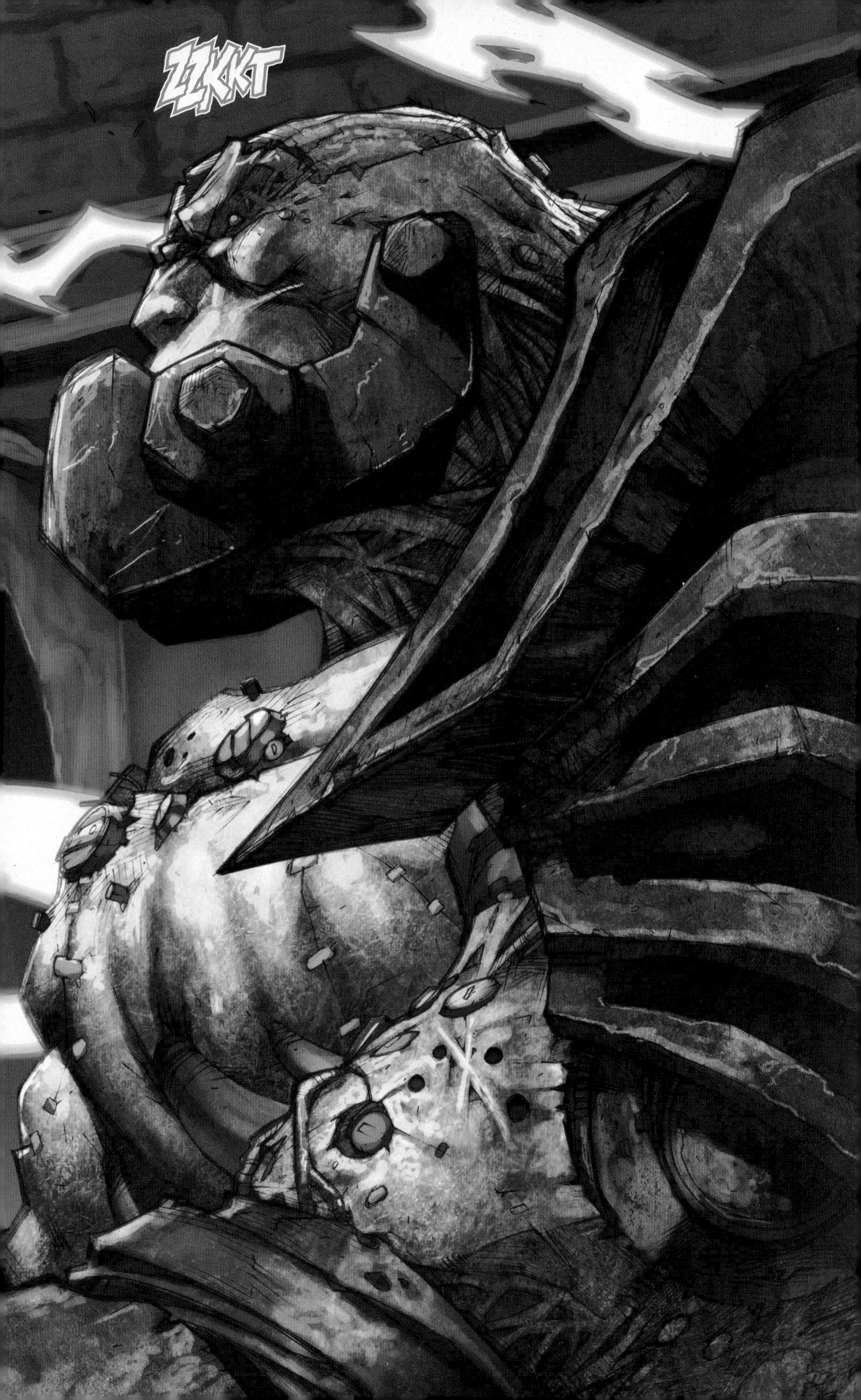
ZZKKT

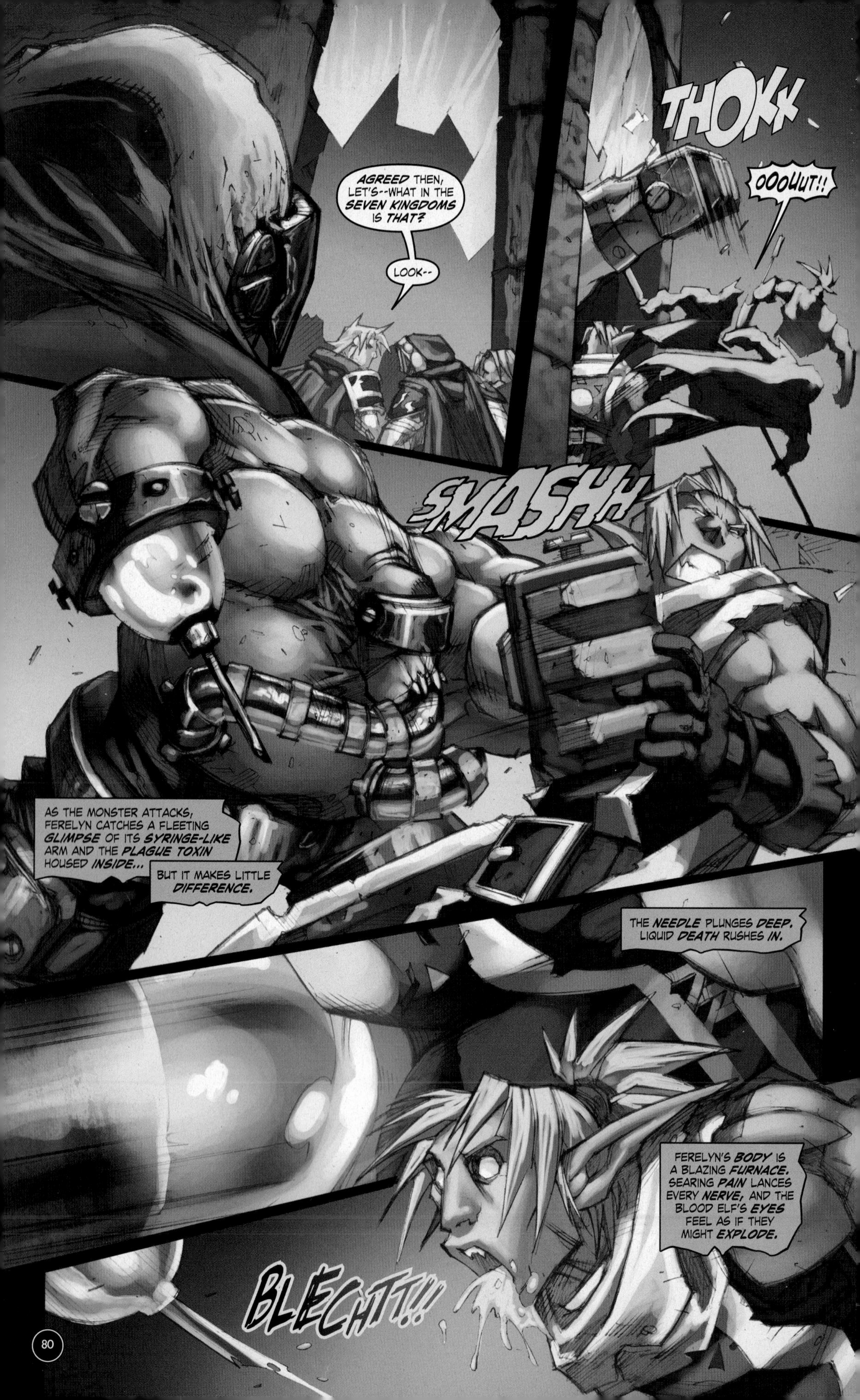
AGREED THEN, LET'S--WHAT IN THE SEVEN KINGDOMS IS THAT?
LOOK--
THOKK
OOOUUT!!
SMASHH
AS THE MONSTER ATTACKS, FERELYN CATCHES A FLEETING GLIMPSE OF ITS SYRINGE-LIKE ARM AND THE PLAGUE TOXIN HOUSED INSIDE...
BUT IT MAKES LITTLE DIFFERENCE.
THE NEEDLE PLUNGES DEEP. LIQUID DEATH RUSHES IN.
FERELYN'S BODY IS A BLAZING FURNACE. SEARING PAIN LANCES EVERY NERVE, AND THE BLOOD ELF'S EYES FEEL AS IF THEY MIGHT EXPLODE.
BLECHTT!!

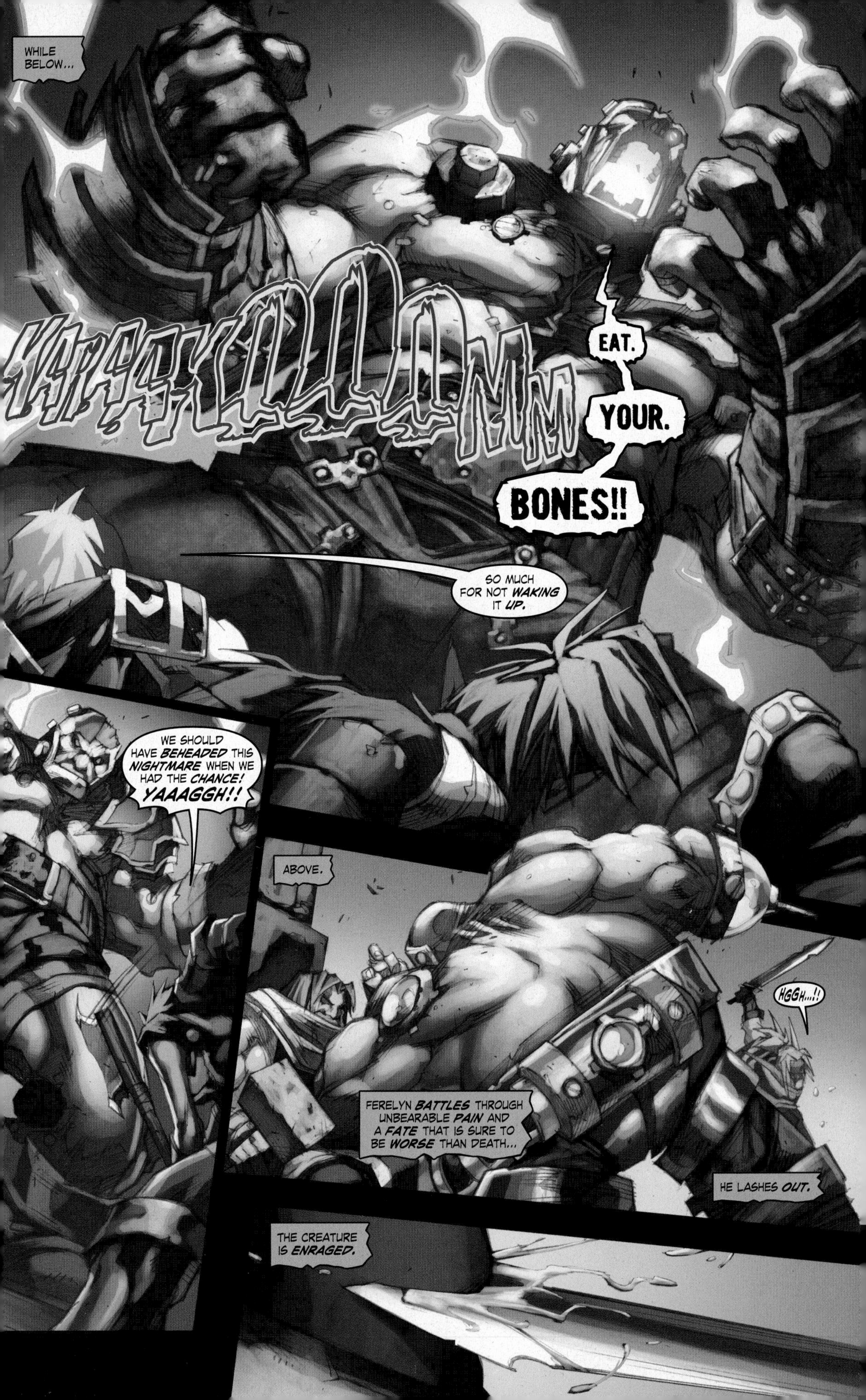
WHILE BELOW...
EAT.
YOUR.
BONES!!
SO MUCH FOR NOT *WAKING* IT *UP*.
WE SHOULD HAVE *BEHEADED* THIS *NIGHTMARE* WHEN WE HAD THE *CHANCE!* *YAAAGGH!!*
ABOVE.
HGGH...!!
FERELYN *BATTLES* THROUGH UNBEARABLE *PAIN* AND A *FATE* THAT IS SURE TO BE *WORSE* THAN DEATH...
HE LASHES *OUT.*
THE CREATURE IS *ENRAGED.*

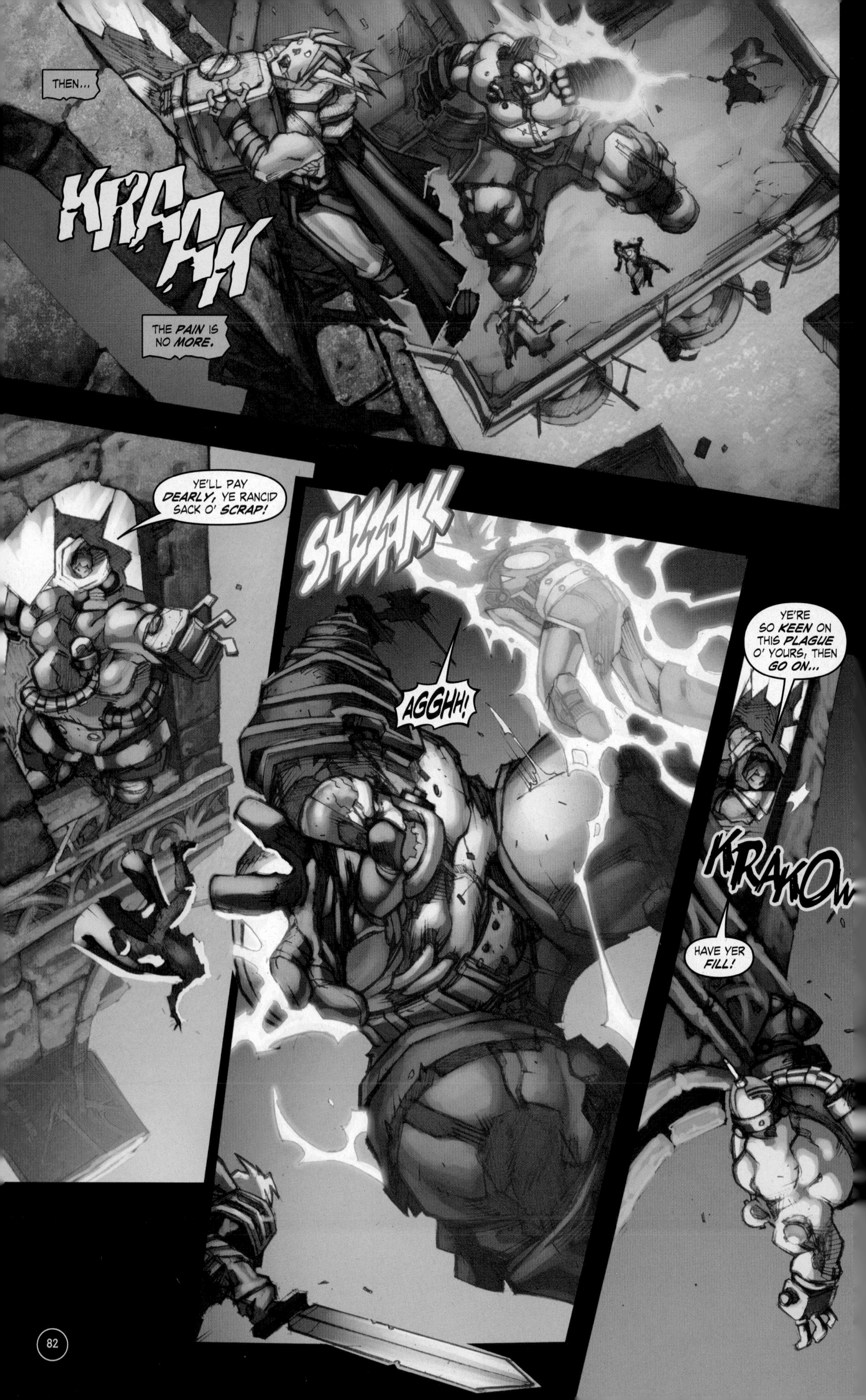
THEN...
KRAAAKK
THE PAIN IS NO MORE.
YE'LL PAY DEARLY, YE RANCID SACK O' SCRAP!
SHAAK!
AGGHH!
YE'RE SO KEEN ON THIS PLAGUE O' YOURS, THEN GO ON...
KRAKOW
HAVE YER FILL!

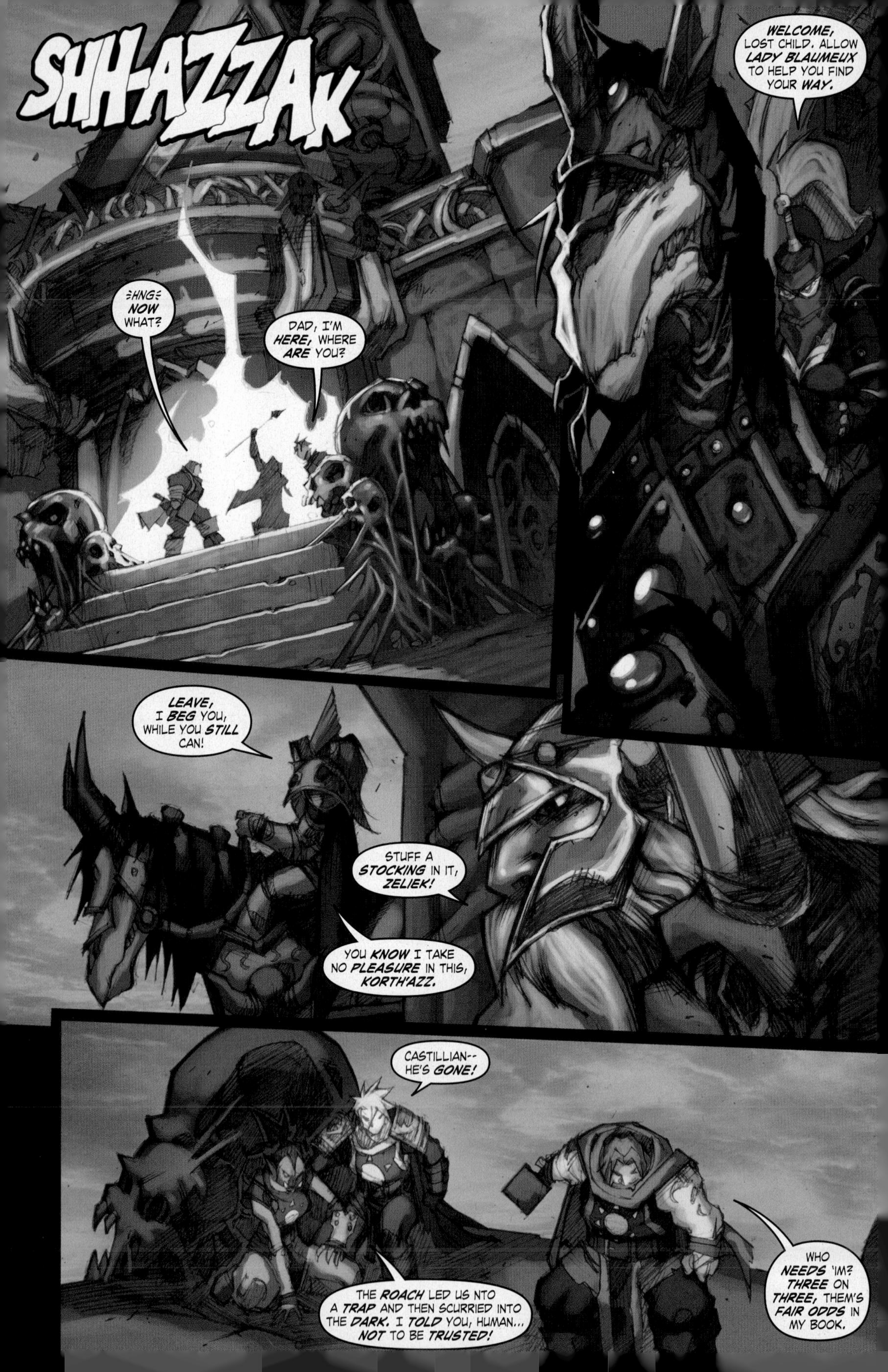
SHH-AZZAK
≷HNG≶ NOW WHAT?
DAD, I'M HERE, WHERE ARE YOU?
WELCOME, LOST CHILD. ALLOW LADY BLAUMEUX TO HELP YOU FIND YOUR WAY.
LEAVE, I BEG YOU, WHILE YOU STILL CAN!
STUFF A STOCKING IN IT, ZELIEK!
YOU KNOW I TAKE NO PLEASURE IN THIS, KORTH'AZZ.
CASTILLIAN-- HE'S GONE!
THE ROACH LED US NTO A TRAP AND THEN SCURRIED INTO THE DARK. I TOLD YOU, HUMAN... NOT TO BE TRUSTED!
WHO NEEDS 'IM? THREE ON THREE, THEM'S FAIR ODDS IN MY BOOK.

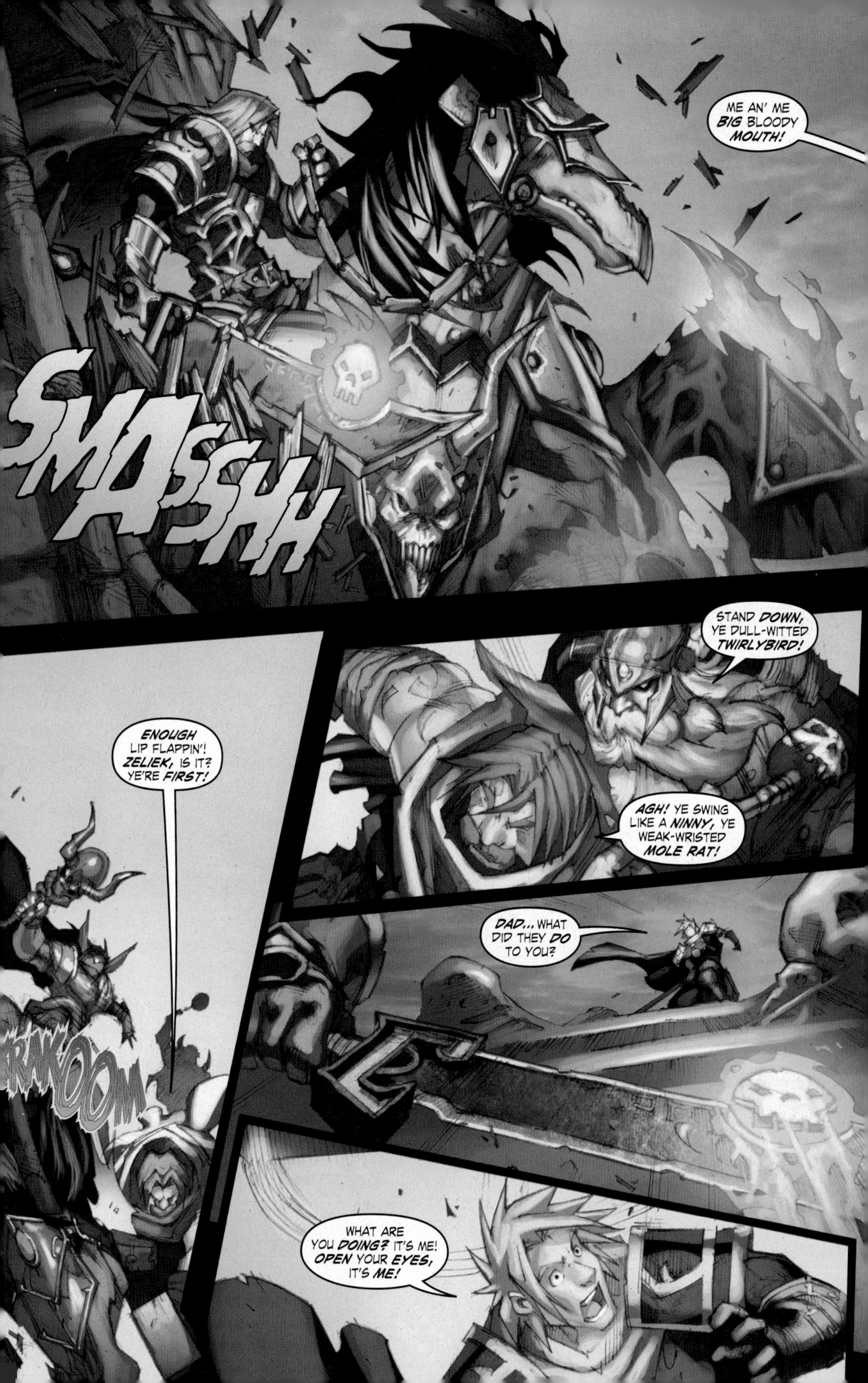
ME AN' ME BIG BLOODY MOUTH!
SMASSHH
STAND DOWN, YE DULL-WITTED TWIRLYBIRD!
ENOUGH LIP FLAPPIN'! ZELIEK, IS IT? YE'RE FIRST!
AGH! YE SWING LIKE A NINNY, YE WEAK-WRISTED MOLE RAT!
DAD... WHAT DID THEY DO TO YOU?
RAKOOOM
WHAT ARE YOU DOING? IT'S ME! OPEN YOUR EYES, IT'S ME!

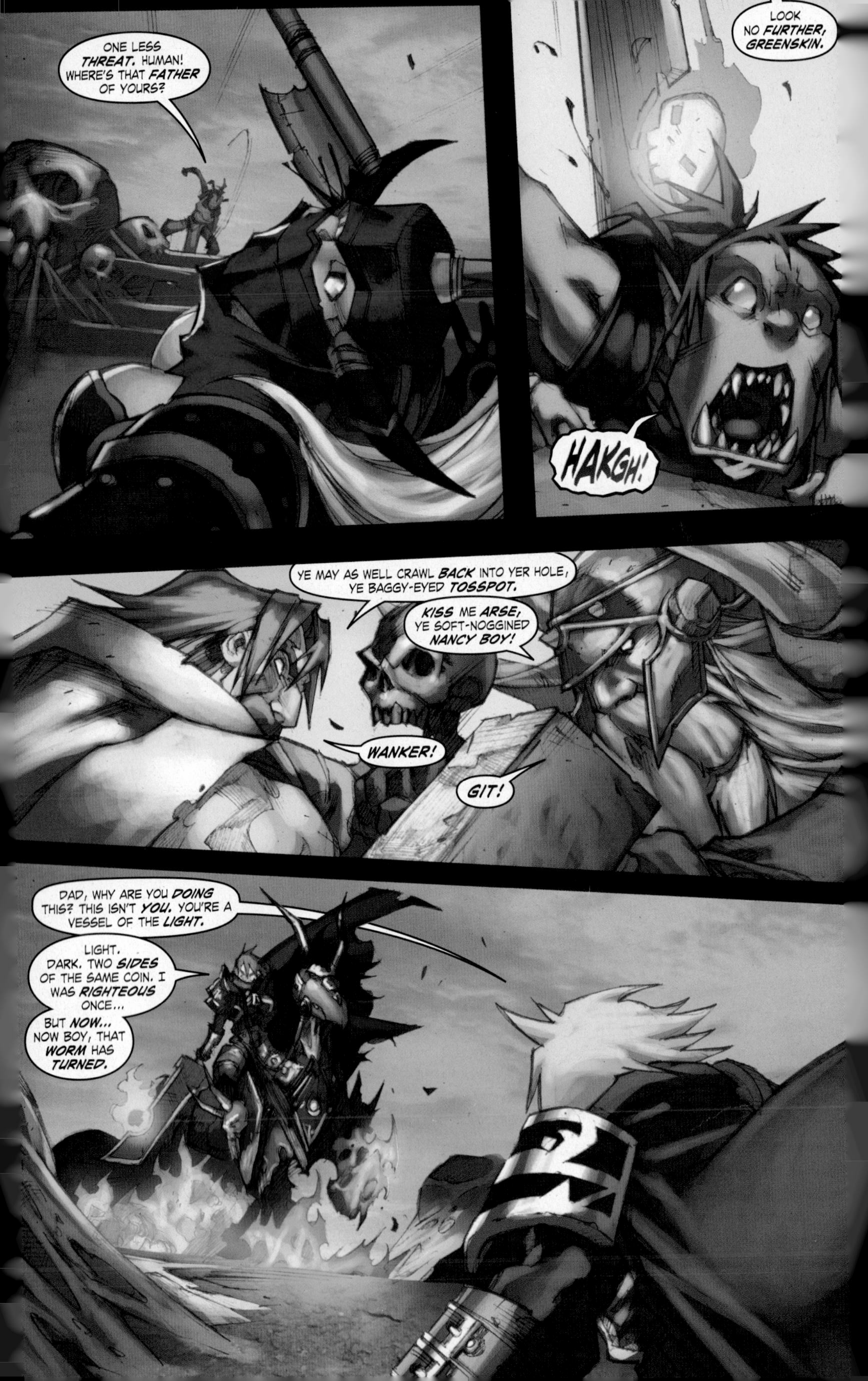
ONE LESS THREAT. HUMAN! WHERE'S THAT FATHER OF YOURS?
LOOK NO FURTHER, GREENSKIN.
HAKGH!
YE MAY AS WELL CRAWL BACK INTO YER HOLE, YE BAGGY-EYED TOSSPOT.
KISS ME ARSE, YE SOFT-NOGGINED NANCY BOY!
WANKER!
GIT!
DAD, WHY ARE YOU DOING THIS? THIS ISN'T YOU. YOU'RE A VESSEL OF THE LIGHT.
LIGHT. DARK. TWO SIDES OF THE SAME COIN. I WAS RIGHTEOUS ONCE...
BUT NOW... NOW BOY, THAT WORM HAS TURNED.

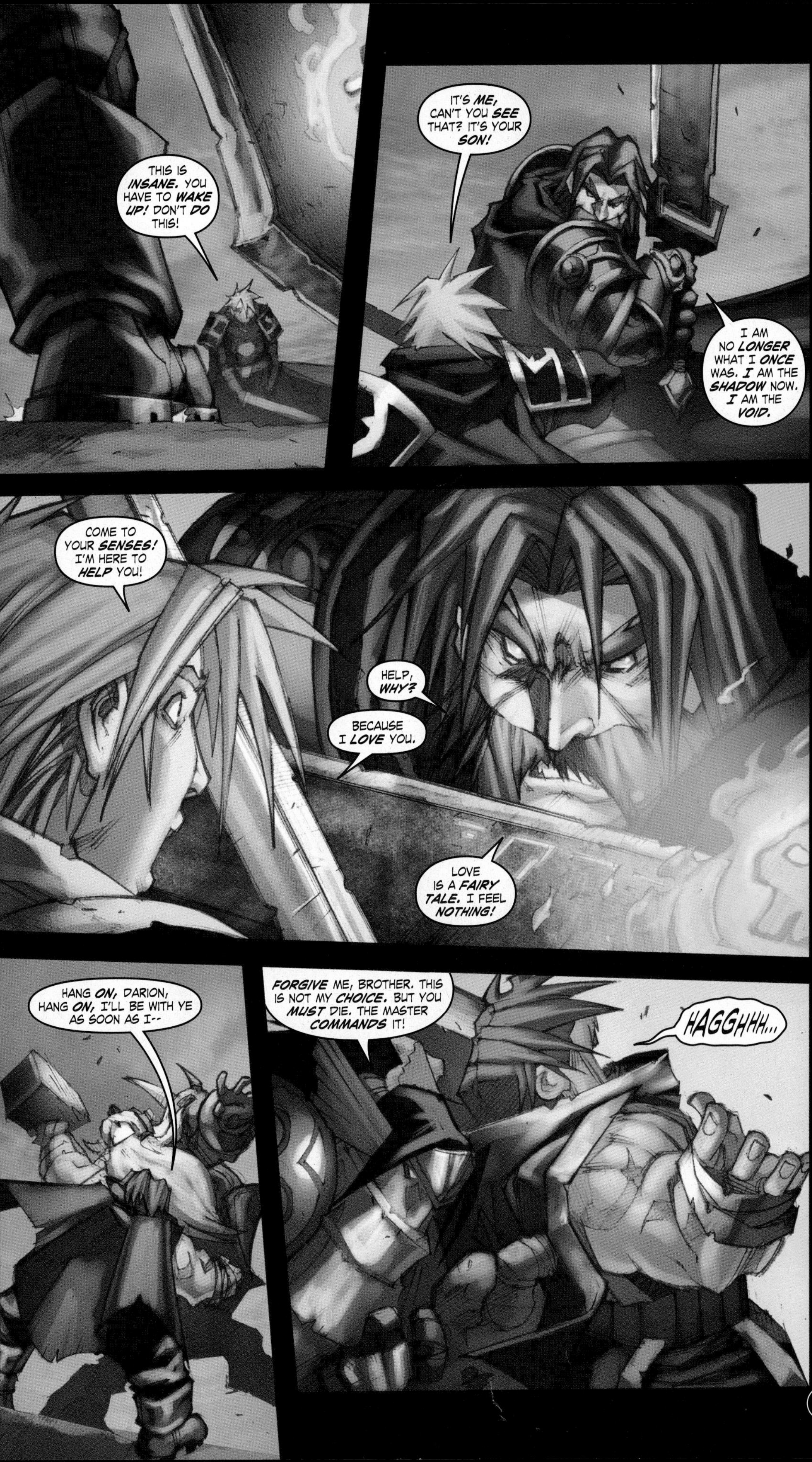
THIS IS INSANE. YOU HAVE TO WAKE UP! DON'T DO THIS!
IT'S ME, CAN'T YOU SEE THAT? IT'S YOUR SON!
I AM NO LONGER WHAT I ONCE WAS. I AM THE SHADOW NOW. I AM THE VOID.
COME TO YOUR SENSES! I'M HERE TO HELP YOU!
HELP, WHY?
BECAUSE I LOVE YOU.
LOVE IS A FAIRY TALE. I FEEL NOTHING!
HANG ON, DARION, HANG ON, I'LL BE WITH YE AS SOON AS I--
FORGIVE ME, BROTHER. THIS IS NOT MY CHOICE. BUT YOU MUST DIE. THE MASTER COMMANDS IT!
HAGGHHH...

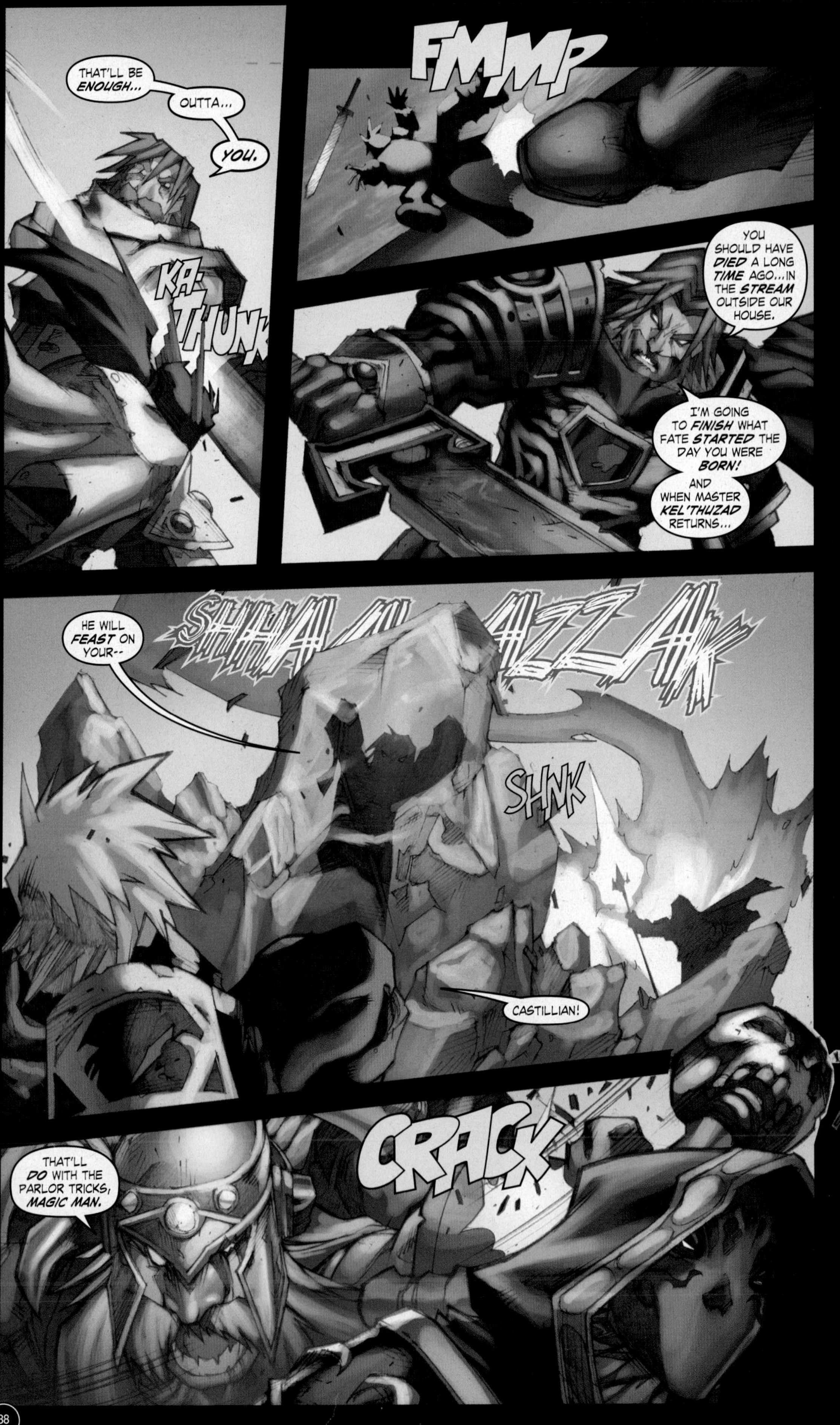
THAT'LL BE ENOUGH...
OUTTA...
YOU.
FMMP
KA-THUNK
YOU SHOULD HAVE DIED A LONG TIME AGO...IN THE STREAM OUTSIDE OUR HOUSE.
I'M GOING TO FINISH WHAT FATE STARTED THE DAY YOU WERE BORN!
AND WHEN MASTER KEL'THUZAD RETURNS...
HE WILL FEAST ON YOUR--
SHHAAAAAZZZAK
SHNK
CASTILLIAN!
THAT'LL DO WITH THE PARLOR TRICKS, MAGIC MAN.
CRACK

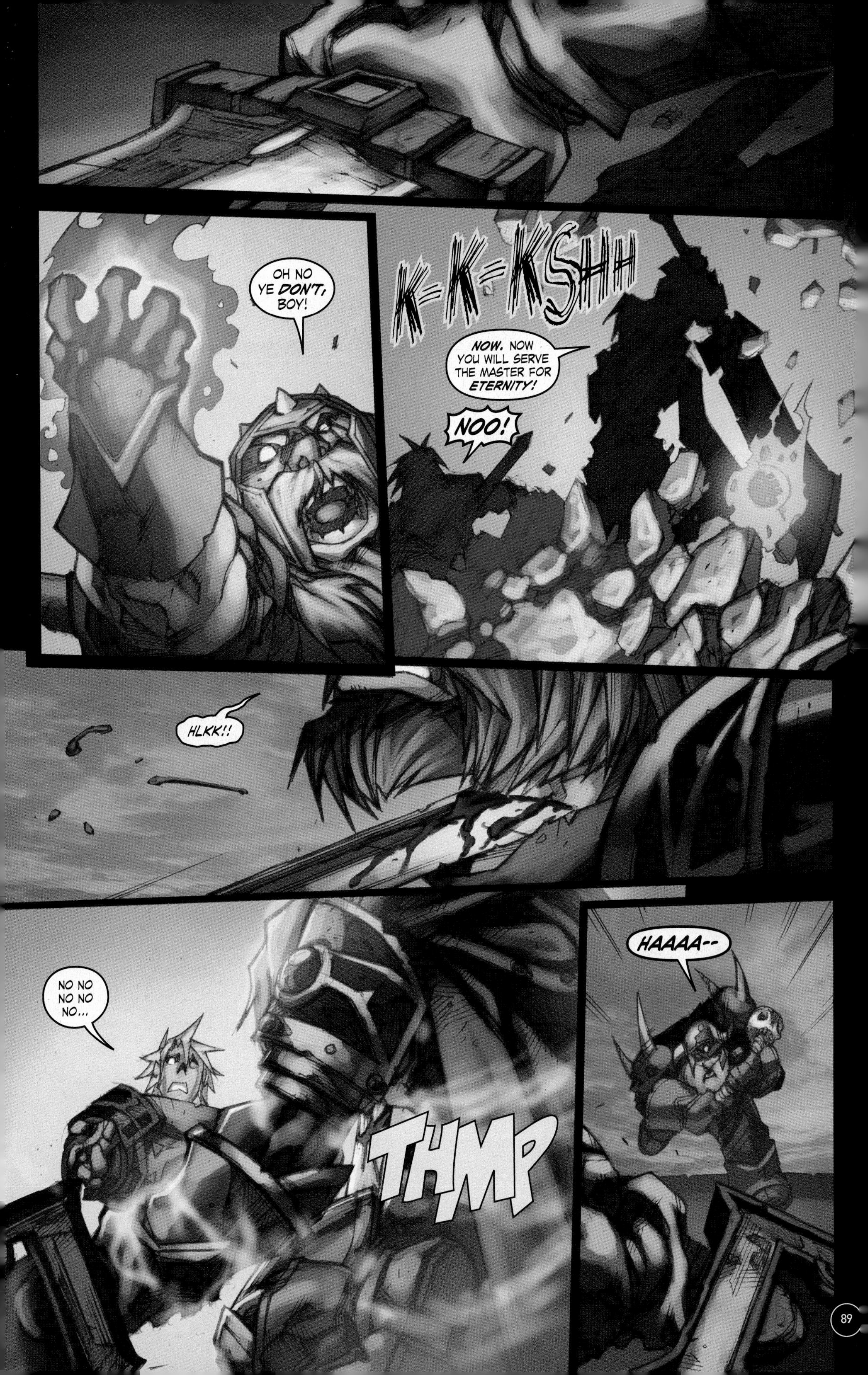
OH NO YE DON'T, BOY!
K-K-KSHH
NOW. NOW YOU WILL SERVE THE MASTER FOR ETERNITY!
NOO!
HLKK!!
NO NO NO NO NO...
THMP
HAAAA--

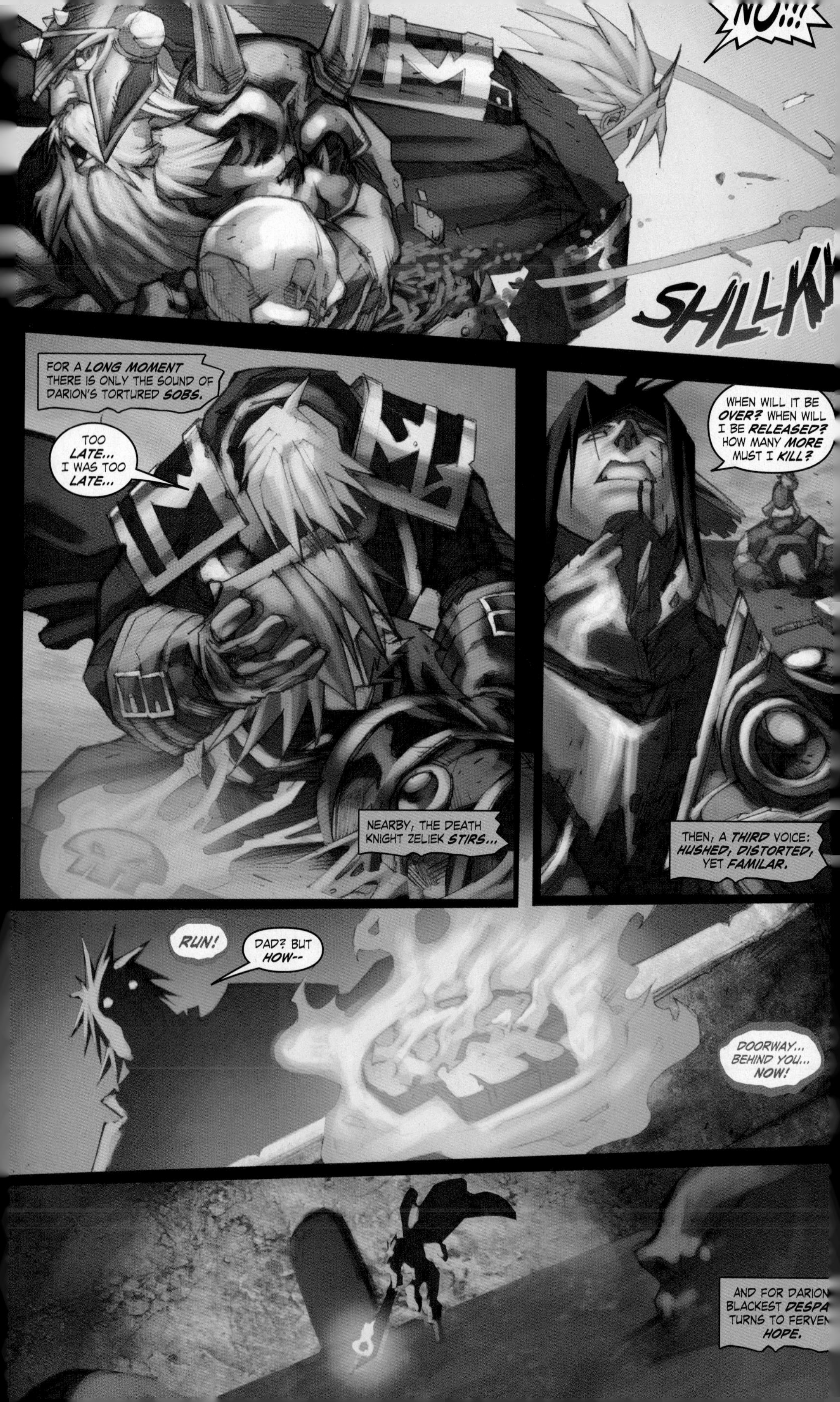
NO!!!
SHLLK
FOR A LONG MOMENT THERE IS ONLY THE SOUND OF DARION'S TORTURED SOBS.
TOO LATE... I WAS TOO LATE...
NEARBY, THE DEATH KNIGHT ZELIEK STIRS...
WHEN WILL IT BE OVER? WHEN WILL I BE RELEASED? HOW MANY MORE MUST I KILL?
THEN, A THIRD VOICE: HUSHED, DISTORTED, YET FAMILAR.
RUN!
DAD? BUT HOW--
DOORWAY... BEHIND YOU... NOW!
AND FOR DARION BLACKEST DESPA TURNS TO FERVEN HOPE.

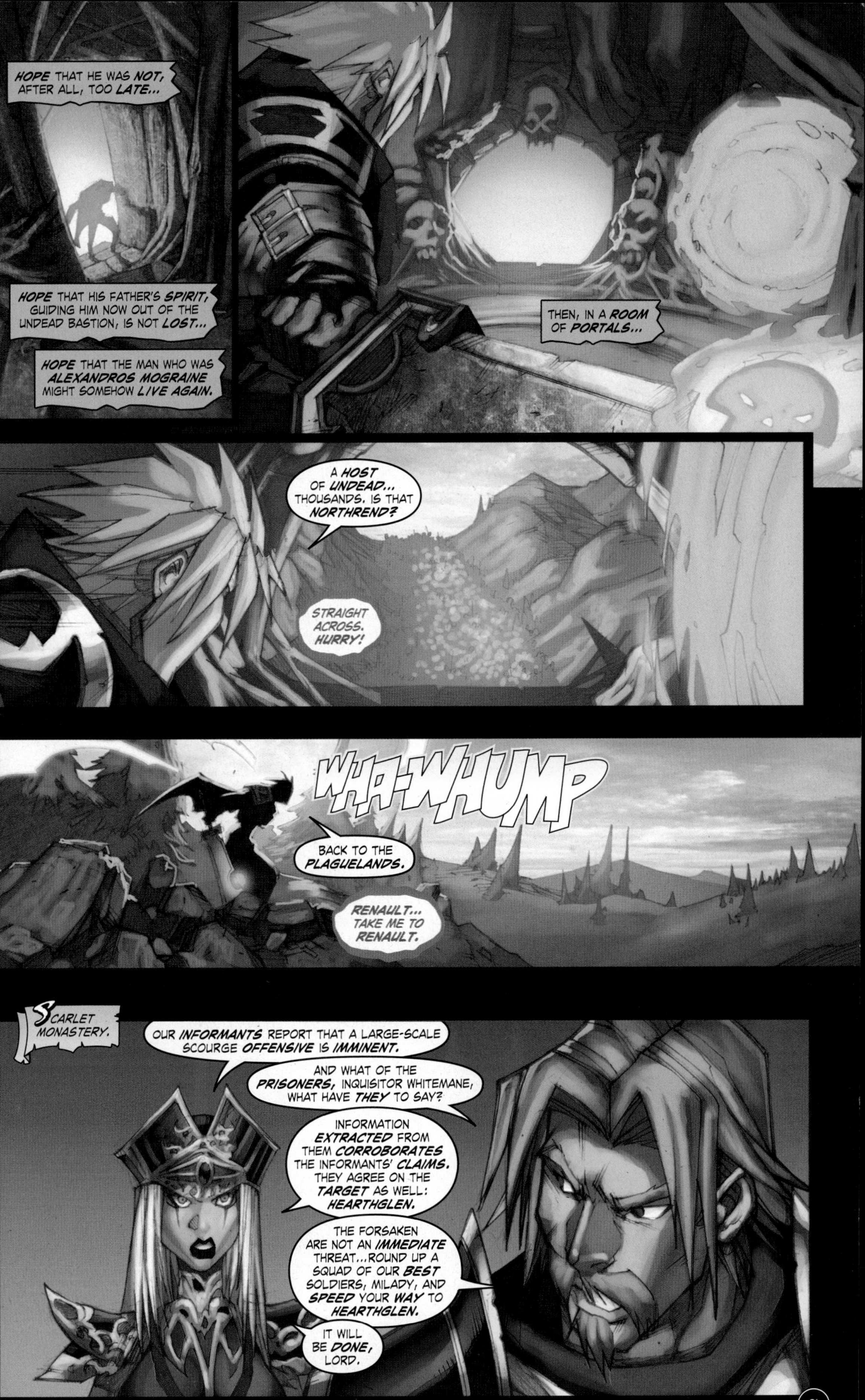

HOPE THAT HE WAS NOT, AFTER ALL, TOO LATE...
HOPE THAT HIS FATHER'S SPIRIT, GUIDING HIM NOW OUT OF THE UNDEAD BASTION, IS NOT LOST...
HOPE THAT THE MAN WHO WAS ALEXANDROS MOGRAINE MIGHT SOMEHOW LIVE AGAIN.
THEN, IN A ROOM OF PORTALS...
A HOST OF UNDEAD... THOUSANDS. IS THAT NORTHREND?
STRAIGHT ACROSS. HURRY!
WHA-WHUMP
BACK TO THE PLAGUELANDS.
RENAULT... TAKE ME TO RENAULT.
SCARLET MONASTERY.
OUR INFORMANTS REPORT THAT A LARGE-SCALE SCOURGE OFFENSIVE IS IMMINENT.
AND WHAT OF THE PRISONERS, INQUISITOR WHITEMANE, WHAT HAVE THEY TO SAY?
INFORMATION EXTRACTED FROM THEM CORROBORATES THE INFORMANTS' CLAIMS. THEY AGREE ON THE TARGET AS WELL: HEARTHGLEN.
THE FORSAKEN ARE NOT AN IMMEDIATE THREAT...ROUND UP A SQUAD OF OUR BEST SOLDIERS, MILADY, AND SPEED YOUR WAY TO HEARTHGLEN.
IT WILL BE DONE, LORD.

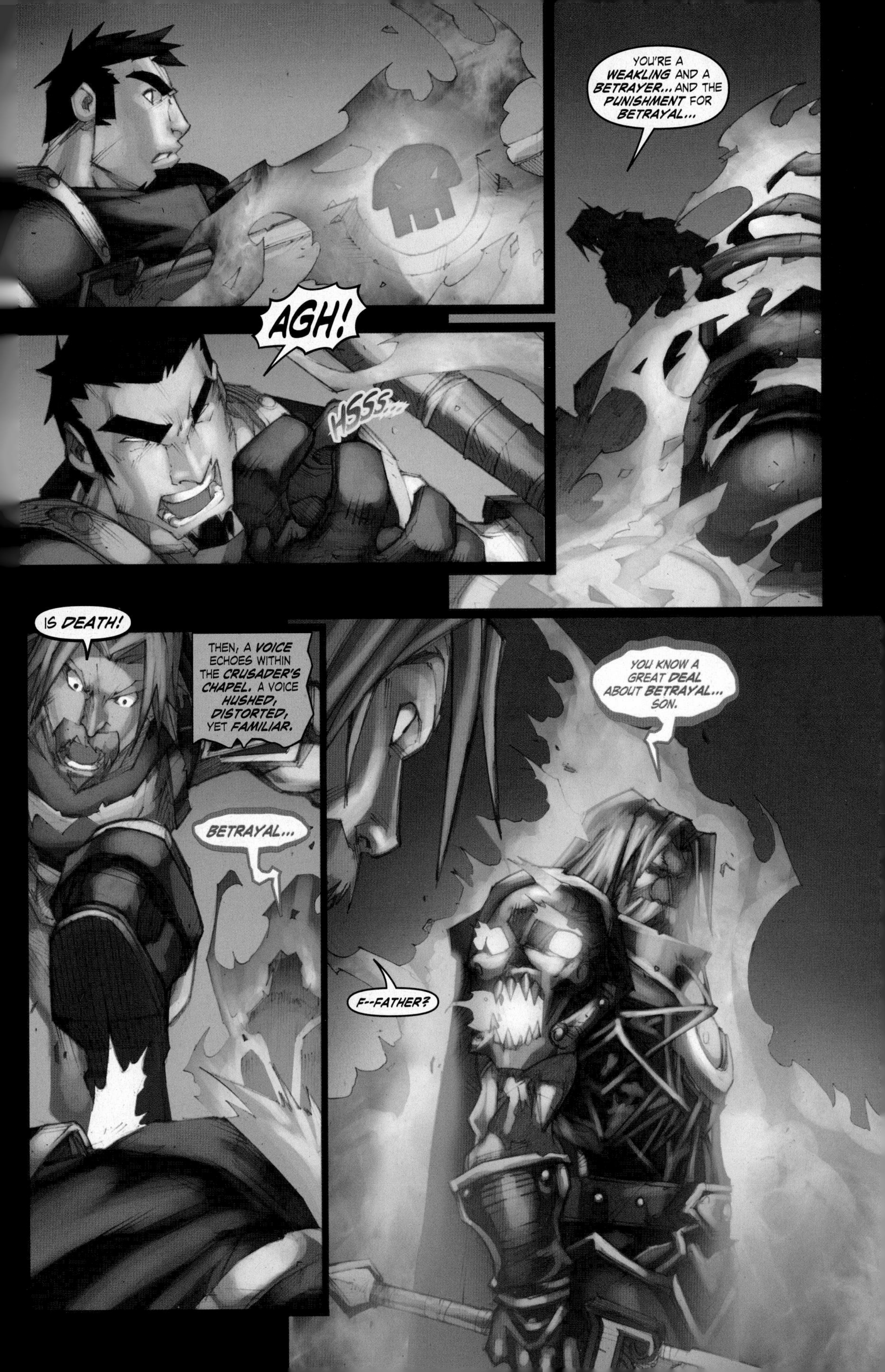
YOU'RE A WEAKLING AND A BETRAYER... AND THE PUNISHMENT FOR BETRAYAL...
AGH!
HSSS...
IS DEATH!
THEN, A VOICE ECHOES WITHIN THE CRUSADER'S CHAPEL. A VOICE HUSHED, DISTORTED, YET FAMILIAR.
BETRAYAL...
YOU KNOW A GREAT DEAL ABOUT BETRAYAL... SON.
F--FATHER?

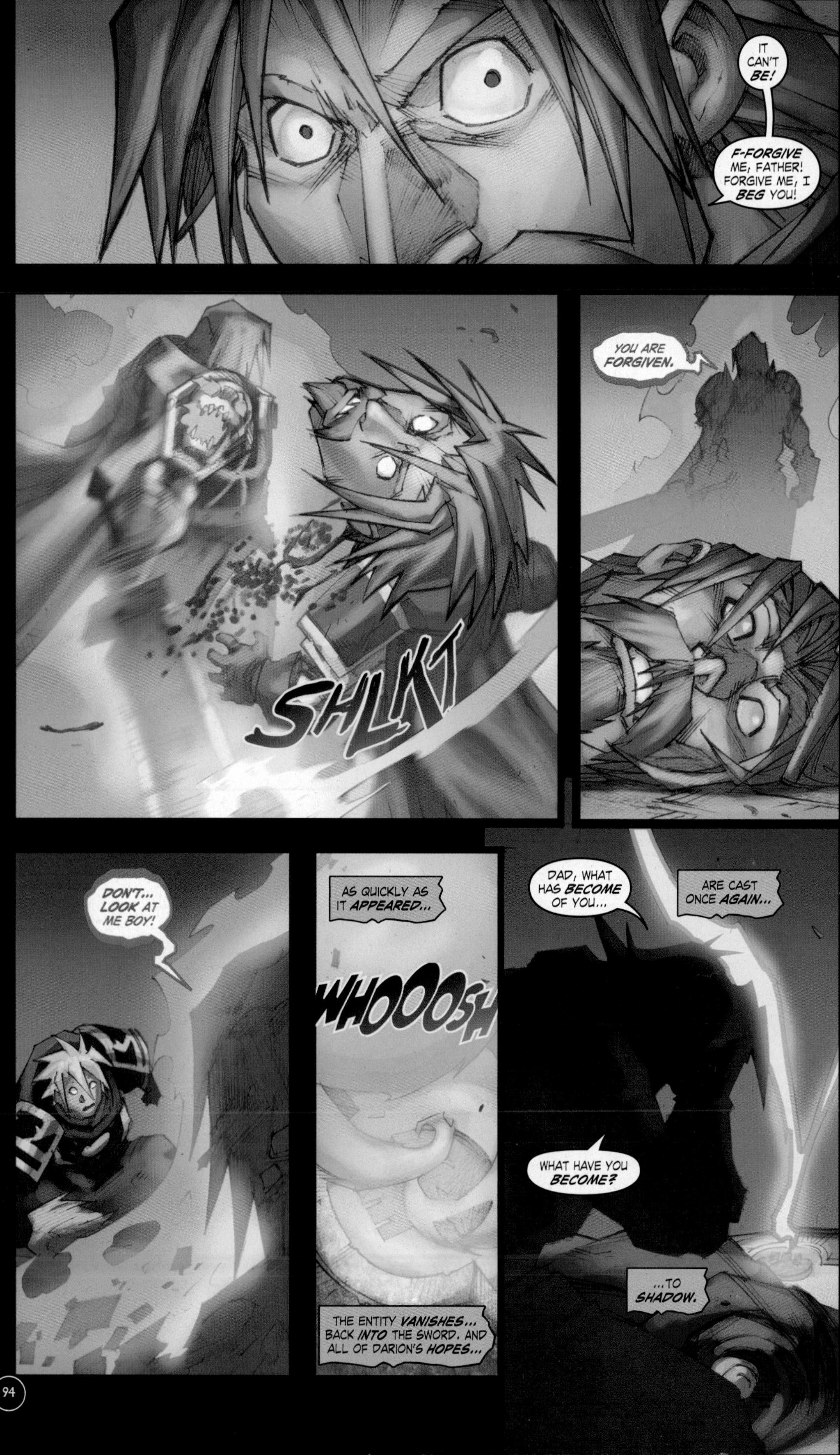
IT CAN'T BE!
F-FORGIVE ME, FATHER! FORGIVE ME, I BEG YOU!
SHLKT
YOU ARE FORGIVEN.
DON'T... LOOK AT ME BOY!
AS QUICKLY AS IT APPEARED...
WHOOOSH
THE ENTITY VANISHES... BACK INTO THE SWORD, AND ALL OF DARION'S HOPES...
DAD, WHAT HAS BECOME OF YOU...
WHAT HAVE YOU BECOME?
ARE CAST ONCE AGAIN...
...TO SHADOW.

CHAPTER 4

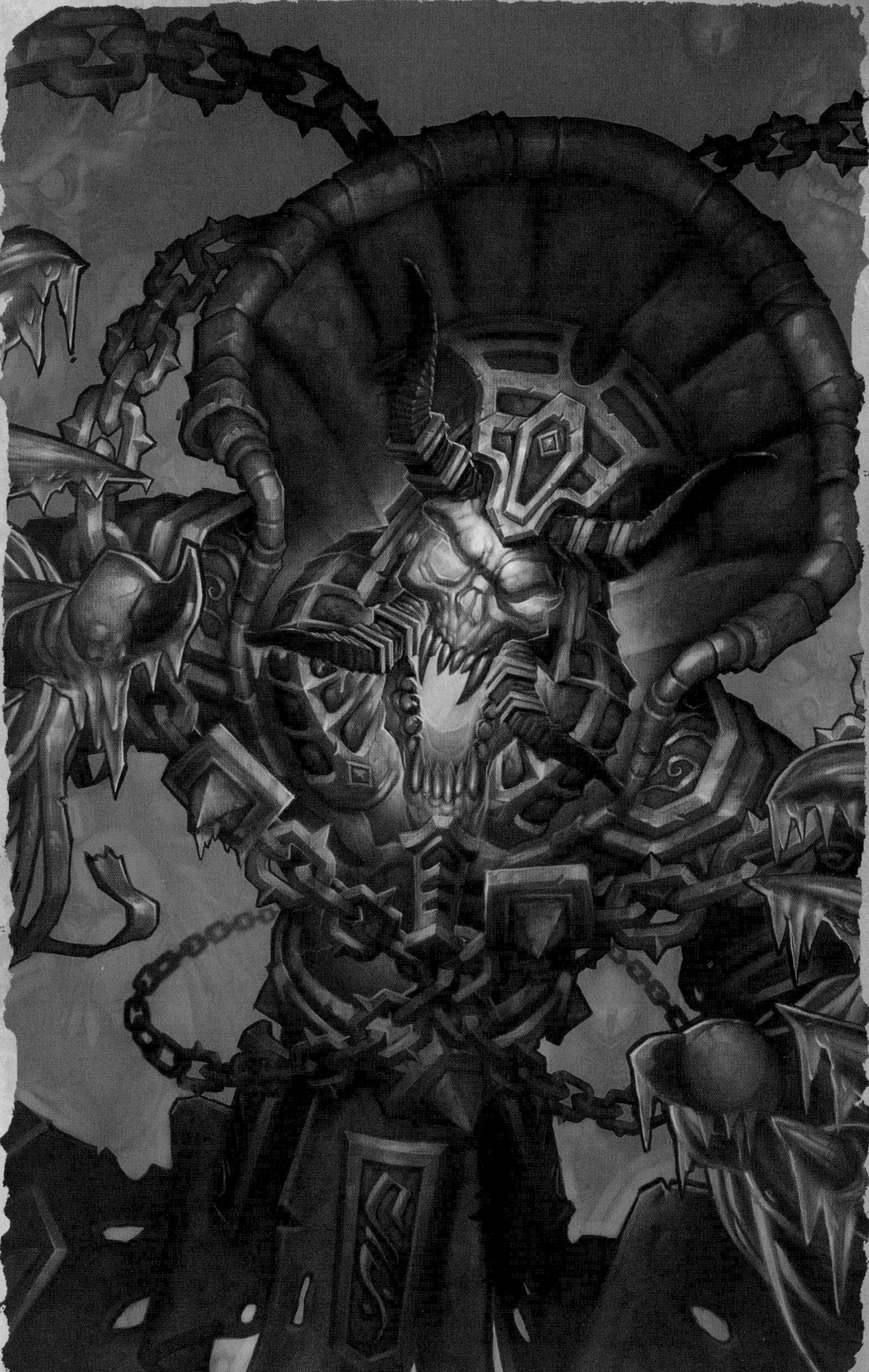

Cover by Chris Robinson

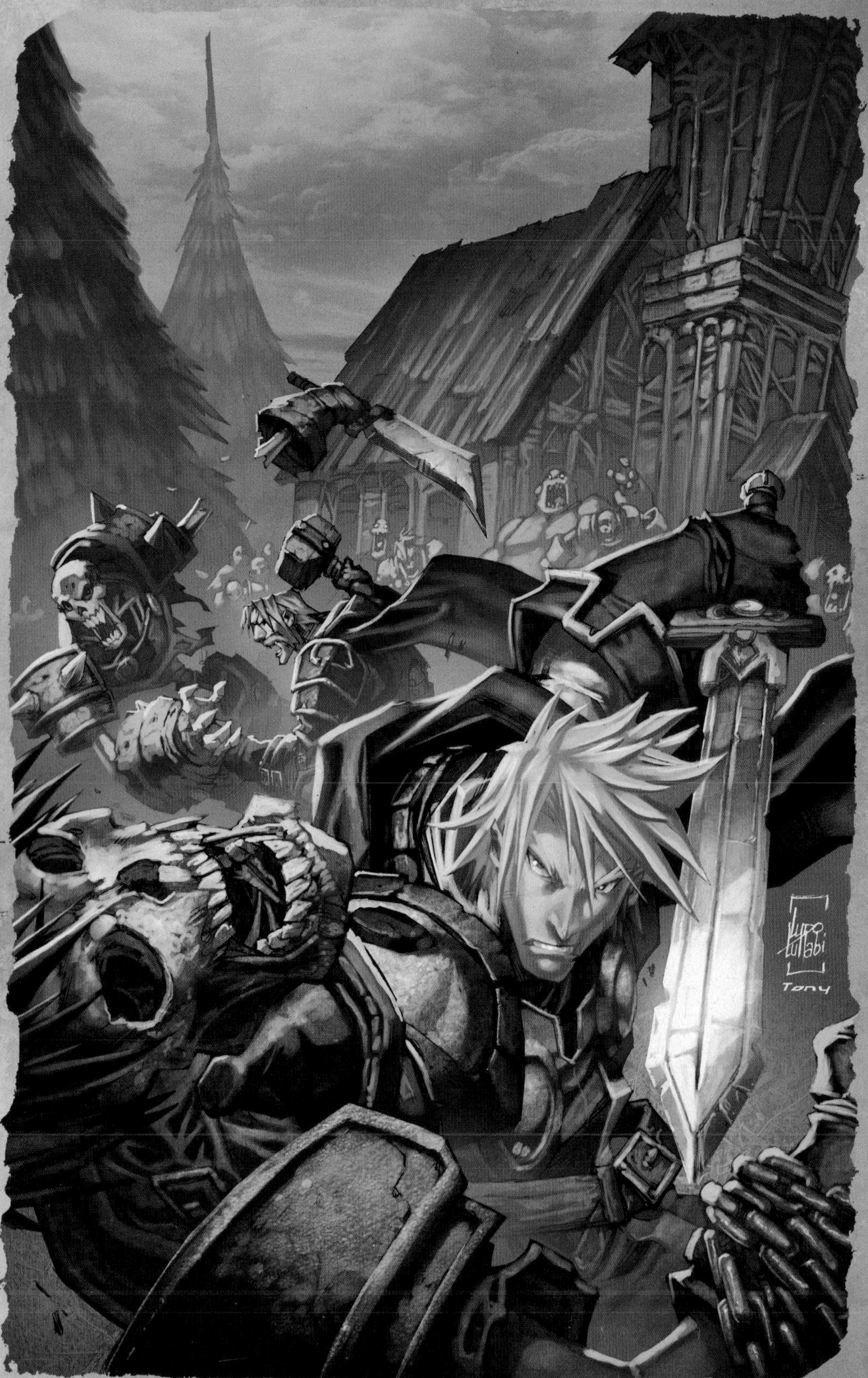

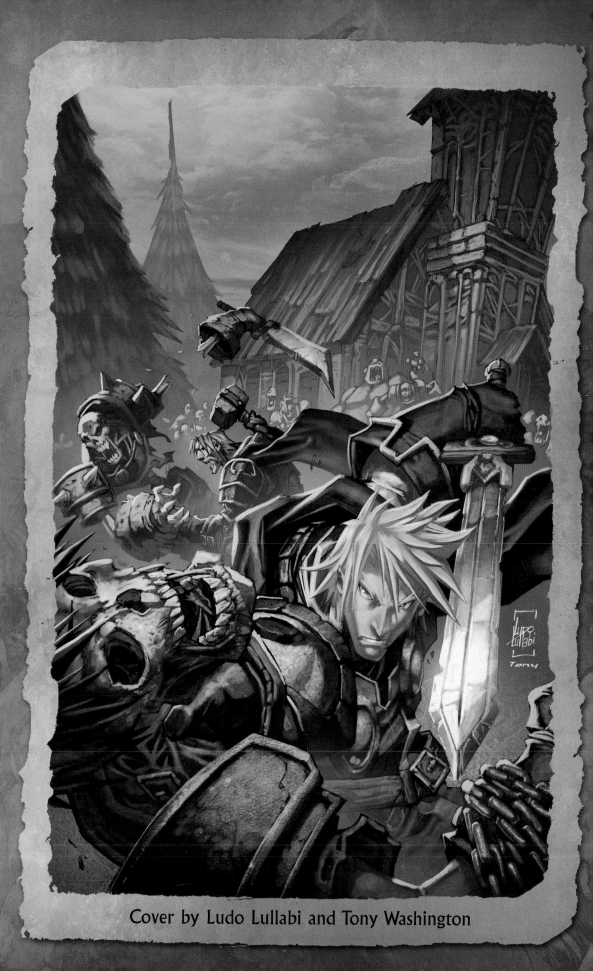

Cover by Ludo Lullabi and Tony Washington

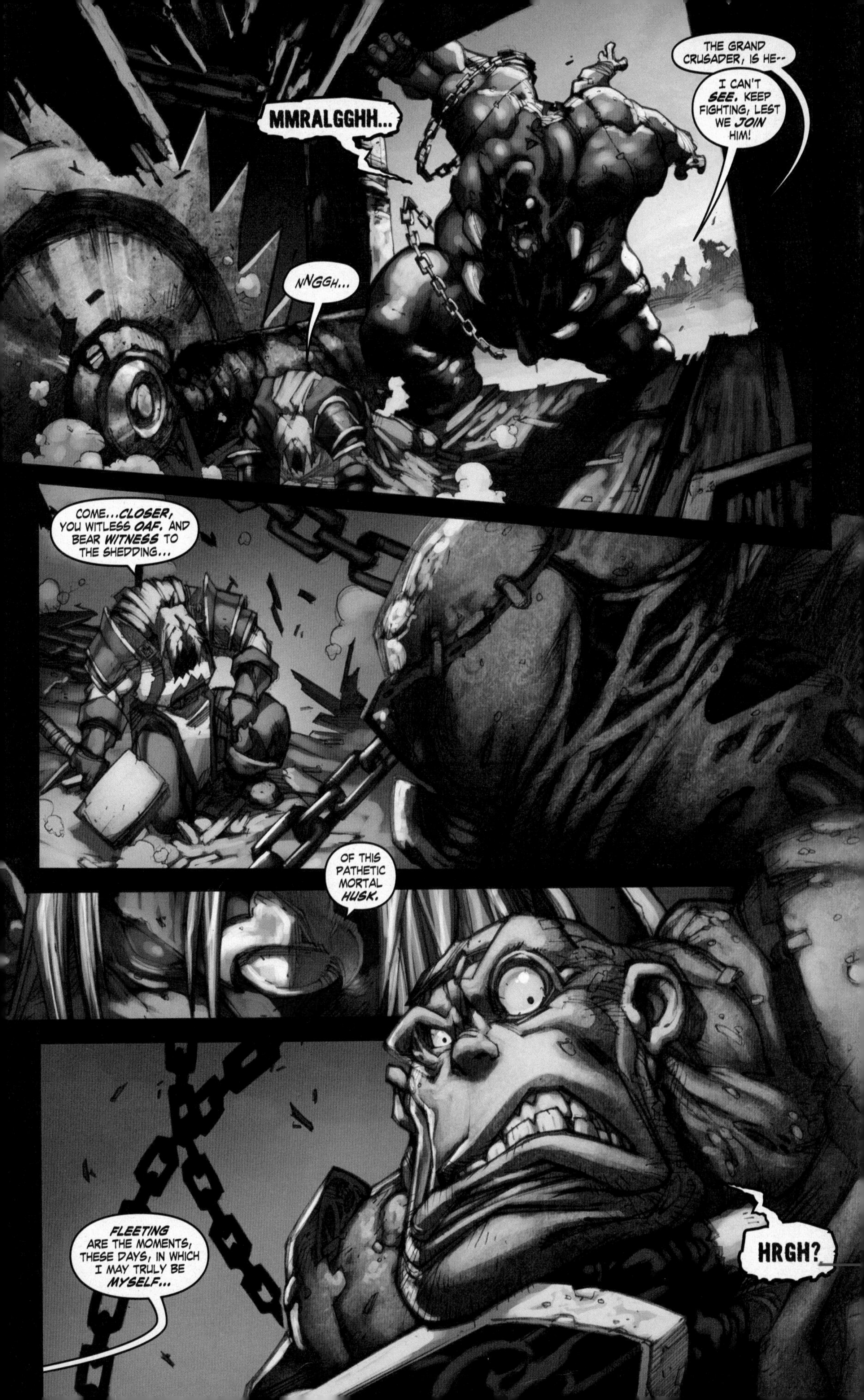
THE GRAND CRUSADER, IS HE--
I CAN'T SEE. KEEP FIGHTING, LEST WE JOIN HIM!
MMRALGGHH...
NNGGH...
COME...CLOSER, YOU WITLESS OAF. AND BEAR WITNESS TO THE SHEDDING...
OF THIS PATHETIC MORTAL HUSK.
FLEETING ARE THE MOMENTS, THESE DAYS, IN WHICH I MAY TRULY BE MYSELF...
HRGH?

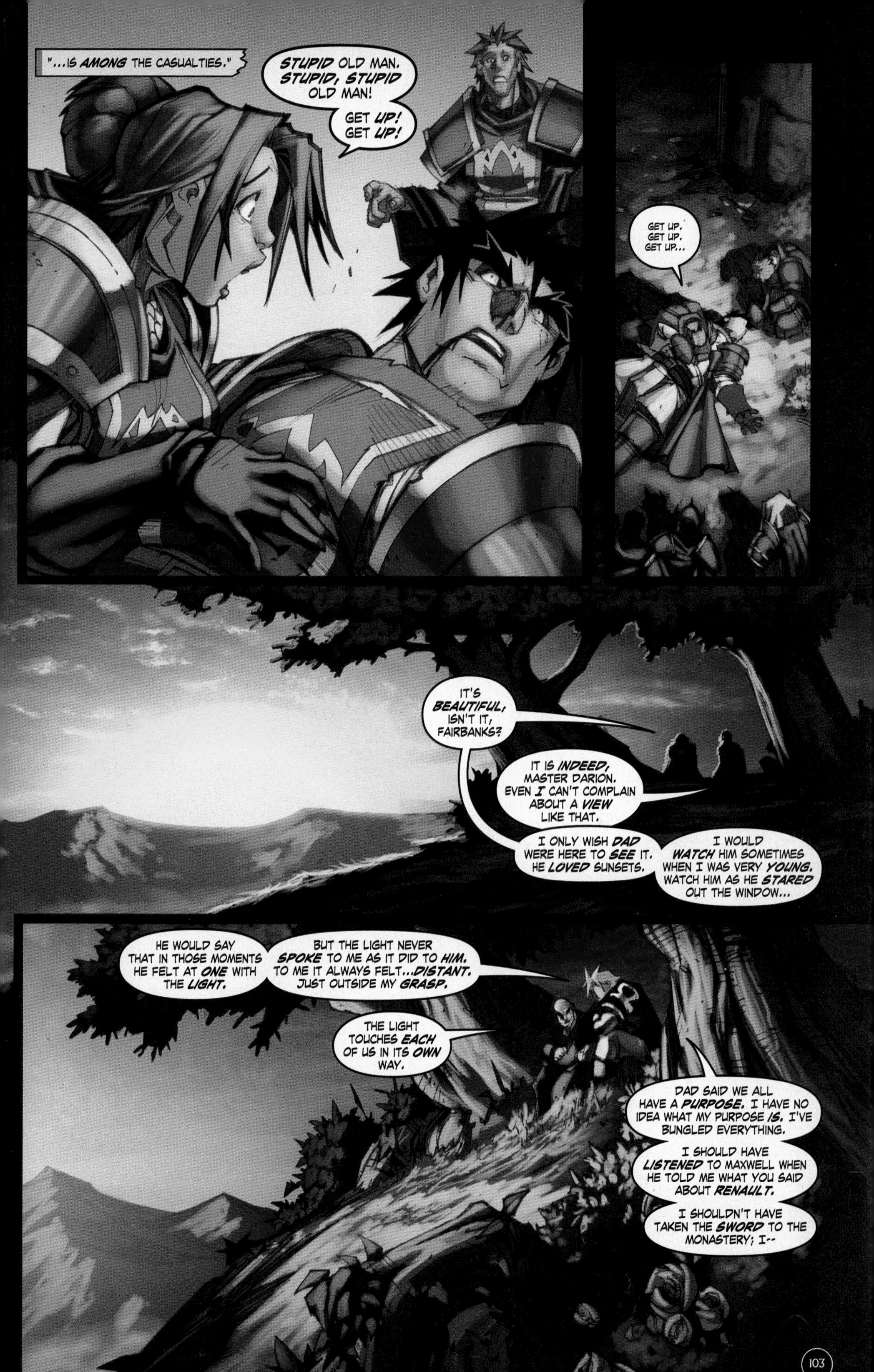
"...IS AMONG THE CASUALTIES."
STUPID OLD MAN. STUPID, STUPID OLD MAN!
GET UP! GET UP!
GET UP. GET UP. GET UP...
IT'S BEAUTIFUL, ISN'T IT, FAIRBANKS?
IT IS INDEED, MASTER DARION. EVEN I CAN'T COMPLAIN ABOUT A VIEW LIKE THAT.
I ONLY WISH DAD WERE HERE TO SEE IT. HE LOVED SUNSETS.
I WOULD WATCH HIM SOMETIMES WHEN I WAS VERY YOUNG. WATCH HIM AS HE STARED OUT THE WINDOW...
HE WOULD SAY THAT IN THOSE MOMENTS HE FELT AT ONE WITH THE LIGHT.
BUT THE LIGHT NEVER SPOKE TO ME AS IT DID TO HIM. TO ME IT ALWAYS FELT...DISTANT. JUST OUTSIDE MY GRASP.
THE LIGHT TOUCHES EACH OF US IN ITS OWN WAY.
DAD SAID WE ALL HAVE A PURPOSE. I HAVE NO IDEA WHAT MY PURPOSE IS. I'VE BUNGLED EVERYTHING.
I SHOULD HAVE LISTENED TO MAXWELL WHEN HE TOLD ME WHAT YOU SAID ABOUT RENAULT.
I SHOULDN'T HAVE TAKEN THE SWORD TO THE MONASTERY; I--

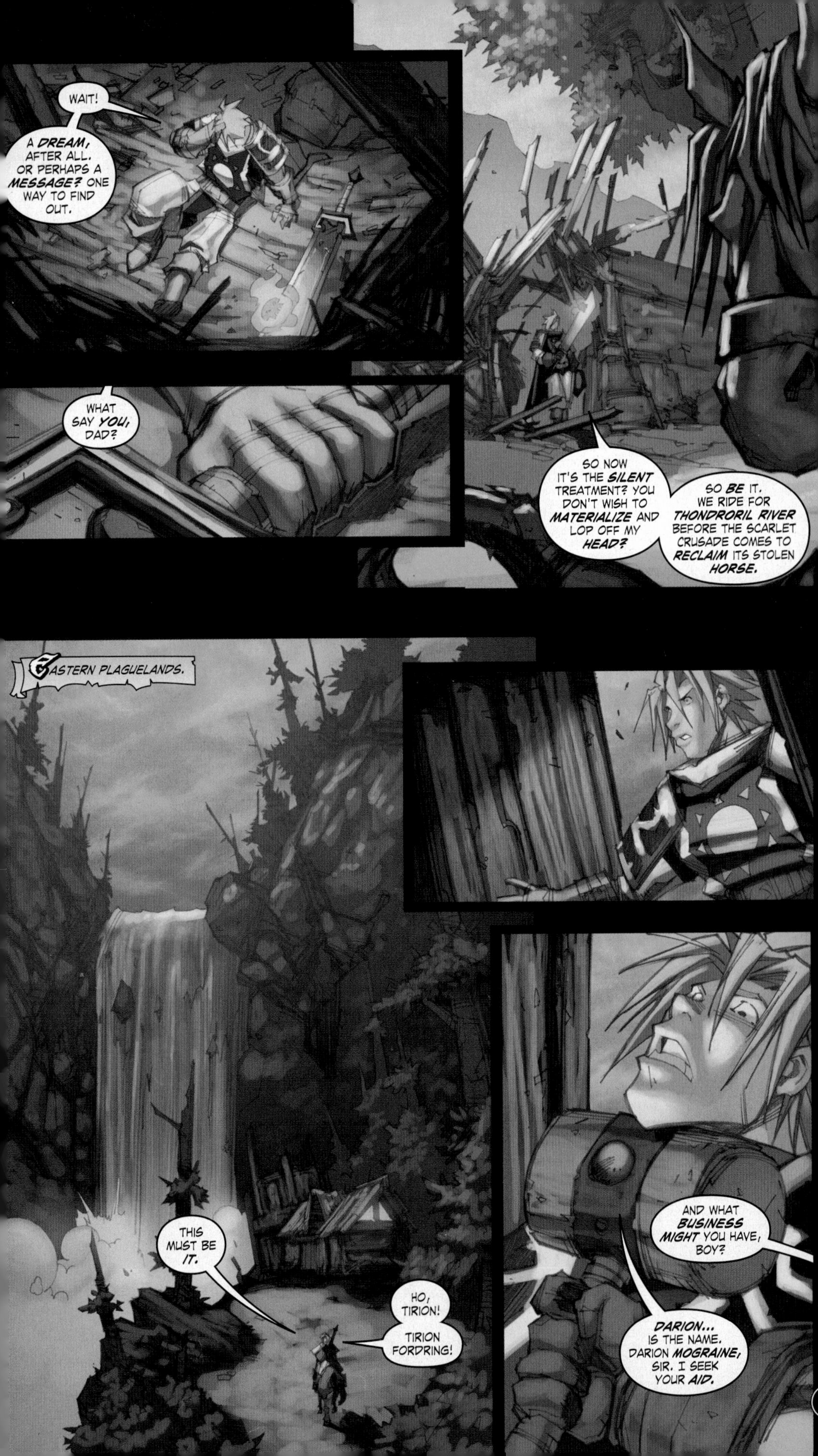
WAIT!
A DREAM, AFTER ALL. OR PERHAPS A MESSAGE? ONE WAY TO FIND OUT.
WHAT SAY YOU, DAD?
SO NOW IT'S THE SILENT TREATMENT? YOU DON'T WISH TO MATERIALIZE AND LOP OFF MY HEAD?
SO BE IT. WE RIDE FOR THONDRORIL RIVER BEFORE THE SCARLET CRUSADE COMES TO RECLAIM ITS STOLEN HORSE.
EASTERN PLAGUELANDS.
THIS MUST BE IT.
HO, TIRION!
TIRION FORDRING!
AND WHAT BUSINESS MIGHT YOU HAVE, BOY?
DARION... IS THE NAME. DARION MOGRAINE, SIR. I SEEK YOUR AID.

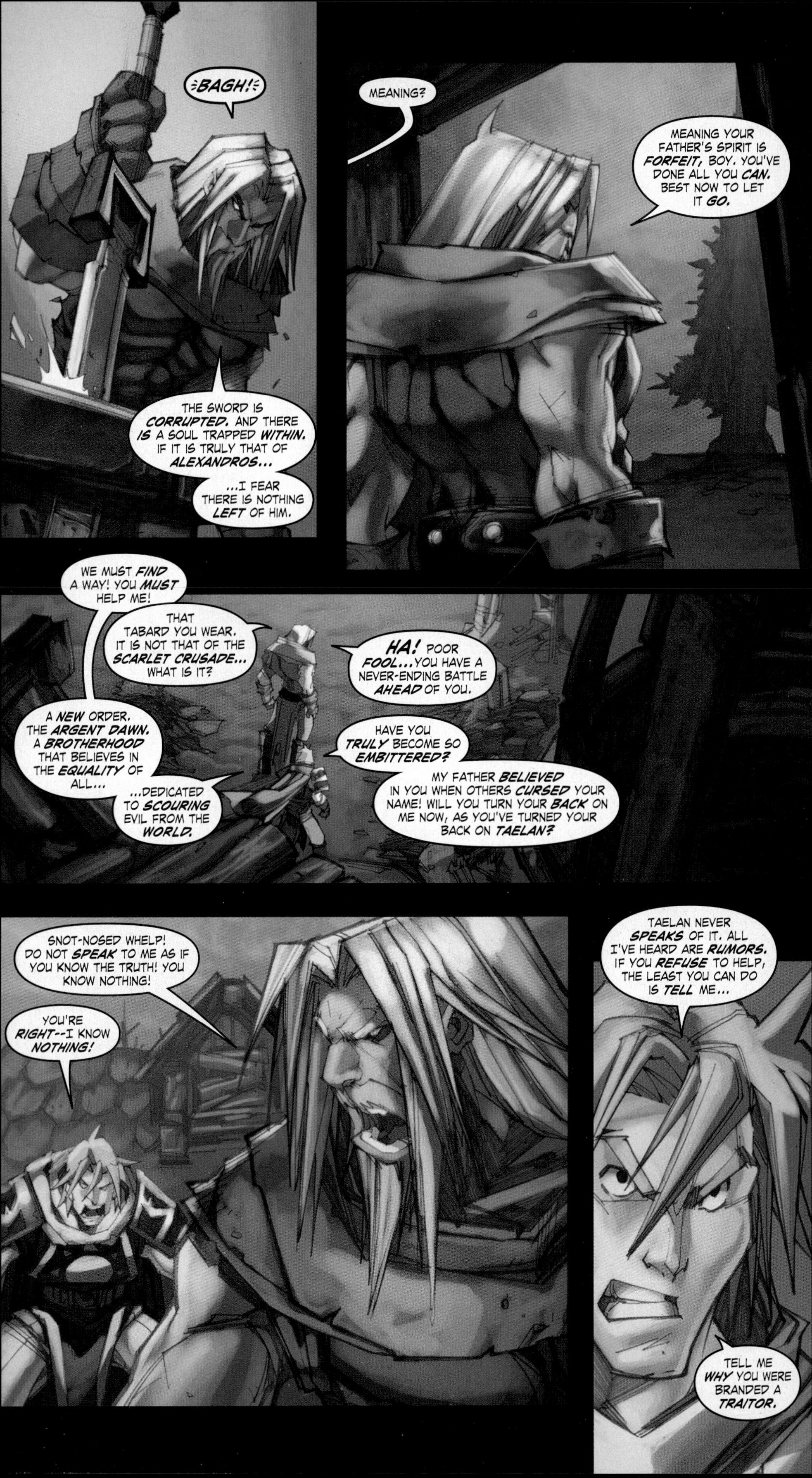
BAGH!
THE SWORD IS CORRUPTED. AND THERE IS A SOUL TRAPPED WITHIN. IF IT IS TRULY THAT OF ALEXANDROS...
...I FEAR THERE IS NOTHING LEFT OF HIM.
MEANING?
MEANING YOUR FATHER'S SPIRIT IS FORFEIT, BOY. YOU'VE DONE ALL YOU CAN. BEST NOW TO LET IT GO.
WE MUST FIND A WAY! YOU MUST HELP ME!
THAT TABARD YOU WEAR. IT IS NOT THAT OF THE SCARLET CRUSADE... WHAT IS IT?
A NEW ORDER. THE ARGENT DAWN. A BROTHERHOOD THAT BELIEVES IN THE EQUALITY OF ALL...
...DEDICATED TO SCOURING EVIL FROM THE WORLD.
HA! POOR FOOL...YOU HAVE A NEVER-ENDING BATTLE AHEAD OF YOU.
HAVE YOU TRULY BECOME SO EMBITTERED?
MY FATHER BELIEVED IN YOU WHEN OTHERS CURSED YOUR NAME! WILL YOU TURN YOUR BACK ON ME NOW, AS YOU'VE TURNED YOUR BACK ON TAELAN?
SNOT-NOSED WHELP! DO NOT SPEAK TO ME AS IF YOU KNOW THE TRUTH! YOU KNOW NOTHING!
YOU'RE RIGHT--I KNOW NOTHING!
TAELAN NEVER SPEAKS OF IT. ALL I'VE HEARD ARE RUMORS. IF YOU REFUSE TO HELP, THE LEAST YOU CAN DO IS TELL ME...
TELL ME WHY YOU WERE BRANDED A TRAITOR.

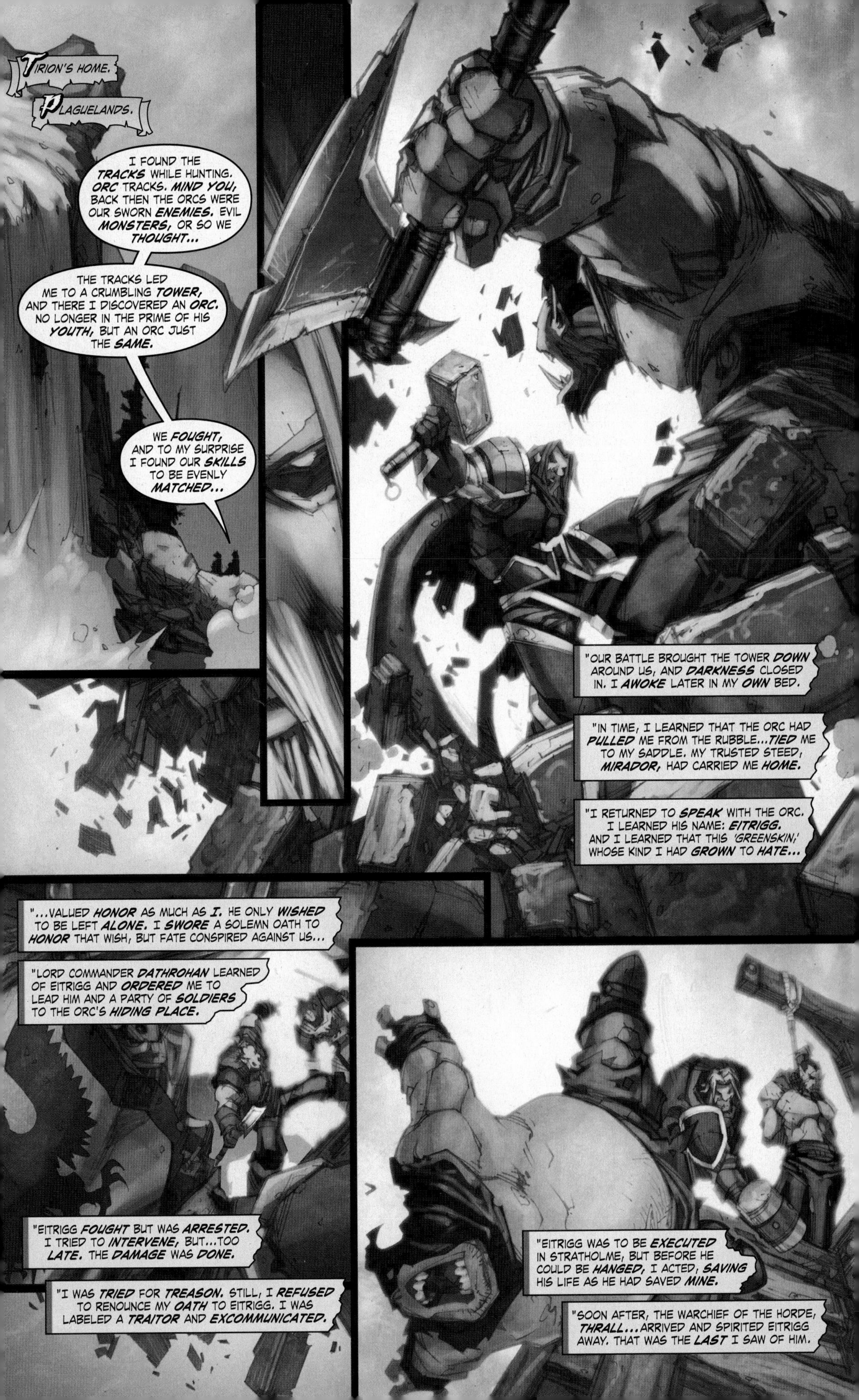
TIRION'S HOME.
PLAGUELANDS.
I FOUND THE TRACKS WHILE HUNTING. ORC TRACKS. MIND YOU, BACK THEN THE ORCS WERE OUR SWORN ENEMIES. EVIL MONSTERS, OR SO WE THOUGHT...
THE TRACKS LED ME TO A CRUMBLING TOWER, AND THERE I DISCOVERED AN ORC. NO LONGER IN THE PRIME OF HIS YOUTH, BUT AN ORC JUST THE SAME.
WE FOUGHT, AND TO MY SURPRISE I FOUND OUR SKILLS TO BE EVENLY MATCHED...
"OUR BATTLE BROUGHT THE TOWER DOWN AROUND US, AND DARKNESS CLOSED IN. I AWOKE LATER IN MY OWN BED.
"IN TIME, I LEARNED THAT THE ORC HAD PULLED ME FROM THE RUBBLE...TIED ME TO MY SADDLE. MY TRUSTED STEED, MIRADOR, HAD CARRIED ME HOME.
"I RETURNED TO SPEAK WITH THE ORC. I LEARNED HIS NAME: EITRIGG. AND I LEARNED THAT THIS 'GREENSKIN,' WHOSE KIND I HAD GROWN TO HATE...
"...VALUED HONOR AS MUCH AS I. HE ONLY WISHED TO BE LEFT ALONE. I SWORE A SOLEMN OATH TO HONOR THAT WISH, BUT FATE CONSPIRED AGAINST US...
"LORD COMMANDER DATHROHAN LEARNED OF EITRIGG AND ORDERED ME TO LEAD HIM AND A PARTY OF SOLDIERS TO THE ORC'S HIDING PLACE.
"EITRIGG FOUGHT BUT WAS ARRESTED. I TRIED TO INTERVENE, BUT...TOO LATE. THE DAMAGE WAS DONE.
"I WAS TRIED FOR TREASON. STILL, I REFUSED TO RENOUNCE MY OATH TO EITRIGG. I WAS LABELED A TRAITOR AND EXCOMMUNICATED.
"EITRIGG WAS TO BE EXECUTED IN STRATHOLME, BUT BEFORE HE COULD BE HANGED, I ACTED, SAVING HIS LIFE AS HE HAD SAVED MINE.
"SOON AFTER, THE WARCHIEF OF THE HORDE, THRALL...ARRIVED AND SPIRITED EITRIGG AWAY. THAT WAS THE LAST I SAW OF HIM.

IT WAS A MATTER OF **HONOR**. A MAN HAS **NOTHING** IF HE HAS NOT HONOR.

OF COURSE, UTHER, DATHROHAN, AND THE OTHERS DIDN'T **SEE** IT THAT WAY. DESPITE MY "OUTCAST" STATUS, I'VE KEPT **WATCH** THROUGH THE YEARS...

THE DAY TAELAN WAS **KNIGHTED**, I **SNUCK** INTO THE CEREMONY. I WAS SO **PROUD** OF HIM...

BUT **NOW**... NOW HE CASTS HIS LOT WITH THIS **SCARLET CRUSADE**...

A CORRUPT **TRAVESTY** THAT'S AS MUCH A **BLIGHT** UPON THE LAND AS THE **PLAGUE** ITSELF.

TAELAN ISN'T **LIKE** THE OTHERS. IF I HAD TO **GUESS**, I'D SAY THAT MAYBE HE'S LOST HIS **WAY**...

I **UNDERSTAND** WHAT HE'S **GOING** THROUGH. I KNOW WHAT IT'S LIKE...

...TO LOSE A **FATHER**.

THANK YOU FOR SHARING YOUR **TALE**, BROTHER TIRION. I **REALIZE** NOW THAT YOU WERE FACED WITH AN **IMPOSSIBLE** CHOICE...

AND YOU MADE THE ONLY **DECISION** YOU COULD. JUST AS I'VE MADE **MINE**: I MUST SET OFF TO MEET THE **OTHERS** AT **LIGHT'S HOPE**...

...AND **CONTINUE** MY QUEST.

AN ACT OF LOVE.

I'VE BEEN GIVING IT CAREFUL **CONSIDERATION**...

I BELIEVE THAT ONLY AN ACT OF LOVE **GREATER** THAN THE ACT OF **EVIL** THAT CORRUPTED THE SWORD WILL BE **POWERFUL** ENOUGH TO FREE YOUR FATHER'S **SOUL**.

WHAT?

BUT BE **WARNED**: SUCH AN ACT IS OFTEN THE **ULTIMATE** TEST OF **FAITH**.

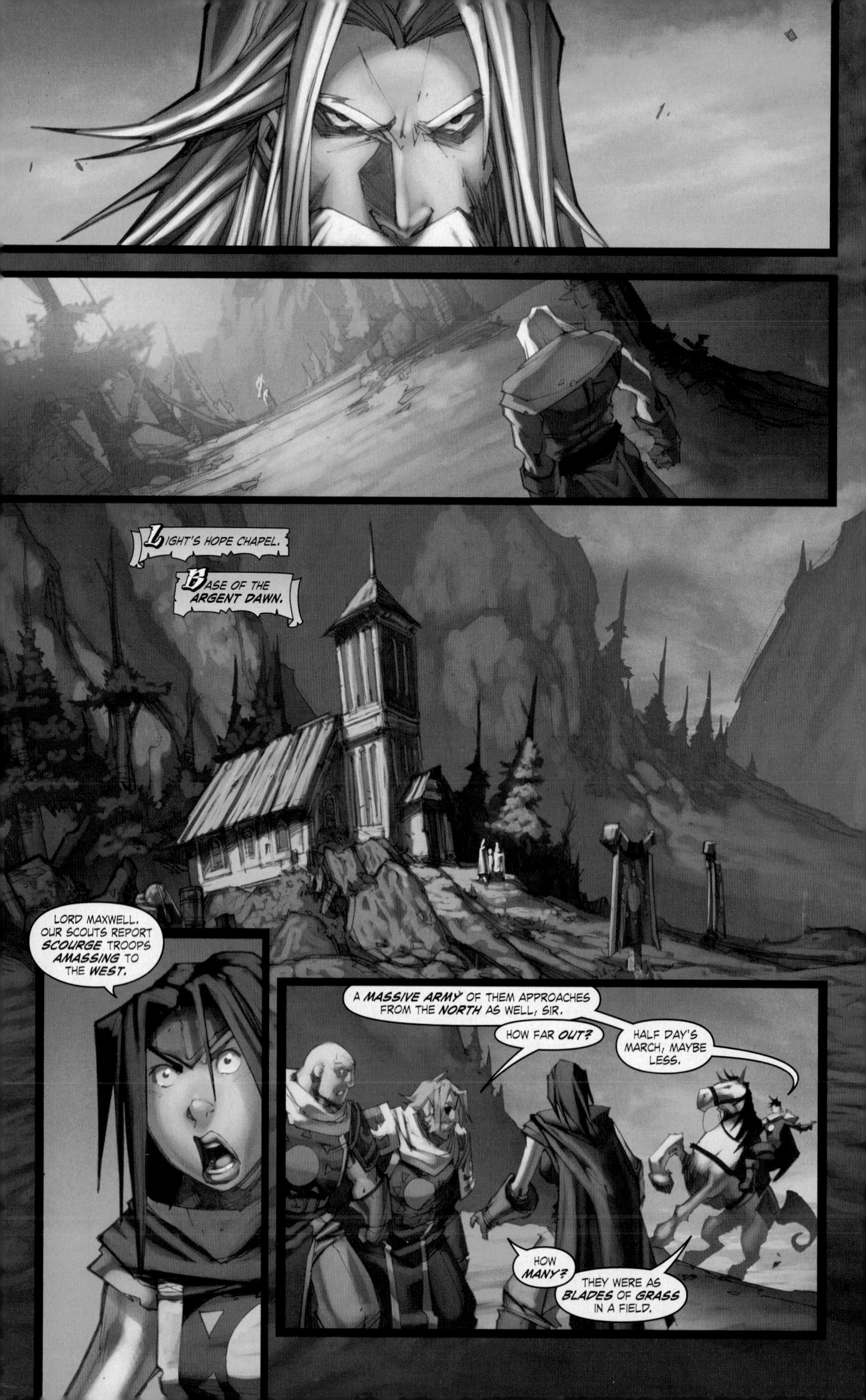
LIGHT'S HOPE CHAPEL.
BASE OF THE ARGENT DAWN.
LORD MAXWELL. OUR SCOUTS REPORT SCOURGE TROOPS AMASSING TO THE WEST.
A MASSIVE ARMY OF THEM APPROACHES FROM THE NORTH AS WELL, SIR.
HOW FAR OUT?
HALF DAY'S MARCH, MAYBE LESS.
HOW MANY?
THEY WERE AS BLADES OF GRASS IN A FIELD.

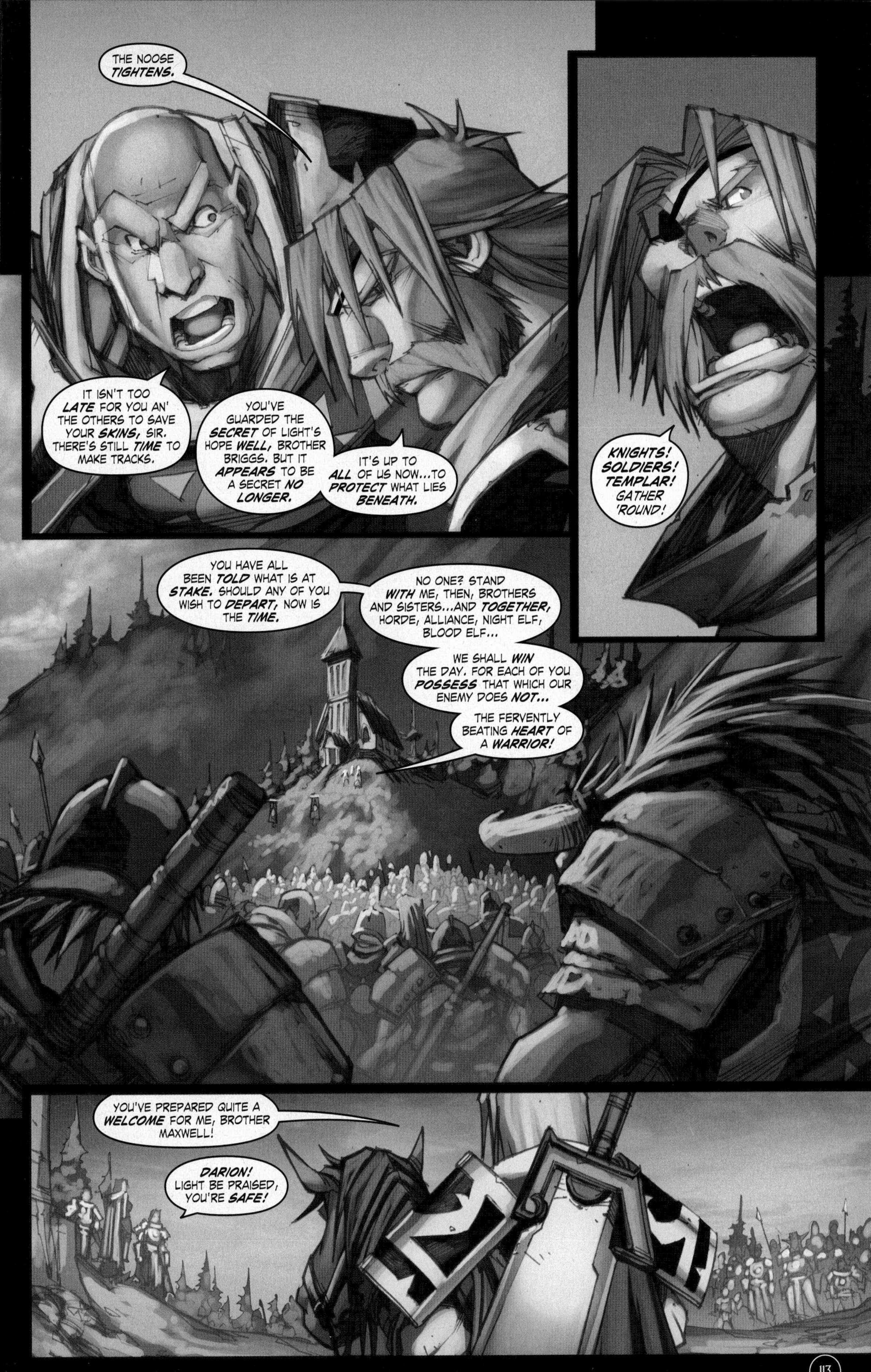
THE NOOSE TIGHTENS.
IT ISN'T TOO LATE FOR YOU AN' THE OTHERS TO SAVE YOUR SKINS, SIR. THERE'S STILL TIME TO MAKE TRACKS.
YOU'VE GUARDED THE SECRET OF LIGHT'S HOPE WELL, BROTHER BRIGGS. BUT IT APPEARS TO BE A SECRET NO LONGER.
IT'S UP TO ALL OF US NOW...TO PROTECT WHAT LIES BENEATH.
KNIGHTS! SOLDIERS! TEMPLAR! GATHER 'ROUND!
YOU HAVE ALL BEEN TOLD WHAT IS AT STAKE. SHOULD ANY OF YOU WISH TO DEPART, NOW IS THE TIME.
NO ONE? STAND WITH ME, THEN, BROTHERS AND SISTERS...AND TOGETHER, HORDE, ALLIANCE, NIGHT ELF, BLOOD ELF...
WE SHALL WIN THE DAY. FOR EACH OF YOU POSSESS THAT WHICH OUR ENEMY DOES NOT...
THE FERVENTLY BEATING HEART OF A WARRIOR!
YOU'VE PREPARED QUITE A WELCOME FOR ME, BROTHER MAXWELL!
DARION! LIGHT BE PRAISED, YOU'RE SAFE!

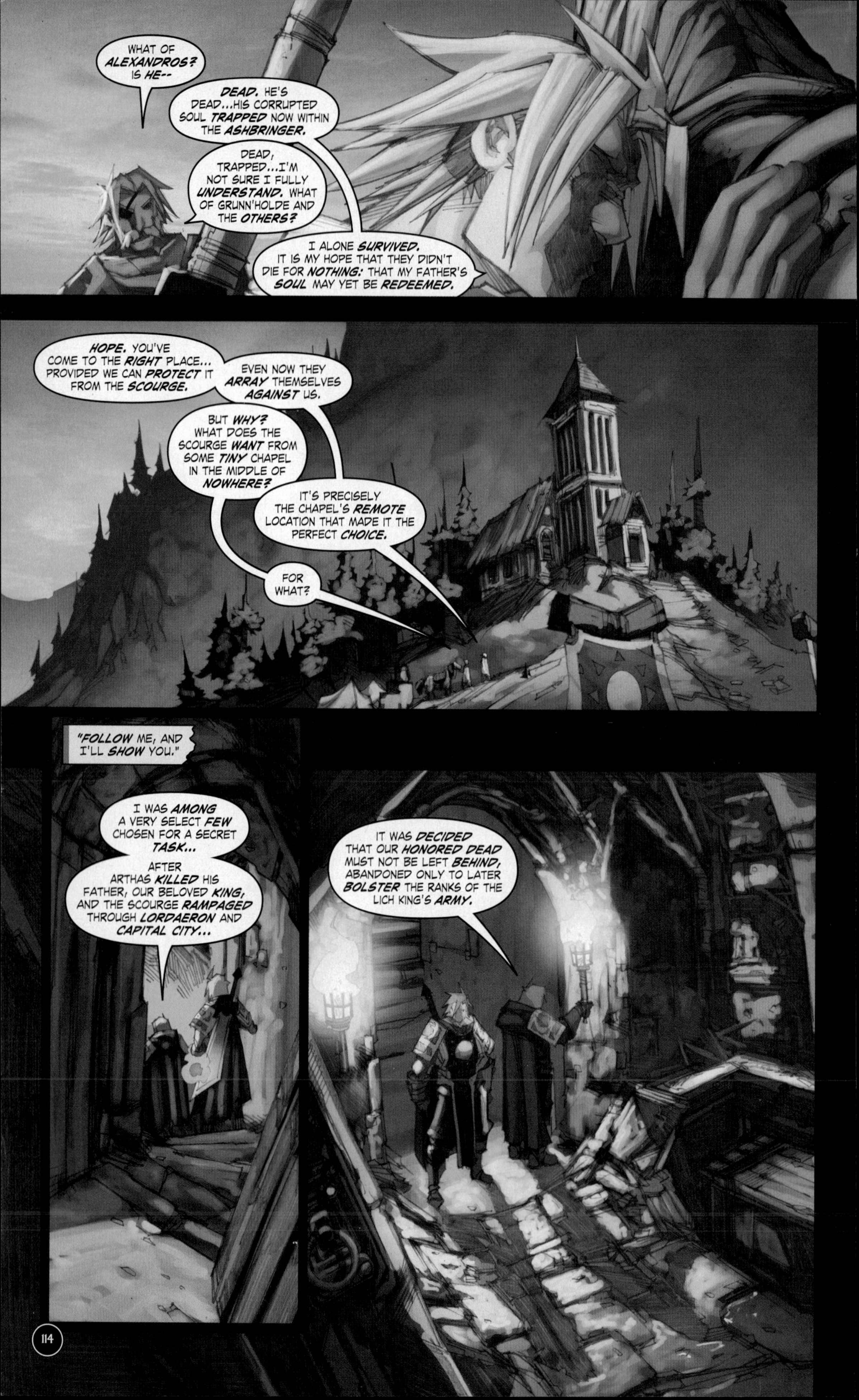
WHAT OF ALEXANDROS? IS HE--
DEAD. HE'S DEAD...HIS CORRUPTED SOUL TRAPPED NOW WITHIN THE ASHBRINGER.
DEAD, TRAPPED...I'M NOT SURE I FULLY UNDERSTAND. WHAT OF GRUNN'HOLDE AND THE OTHERS?
I ALONE SURVIVED. IT IS MY HOPE THAT THEY DIDN'T DIE FOR NOTHING: THAT MY FATHER'S SOUL MAY YET BE REDEEMED.
HOPE. YOU'VE COME TO THE RIGHT PLACE... PROVIDED WE CAN PROTECT IT FROM THE SCOURGE.
EVEN NOW THEY ARRAY THEMSELVES AGAINST US.
BUT WHY? WHAT DOES THE SCOURGE WANT FROM SOME TINY CHAPEL IN THE MIDDLE OF NOWHERE?
IT'S PRECISELY THE CHAPEL'S REMOTE LOCATION THAT MADE IT THE PERFECT CHOICE.
FOR WHAT?
"FOLLOW ME, AND I'LL SHOW YOU."
I WAS AMONG A VERY SELECT FEW CHOSEN FOR A SECRET TASK...
AFTER ARTHAS KILLED HIS FATHER, OUR BELOVED KING, AND THE SCOURGE RAMPAGED THROUGH LORDAERON AND CAPITAL CITY...
IT WAS DECIDED THAT OUR HONORED DEAD MUST NOT BE LEFT BEHIND, ABANDONED ONLY TO LATER BOLSTER THE RANKS OF THE LICH KING'S ARMY.

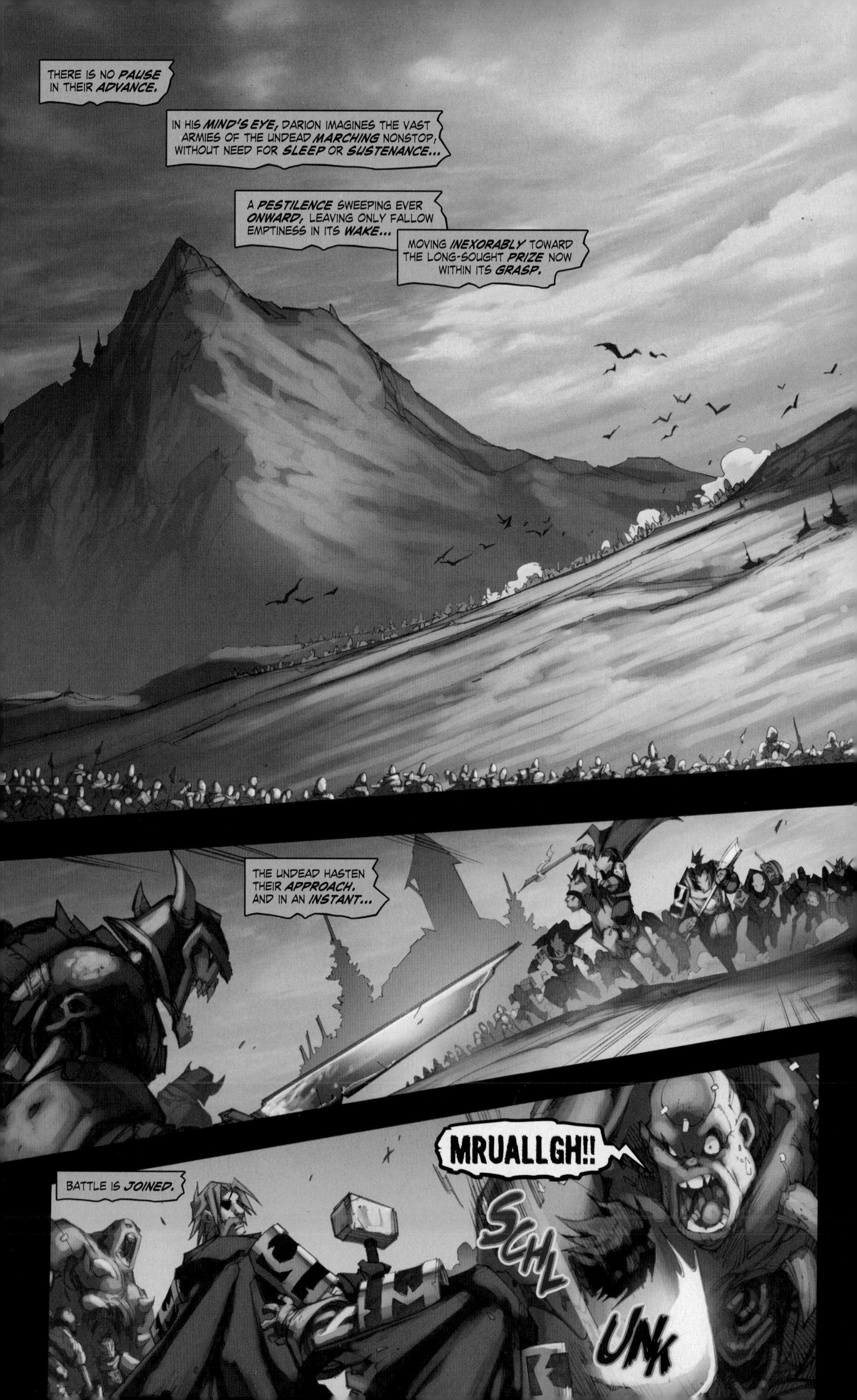
THERE IS NO PAUSE IN THEIR ADVANCE.
IN HIS MIND'S EYE, DARION IMAGINES THE VAST ARMIES OF THE UNDEAD MARCHING NONSTOP, WITHOUT NEED FOR SLEEP OR SUSTENANCE...
A PESTILENCE SWEEPING EVER ONWARD, LEAVING ONLY FALLOW EMPTINESS IN ITS WAKE...
MOVING INEXORABLY TOWARD THE LONG-SOUGHT PRIZE NOW WITHIN ITS GRASP.
THE UNDEAD HASTEN THEIR APPROACH. AND IN AN INSTANT...
BATTLE IS JOINED.
MRUALLGH!!
SCHLUNK

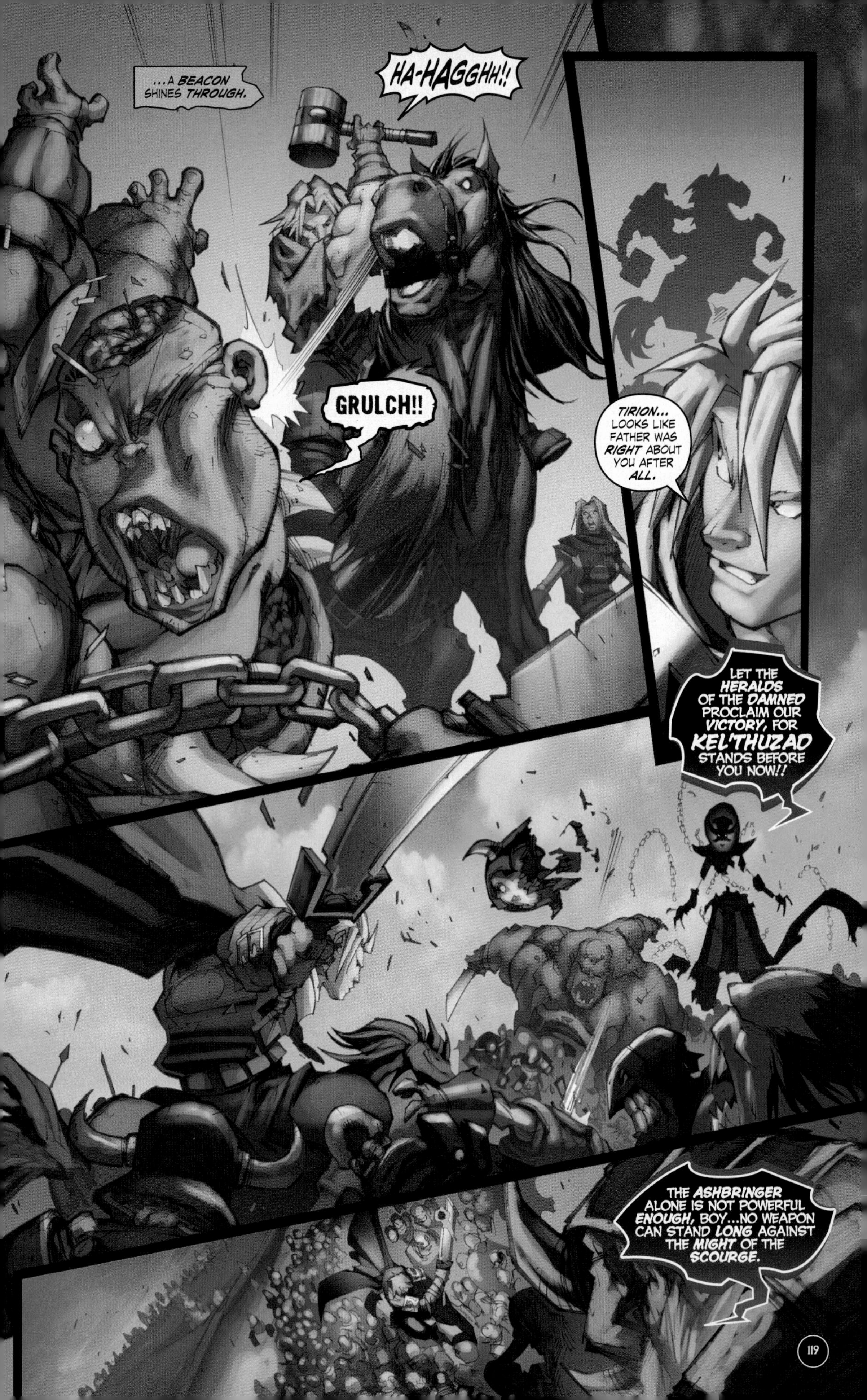
...A BEACON SHINES THROUGH.
HA-HAGGHH!!
GRULCH!!
TIRION... LOOKS LIKE FATHER WAS RIGHT ABOUT YOU AFTER ALL.
LET THE HERALDS OF THE DAMNED PROCLAIM OUR VICTORY, FOR KEL'THUZAD STANDS BEFORE YOU NOW!!
THE ASHBRINGER ALONE IS NOT POWERFUL ENOUGH, BOY...NO WEAPON CAN STAND LONG AGAINST THE MIGHT OF THE SCOURGE.

THIS IS MY PURPOSE, THEN. SO BE IT.
MY SOUL FOR YOURS.
I LOVE YOU, DAD.
THE ULTIMATE TEST OF FAITH...
AN ACT OF LOVE.
DARION...
SCHLUNKT
ONCE AGAIN, DARION IS OVERWHELMED BY A SENSATION OF SINKING BENEATH MURKY FATHOMS, OF STRUGGLING FOR BREATH...
YET EVEN AS OBLIVION BECKONS, HE IS ABLE TO CATCH A BRIEF GLIMPSE...

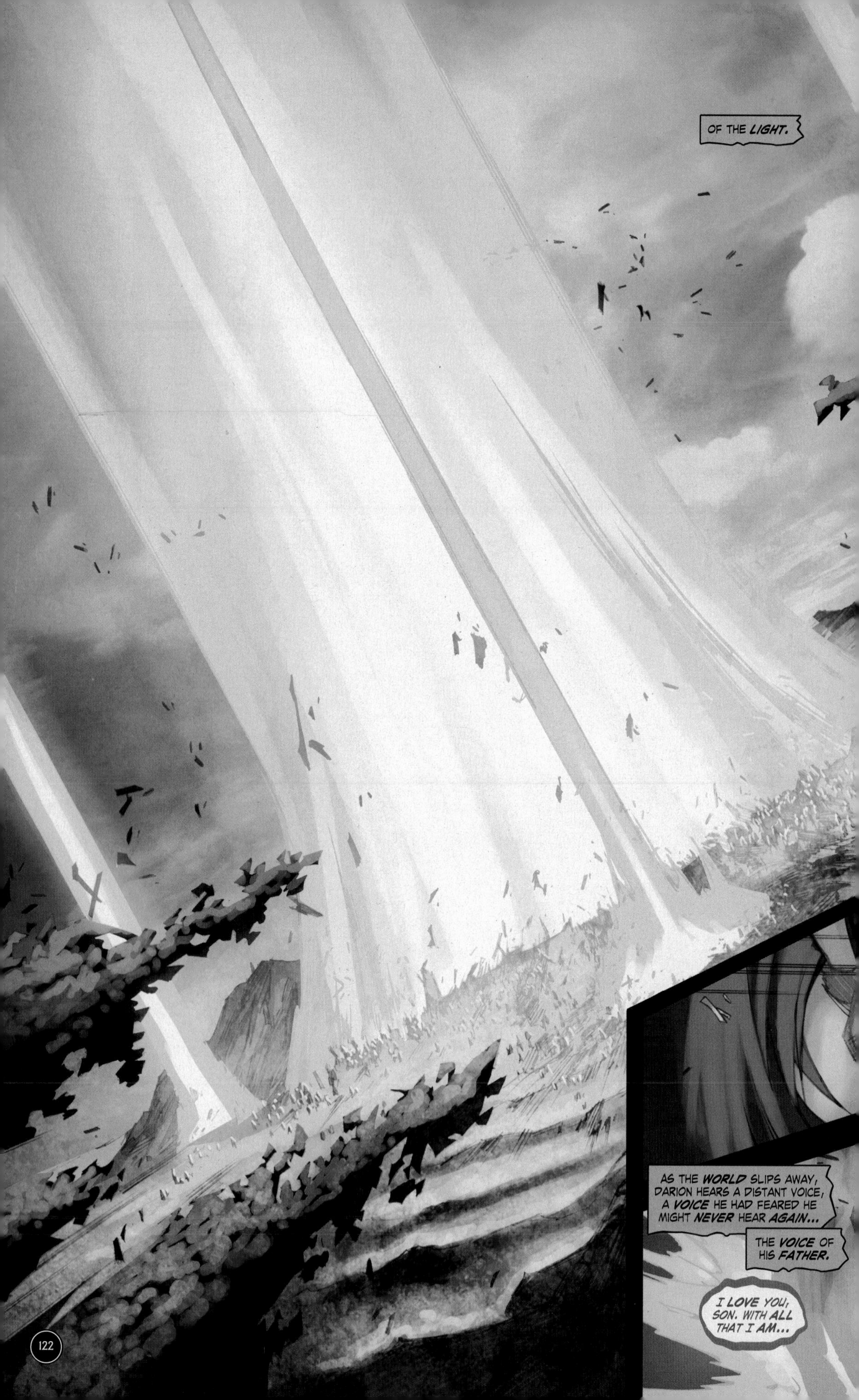

OF THE LIGHT.
AS THE WORLD SLIPS AWAY, DARION HEARS A DISTANT VOICE, A VOICE HE HAD FEARED HE MIGHT NEVER HEAR AGAIN...
THE VOICE OF HIS FATHER.
I LOVE YOU, SON. WITH ALL THAT I AM...

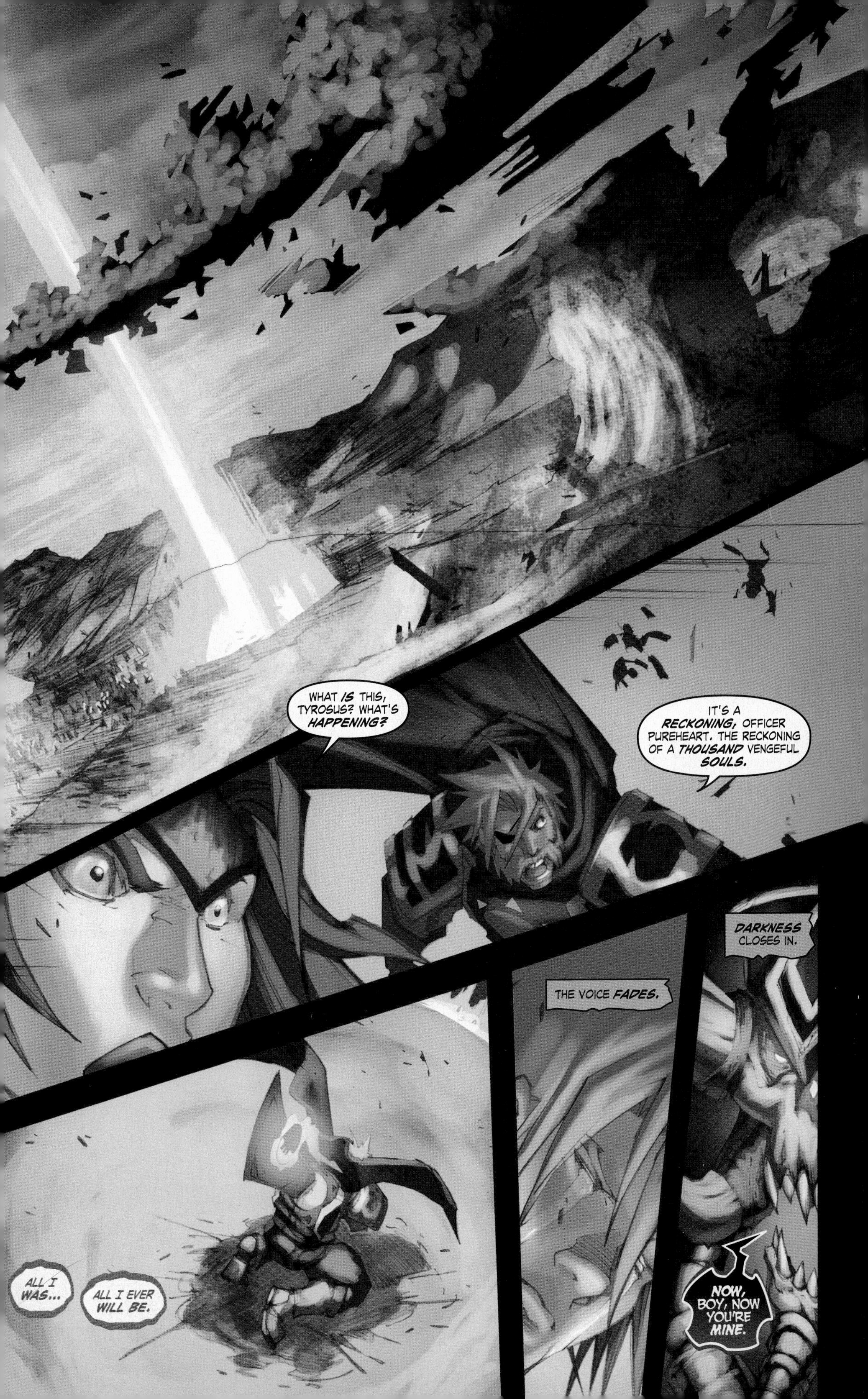
WHAT *IS* THIS, TYROSUS? WHAT'S *HAPPENING?*
IT'S A *RECKONING,* OFFICER PUREHEART. THE RECKONING OF A *THOUSAND* VENGEFUL *SOULS.*
ALL I WAS...
ALL I EVER WILL BE.
THE VOICE *FADES.*
DARKNESS CLOSES IN.
NOW, BOY, NOW YOU'RE *MINE.*

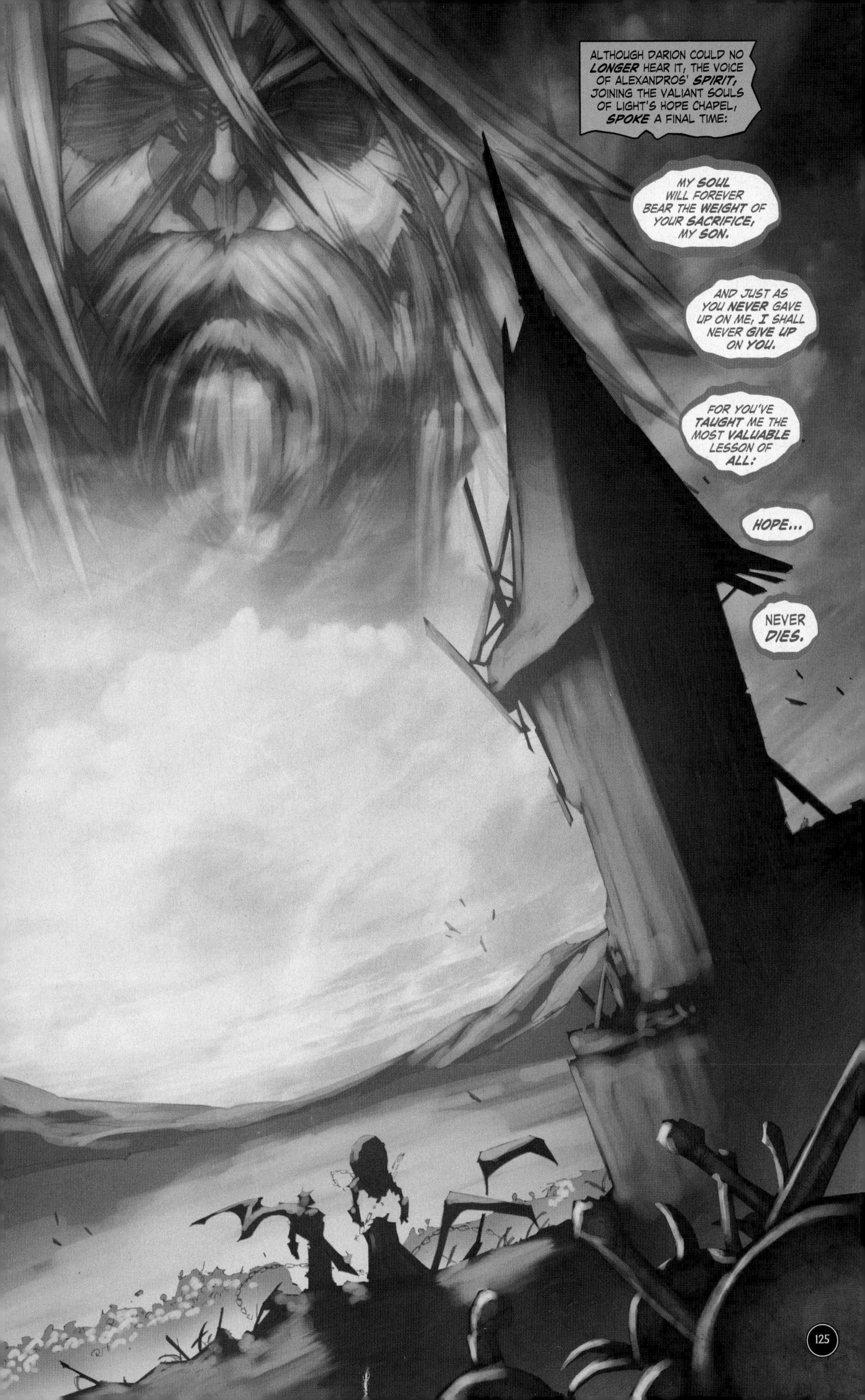
ALTHOUGH DARION COULD NO LONGER HEAR IT, THE VOICE OF ALEXANDROS' SPIRIT, JOINING THE VALIANT SOULS OF LIGHT'S HOPE CHAPEL, SPOKE A FINAL TIME:
MY SOUL WILL FOREVER BEAR THE WEIGHT OF YOUR SACRIFICE, MY SON.
AND JUST AS YOU NEVER GAVE UP ON ME, I SHALL NEVER GIVE UP ON YOU.
FOR YOU'VE TAUGHT ME THE MOST VALUABLE LESSON OF ALL:
HOPE...
NEVER DIES.

EPILOGUE

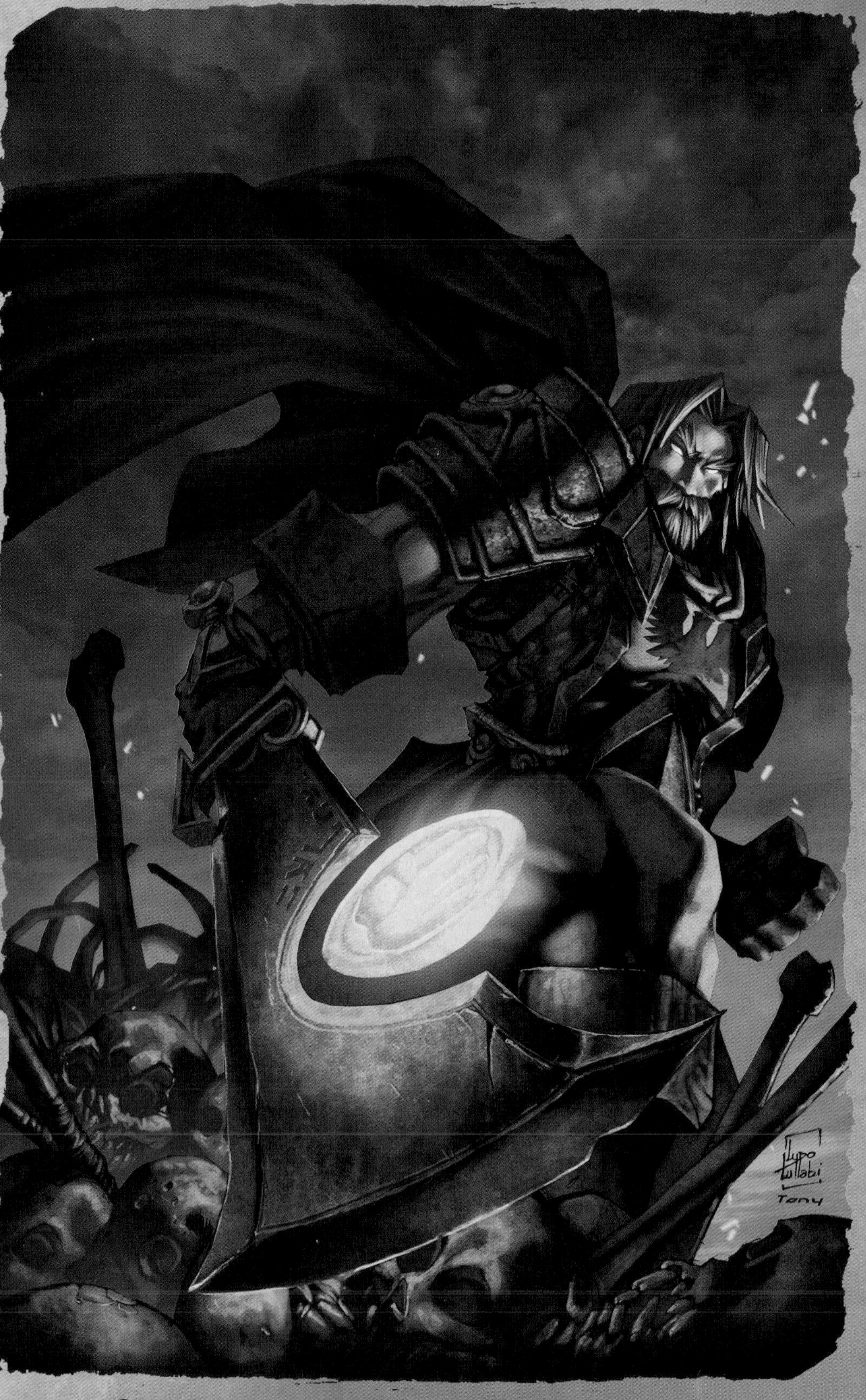
Ludo
Lullabi
Tony

Cover #1 by Ludo Lullabi and Tony Washington

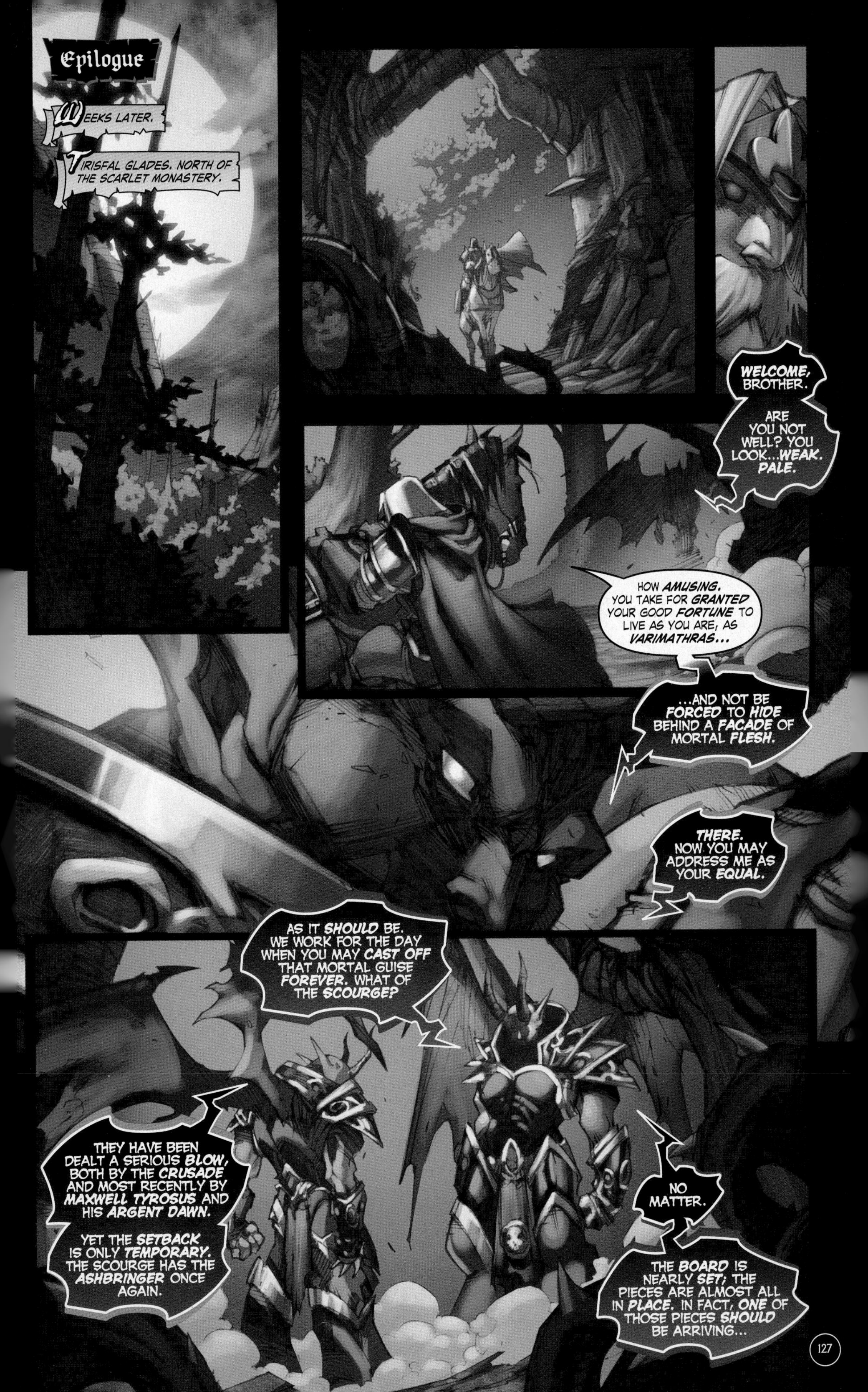
Epilogue
WEEKS LATER.
TIRISFAL GLADES. NORTH OF THE SCARLET MONASTERY.
WELCOME, BROTHER.
ARE YOU NOT WELL? YOU LOOK...WEAK. PALE.
HOW AMUSING. YOU TAKE FOR GRANTED YOUR GOOD FORTUNE TO LIVE AS YOU ARE; AS VARIMATHRAS...
...AND NOT BE FORCED TO HIDE BEHIND A FACADE OF MORTAL FLESH.
THERE. NOW YOU MAY ADDRESS ME AS YOUR EQUAL.
AS IT SHOULD BE. WE WORK FOR THE DAY WHEN YOU MAY CAST OFF THAT MORTAL GUISE FOREVER. WHAT OF THE SCOURGE?
THEY HAVE BEEN DEALT A SERIOUS BLOW, BOTH BY THE CRUSADE AND MOST RECENTLY BY MAXWELL TYROSUS AND HIS ARGENT DAWN.
YET THE SETBACK IS ONLY TEMPORARY. THE SCOURGE HAS THE ASHBRINGER ONCE AGAIN.
NO MATTER.
THE BOARD IS NEARLY SET; THE PIECES ARE ALMOST ALL IN PLACE. IN FACT, ONE OF THOSE PIECES SHOULD BE ARRIVING...

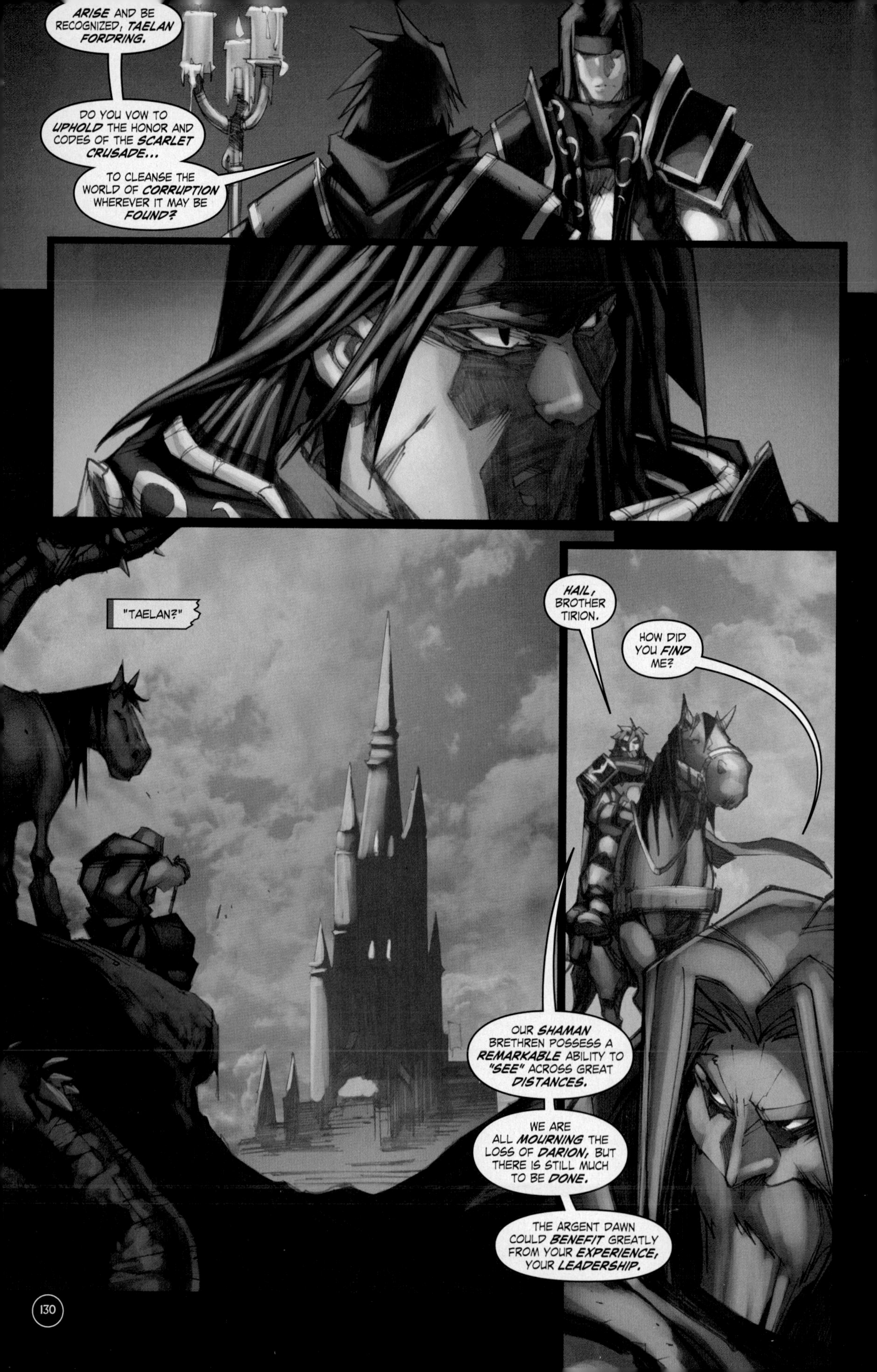
ARISE AND BE RECOGNIZED, TAELAN FORDRING.
DO YOU VOW TO UPHOLD THE HONOR AND CODES OF THE SCARLET CRUSADE...
TO CLEANSE THE WORLD OF CORRUPTION WHEREVER IT MAY BE FOUND?
"TAELAN?"
HAIL, BROTHER TIRION.
HOW DID YOU FIND ME?
OUR SHAMAN BRETHREN POSSESS A REMARKABLE ABILITY TO "SEE" ACROSS GREAT DISTANCES.
WE ARE ALL MOURNING THE LOSS OF DARION, BUT THERE IS STILL MUCH TO BE DONE.
THE ARGENT DAWN COULD BENEFIT GREATLY FROM YOUR EXPERIENCE, YOUR LEADERSHIP.

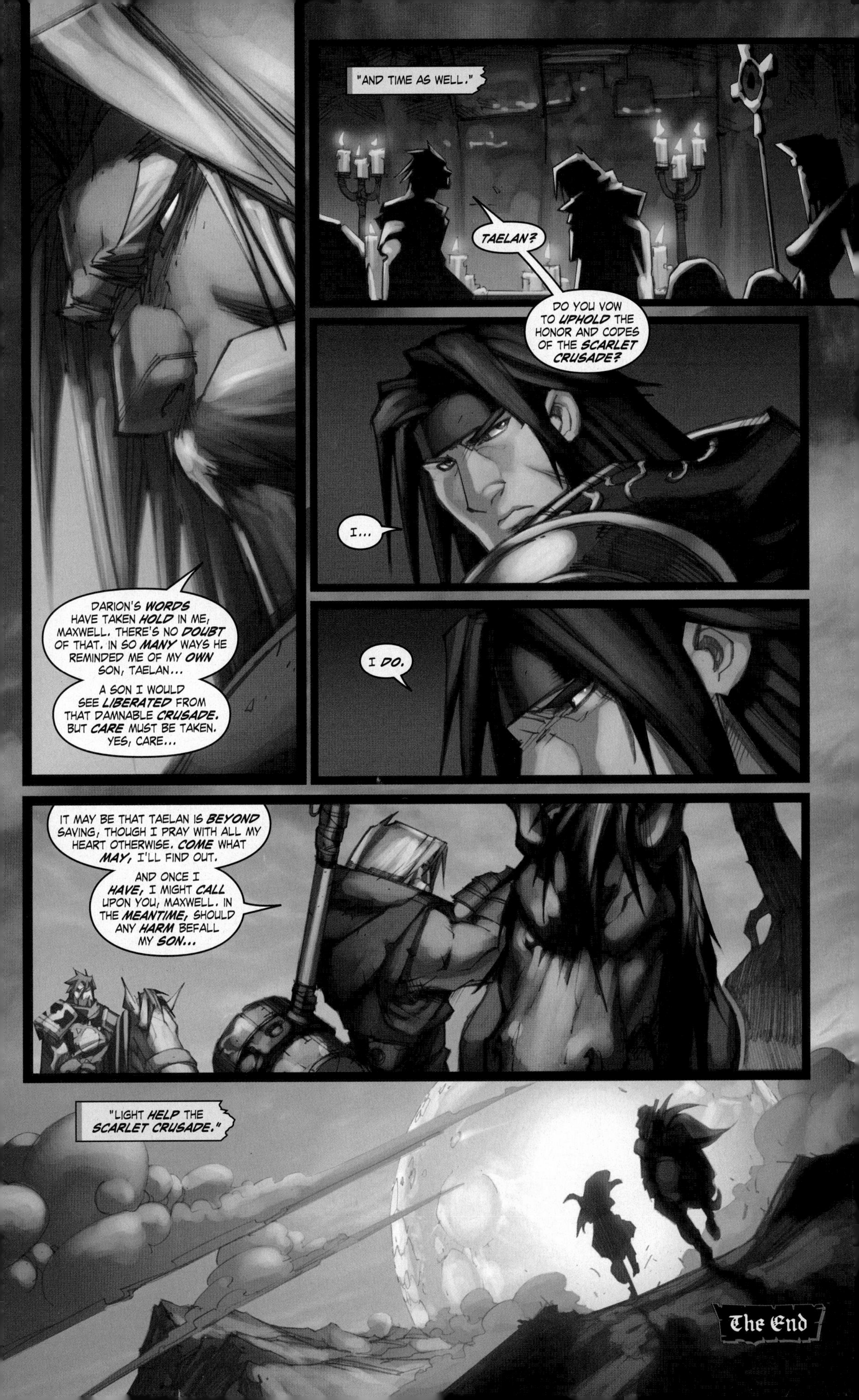
"AND TIME AS WELL."
TAELAN?
DO YOU VOW TO UPHOLD THE HONOR AND CODES OF THE SCARLET CRUSADE?
I...
I DO.
DARION'S WORDS HAVE TAKEN HOLD IN ME, MAXWELL. THERE'S NO DOUBT OF THAT. IN SO MANY WAYS HE REMINDED ME OF MY OWN SON, TAELAN...
A SON I WOULD SEE LIBERATED FROM THAT DAMNABLE CRUSADE. BUT CARE MUST BE TAKEN. YES, CARE...
IT MAY BE THAT TAELAN IS BEYOND SAVING, THOUGH I PRAY WITH ALL MY HEART OTHERWISE. COME WHAT MAY, I'LL FIND OUT.
AND ONCE I HAVE, I MIGHT CALL UPON YOU, MAXWELL. IN THE MEANTIME, SHOULD ANY HARM BEFALL MY SON...
"LIGHT HELP THE SCARLET CRUSADE."
The End

Creating A Page:
PENCILS

Stage 1: Roughed in
Ludo starts by breaking the page into panels, and laying out the figures. In page 1, panel 1, you can see that he's broken out the markers to place the trees against the moon.

Stage 2: Tightened Sketches
For these pages, Ludo chose to re-do the sketches and tighten them up before moving to the final boards with his pencils. Page 2, panel 2 is almost complete, but panel 3 shows that he's still working out how the shadows fall on Balnazzar's wings--gray markers this time!

Stage 3: Final Pencils
This is the final stage before we send them off to Tony. Pencils only, drawn on Strathmore art boards, working area approximately 11" x 17". Of course, Ludo has to draw on the reverse of our regular boards, so the scanner doesn't pick up the live area and crop lines.

PAGE ONE

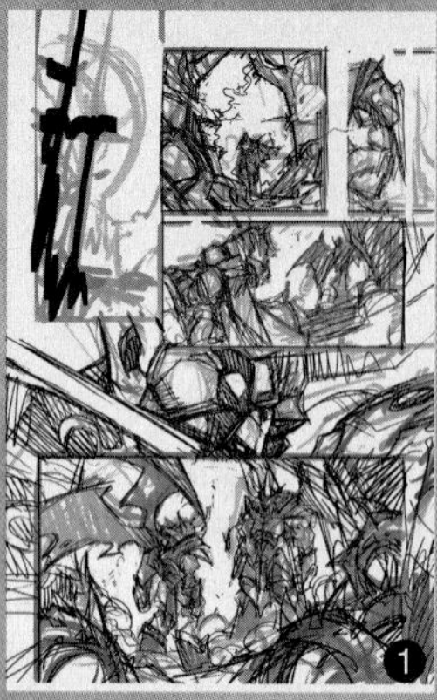

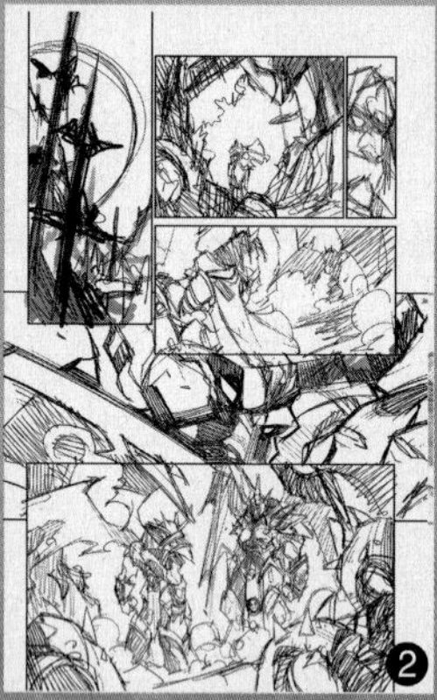

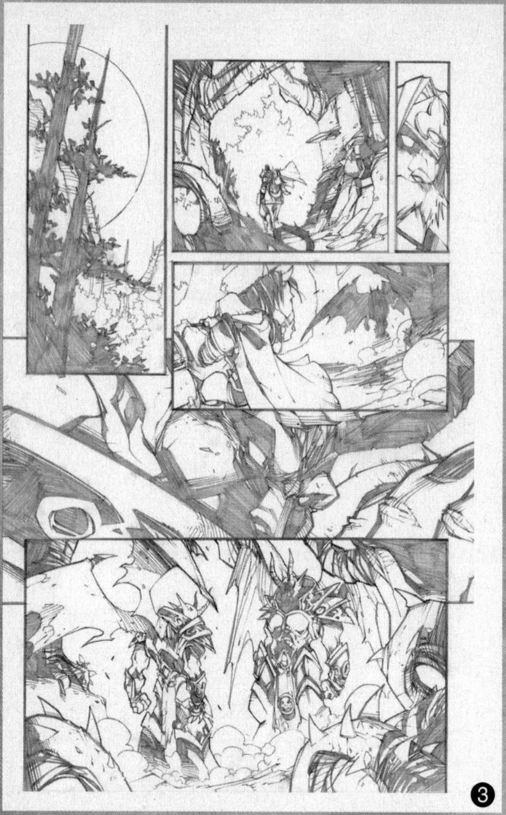

PAGE TWO

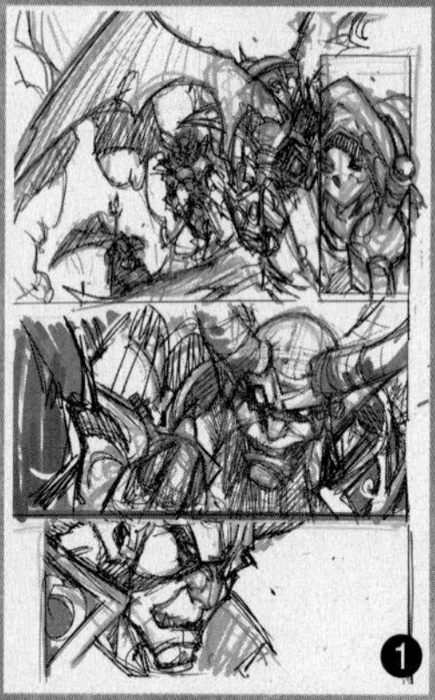

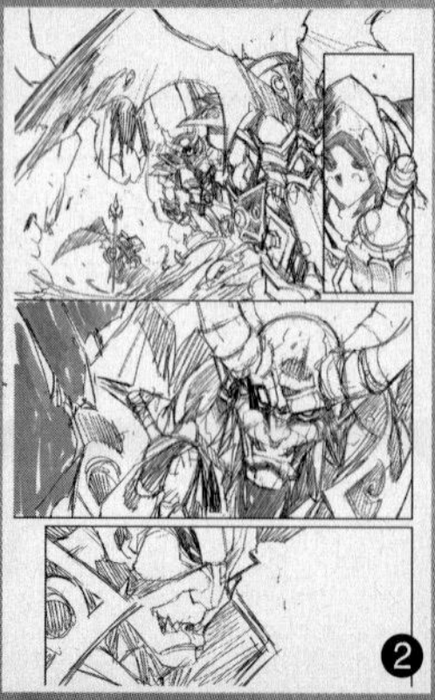

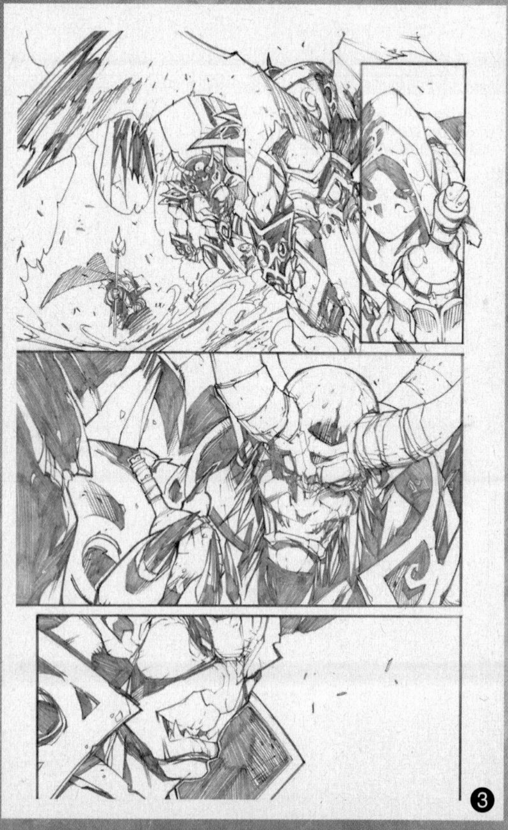

PAGE ONE

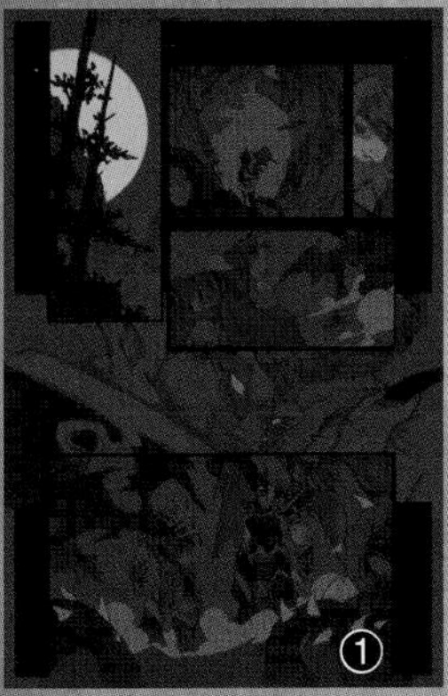

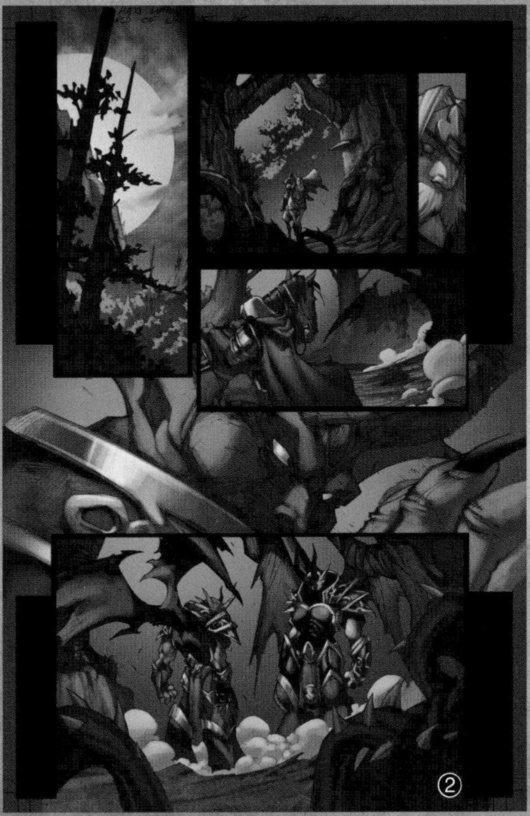

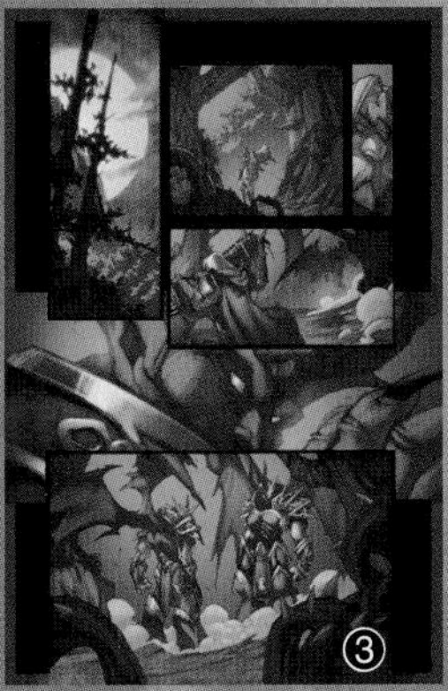

Creating A Page: COLORS

Stage 1: Flats

The first step in digital coloring is flatting. You select the main shapes and assign them a color—but overall, the piece stays dark. Tony's a glutton for punishment and handles this himself, though a lot of pro colorists opt to have an assistant take care of this step.

Stage 2: Rendering

This is where you see most of the change happening. Background trees reappear in page 1, panel 2. Dathrohan's hair and skin tones are refined to match his regular appearance. Overall, this is where all the details take shape.

Stage 3: Effects

By this point, the changes are all subtle. Looking at page 2, panel 1, Castillian's arrival goes from a harsh tan blob in stage 1, to a fiery yellow-orange in stage 2, to a glowing fire-burst in stage 3. Suddenly, he's not "just" stepping out of a yellow glare. The light reflects off his cloak and staff, and the glow hits Balnazzar's wings—but not as obviously, increasing the distance between them, which is a nice trick when you're coloring on a flat plane.

Stage 4: Final colors

If you turn back to pages 127 and 128, you can see the final colors for these pages. There are changes, because while Tony's good, with this many characters in play, the editors occasionally do have to request tweaks to make sure we're consistent with previous appearances.

PAGE TWO

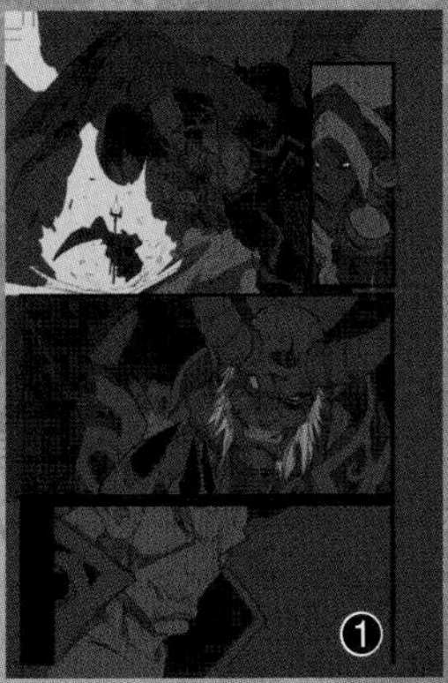

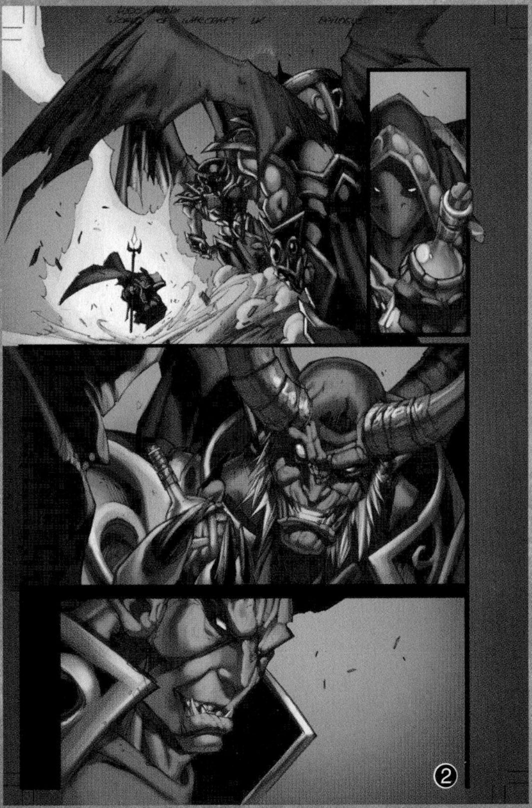

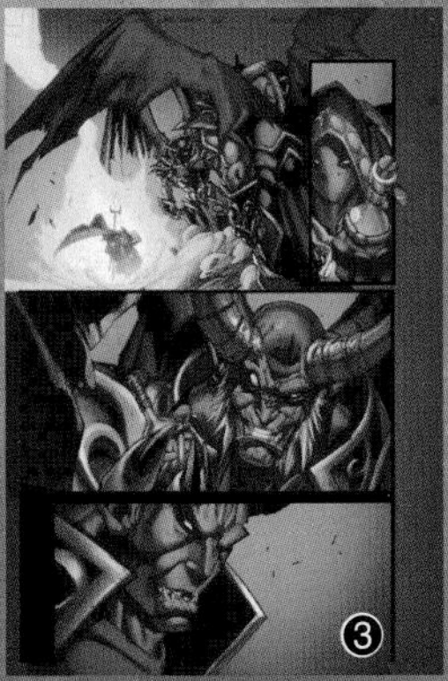

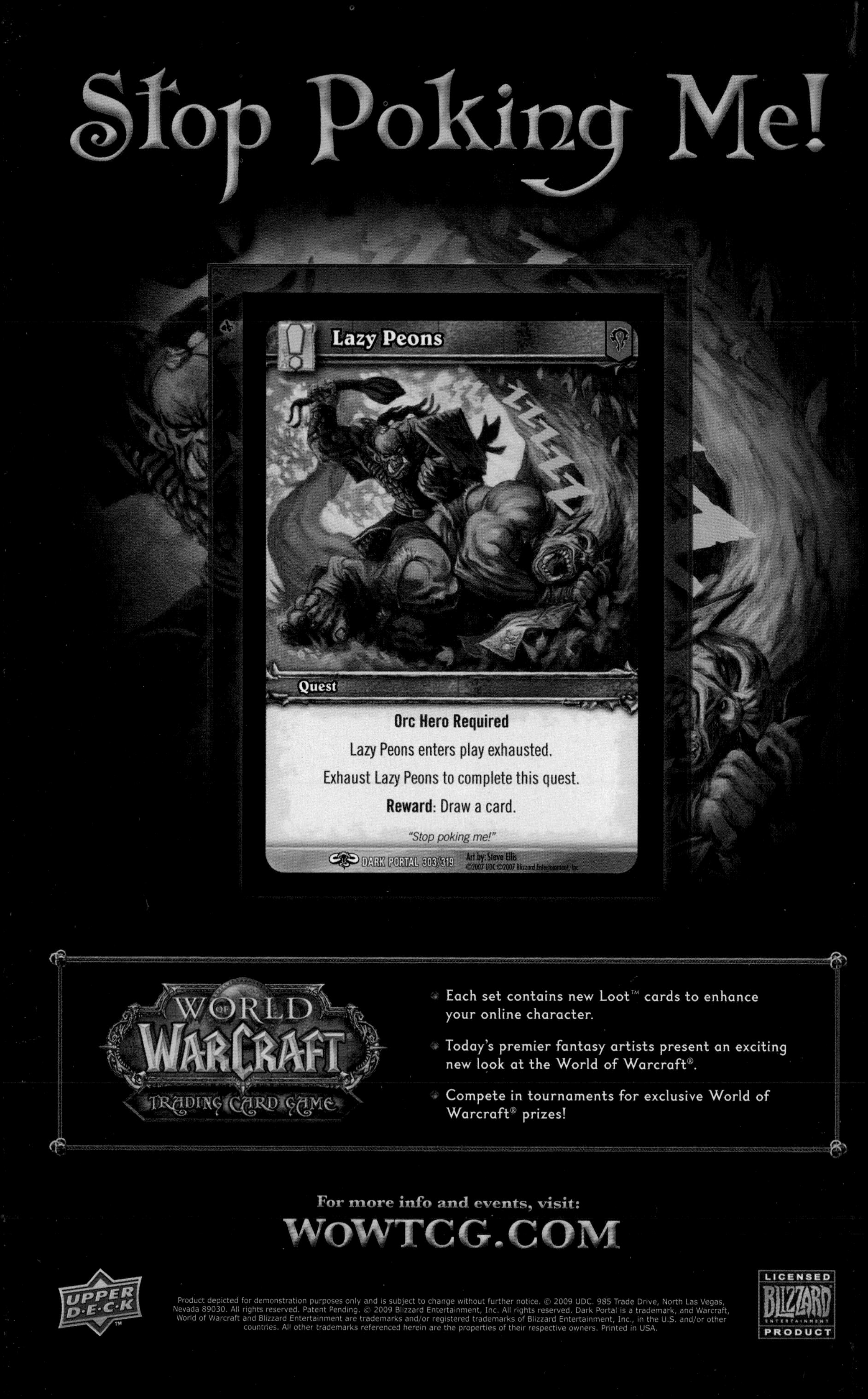
Stop Poking Me!
Lazy Peons
Quest
Orc Hero Required
Lazy Peons enters play exhausted.
Exhaust Lazy Peons to complete this quest.
Reward: Draw a card.
"Stop poking me!"
DARK PORTAL 303/319
Art by: Steve Ellis
©2007 UDC ©2007 Blizzard Entertainment, Inc.
WORLD OF WARCRAFT
TRADING CARD GAME
Each set contains new Loot™ cards to enhance your online character.
Today's premier fantasy artists present an exciting new look at the World of Warcraft®.
Compete in tournaments for exclusive World of Warcraft® prizes!
For more info and events, visit:
WOWTCG.COM
UPPER DECK
Product depicted for demonstration purposes only and is subject to change without further notice. © 2009 UDC. 985 Trade Drive, North Las Vegas, Nevada 89030. All rights reserved. Patent Pending. © 2009 Blizzard Entertainment, Inc. All rights reserved. Dark Portal is a trademark, and Warcraft, World of Warcraft and Blizzard Entertainment are trademarks and/or registered trademarks of Blizzard Entertainment, Inc., in the U.S. and/or other countries. All other trademarks referenced herein are the properties of their respective owners. Printed in USA.
LICENSED
BLIZZARD
ENTERTAINMENT
PRODUCT

WORLD OF WARCRAFT
BOOK 1

An amnesiac washes up on the shores of Kalimdor, starting the epic quest of the warrior Lo'Gosh, and his unlikely allies Broll Bearmantle and Valeera Sanguinar. Striking uneasy relationships with other races, as well as each other, they must fight both the Alliance and the Horde as they struggle to uncover the secrets of Lo'Gosh's past! Written by Walter Simonson (THE JUDAS COIN, *Thor*) and illustrated by Ludo Lullabi (*Lanfeust Quest*) and Sandra Hope (JUSTICE LEAGUE OF AMERICA), this is the latest saga set in the World of Warcraft!

**WORLD OF WARCRAFT
BOOK TWO
•Available August 2009•**

**Simonson
Buran • Bowden**

**WORLD OF WARCRAFT
THE MONTHLY SERIES**

Simonson • Bowden

Familiar faces from WildStorm!

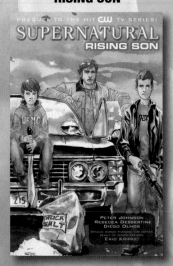